ecpr PRESS

I0094625

great expectations, slow transformations

incremental change in post-crisis regulation

Edited by

Manuela Moschella
and Eleni Tsingou

© M. Moschella and E. Tsingou 2013

First published by the ECPR Press in 2013

The ECPR Press is the publishing imprint of the European Consortium for Political Research (ECPR), a scholarly association, which supports and encourages the training, research and cross-national co-operation of political scientists in institutions throughout Europe and beyond.

ECPR Press
University of Essex
Wivenhoe Park
Colchester
CO4 3SQ
UK

All rights reserved. No part of this book may be reprinted or reproduced or utilised in any form or by any electronic, mechanical, or other means, now known or hereafter invented, including photocopying and recording, or in any information storage or retrieval system, without permission in writing from the publishers.

Typeset by Anvi

Printed and bound by Lightning Source

British Library Cataloguing in Publication Data

A catalogue record for this book is available from the British Library

Hardback ISBN: 978-1-907301-54-4

www.ecpr.eu/ecprpress

ECPR – *Studies in European Political Science*
Series Editors:
Dario Castiglione (University of Exeter)
Peter Kennealy (European University Institute)
Alexandra Segerberg (Stockholm University)
Peter Triantafillou (Roskilde University)

ECPR – *Studies in European Political Science* is a series of high-quality edited volumes on topics at the cutting edge of current political science and political thought. All volumes are research-based, offering new perspectives in the study of politics with contributions from leading scholars working in the relevant fields. Most of the volumes originate from ECPR events including the Joint Sessions of Workshops, the Research Sessions, and the General Conferences.

contents

| list of figures and tables

Figures

Tables

| contributors

ANDREW BAKER is Reader in Political Economy at Queen's University, Belfast. He is the current lead editor of the *British Journal of Politics and International Relations* and an Honorary Research Fellow of the Sheffield Political Economy Research Institute (SPERI University of Sheffield.) His research interests cover the politics of the financial crisis, Anglo-American political economy, the knowledge systems and professional cultures of leading finance ministries and central banks, and the history of macroprudential ideas. He has published over 25 refereed chapters and articles on financial governance and has authored two books, *The Group of Seven,* and *Governing Financial Globalization*, published by Routledge in 2006 and 2005.

SEBASTIAN BOTZEM is Research Fellow at the Social Science Research Center, Berlin. He studied political science and holds a PhD in business administration. His research focus is on transnational standardisation in accounting, regulation of financial markets, and the role of organisations in international political economy. Recent publications include *The Politics of Accounting Regulation: Organizing transnational standard setting in financial reporting* (Edward Elgar, 2012).

MARTIN CARSTENSEN is Assistant Professor at the Department of Business and Politics, Copenhagen Business School. His primary theoretical interests lie within institutional theory and discursive institutionalism, and he has published articles on the question of how ideas develop over time and after crises, using the financial crisis as a case, in *Political Studies, European Political Science Review* and *New Political Economy*. He is currently working on a three-year post-doctoral project funded by the Carlsberg Fund.

IVER KJAR is a doctoral student at the Department for Business and Politics of the Copenhagen Business School. He holds a Master of Arts in international political economy from the University of Warwick. His research interests are in international political economy and economic sociology and specifically everyday politics, legitimacy, housing, institutional change, and financialisation.

MANUELA MOSCHELLA is Assistant Professor in Political Science at the University of Turin. She is the author of *Governing Risk: The IMF and global financial crises* (Palgrave Macmillan, 2010). Her core research interests include the politics of financial crises and processes of change in global economic governance with a particular focus on the international financial institutions. She has published in *Review of International Political Economy, New Political Economy, Journal of Public Policy, Comparative European Politics*, and *Comparative Economic Studies*. She is currently co-editing the new *Handbook of Global Economic Governance* for Routledge.

STEFANO PAGLIARI is a Lecturer in International Political Economy in the International Politics Department at City University, London. His research interests are in global finance and regulation and his work has been published in *International Organization, New Political Economy, European Law Journal* and *Journal of European Integration.*

LUCIA QUAGLIA is Professor of Political Science at the University of York. Her most recent research monographs are *Governing Financial Services in the European Union* (2010) and *Central Banking Governance in the EU: A comparative analysis* (2008), both published by Routledge. She is also the author with Kenneth Dyson of *European Economic Governance and Policies* (OUP, 2010). She was guest co-editor, with Dermot Hodson, of the 2009 special issue of the *Journal of Common Market Studies* on 'The Global Financial Turmoil: European Perspectives and Lessons'.

THOMAS RIXEN is Professor of Political Science at the University of Bamberg. His research interests are in international and comparative political economy. He is the author of *The Political Economy of International Tax Governance* (Palgrave Macmillan, 2008) and has published in *European Journal of International Relations, Review of International Political Economy* and *Journal of Common Market Studies,* among other journals.

ELENI TSINGOU is Assistant Professor of International Political Economy at the Copenhagen Business School and Senior Research Fellow at the University of Warwick. She is the author of numerous chapters and articles on the governance of global finance and her work has appeared in *Review of International Political Economy, International Politics* and *International Political Sociology.* She was also a member of the Warwick Commission on International Financial Reform.

KEVIN YOUNG is Assistant Professor in the Department of Political Science at the University of Massachusetts, Amherst. His research focuses on the politics of financial regulation, international negotiation theory, transnational policy networks and the role of interest groups in economic policy-making. His published work appears in *Public Administration* and *Review of International Political Economy.*

| acknowledgements

This project started life as a proposal for the revamped Research Sessions of the European Consortium for Political Research (ECPR) in the autumn of 2010. Thinking through the state of play in the reform process in the aftermath of the financial crisis, we found that analyses of the pace and content of reform could greatly benefit from a more comprehensive political economy approach, one that made better use of the richness of international political economy and comparative politics. In particular, we found the language of 'incrementalism', 'change-agents' and 'veto-players' to be especially useful in highlighting the key institutional constraints and in analysing the preferences and strategies of the actors at the centre of reform. Happily, the organisers of the Research Sessions agreed with us and a first meeting took place in Florence in May 2011. We could not have hoped for a better setting to embark on our conversations and are grateful to the ECPR for giving us the opportunity to bring the initial team together in an intensive workshop, which delineated the key debates and allowed us to clarify our conceptual framework significantly.

The enlarged team met again in Copenhagen in December 2011 and we wish to thank the Department of Business and Politics (DBP) of the Copenhagen Business School for financial support for this event. By that stage, we were thrilled by the commitment of participants to the project, a commitment evidenced both by their incredible reliability with writing deadlines and the impressive quality of the original research that they shared with us for this purpose. Working with the contributors to this volume has been a pleasure and a privilege and we wish to thank them for making this such a fun project for us to work on.

Several colleagues commented on one or more of the chapters of this book, and we would like to thank in particular André Broome, Lasse Folke Henriksen, Jens Mortensen, Adriana Nilsson and Sven Steinmo, who took part in one or both of our meetings to discuss the work. Colleagues at DBP and the University of Bologna also commented on early versions of our Introduction and we would like to express our thanks in particular to Hubert Buch-Hansen, Aldo di Virgilio, Daniela Giannetti, Anna Leander, Gianluca Passarelli, James Perry and Leonard Seabrooke. Our Introduction was also considerably strengthened thanks to the comments of Hermot Dobson, Orfeo Fioretos, Randy Germain, Eric Helleiner, Luca Lanzalaco, Tony Porter, Cornelia Woll and Jonathan Zeitlin; all were incredibly generous with their time and gave us very useful feedback at various stages of the project. Financial support from the Bologna Alma Graduate School, within the framework of the 'Nino Andreatta Fellowship' is also gratefully acknowledged.

ECPR Press, and editor Dario Castiglione showed great interest and enthusiasm for the project from the outset. We wish to thank all those at ECPR Press who have made the transition from project to book so smooth. We are also grateful to the reviewer comments for helping us tighten the content and sharpening our contribution.

Finally, we would like to thank our families for their continuous support and good-natured patience. More unusually, perhaps, we would like to take this opportunity to publicly thank each other – while this project has been taking shape, a lot of 'life' has been happening as well, with new jobs, house moves and the arrival of offspring. Commitment to and leadership of the project never wavered, and that has made this collaboration a truly special one.

Manuela Moschella and Eleni Tsingou
Copenhagen and Turin
July 2013

chapter one | introduction: the financial crisis and the politics of reform: explaining incremental change

Manuela Moschella and Eleni Tsingou

The global financial crisis and global financial regulation: big expectations but small change

> One of the things most astonishing to posterity about our own times will be not how much we understood but how much we took for granted. We revel in every new excuse to label our times revolutionary; ours is the atomic/permissive/electronic/affluent/space age. Attention centers on the glittering pageant and dramatic incident, rather than on the elusive processes that evoke the incidents. Revolutions must be visible, palpable, and immediate, although it is the annual change of only one percent that can produce some of the greatest transformations. Paradoxically, a glib preoccupation with the 'revolutionary' has tended to reduce our sensitivity to change itself (Heclo 1974: 1).

Since the onset of the global financial crisis, 'change' has been the catchword in the international regulatory debate. In an attempt to respond to the weaknesses in financial regulation and supervision exposed by the crisis,[1] important legislative changes have been adopted in the world's leading financial centres, notably the Dodd-Frank Act in the United States and European Union legislation mandating the creation of new pan-European regulatory and supervisory authorities. At the international level, the leaders of the Group of 20 (G20) endorsed major reform proposals, partly in conjunction with the revamped Financial Stability Board (FSB) in areas such as banking regulation, compensation practices, resolution regimes, the development of macroprudential frameworks and tools, and the workings of derivatives markets and their infrastructure.[2] Interestingly, the regulatory-reform process has often been presented in terms of a revolutionary transformation. At the height of the crisis, several political leaders suggested

---

1. The literature on the causes of the global financial crisis is already quite large and it is not the purpose of this volume to review it thoroughly. For an introduction to the causes of the crisis from an economics perspective *see*, among others, de Larosière 2009; IMF 2009; Carmassi, Gros and Micossi 2009; Gorton 2008; Obstfeld and Rogoff 2009; Truman 2009.

2. At the time of writing, the latest report assessing the implementation of G20 recommendations for the strengthening of financial stability was issued in June 2012. Financial Stability Board, *FSB Report on the Overview of Progress in the Implementation of the G20 Recommendations for Strengthening Financial Stability*, available at http://www.financialstabilityboard.org/publications/r_120619a.pdf.

comparisons between the current reformist moment and the Bretton Woods moment (Parker and Barber 2008; Porter, Winnett and Harnden 2009), when the creation of new rules and institutions 'revolutionised' international monetary co-operation. Much early emphasis from policy-makers and indeed scholars[3] focused on the potential for significant transformation in global financial regulation. Referring to Peter Hall's (1993) seminal study on the paradigmatic shift in UK economic policy-making, Blyth (2013) laments the absence of third-order change. Nevertheless, as the quotation from Heclo at the start of this section reminds us,[4] the disproportionate attention given to revolutionary change risks reducing our understanding of change itself.

This is important as the process of international financial regulatory-reform as it has evolved, displays few of the revolutionary characteristics that have been touted. For instance, although progress has been made on microprudential banking regulation with the introduction of higher and counter-cyclical buffers into the Basel III accord of the Basel Committee on Banking Supervision (BCBS), Basel III has not altered the practice of allowing banks to measure their own risk when setting capital requirements (Haldane 2012) and there is still no agreement on what should exactly count as liquid assets to satisfy the proposed liquidity standards. Furthermore, a stinging issue throughout the crisis, that of 'too-big-to-fail' financial institutions, remains under-explored and instruments aimed at increasing the loss-absorbency capacity of systemically important financial institutions (SIFIs) have yet to be incorporated into formal and binding rules. As for the development of macroprudential regulation, which aims to preserve the health and stability of the financial system as a whole, agreement on what policy tools fall within its scope is still in its infancy (*see* Baker in this volume). In addition, the creation of an effective cross-border resolution scheme is still on the nominal 'to do' list, as is the regulation of the over-the-counter (OTC) derivatives market and the shadow-banking system (Carstensen and Rixen in this volume). Finally, and despite the criticisms it has attracted, the International Accounting Standards Board (IASB) has displayed remarkable stability in the content of rules, governance structure, and decision-making (*see* Botzem in this volume). In short, the process of international financial reform has fallen short of initial (and proclaimed) expectations of rapid and revolutionary transformation and has instead been characterised by small and incremental changes.

The incremental pattern of change in global financial regulation may also be considered puzzling in theoretical terms – primarily because the conditions for the kind of 'punctuations' that are associated with very large and often very consequential policy shifts appeared to be in place.[5] Indeed, it is often recognised

---

3.   *See*, for example, Posner 2009; Singer 2009.

4.   The quotation is linked to Heclo's study on the evolution of social policy in Britain and Sweden (1974).

5.   According to Baumgartner and Jones (1993) incremental policy-making, while common and dominant most of the time, is only one of two models of policy-making: periods of incremental adjustments are routinely 'punctuated' by short-lived bouts of radical policy change.

that an exogenous shock, such as the one offered by the global financial crisis, is likely to trigger a reaction that overcomes the institutional frictions that usually constrain policy change. Periods of 'normal' marginal adaptation are interrupted by more infrequent and atypical periods of 'non-linear' policy changes (Howlett and Migone 2011: 54). Such changes are more likely to occur when the exogenous shock interacts with heightened public and government attention and with the alteration of the policy subsystem that is involved in decision-making (Baumgartner and Jones 1993, True *et al.* 2007). These are precisely the conditions that characterised the post-crisis environment. Indeed, the crisis catalysed public and policy-makers' attention around financial regulatory issues (*see also* Helleiner, Pagliari and Zimmermann 2009). At the same time, the debate on the content of financial rules became increasingly politicised, as attested by the primary role accorded to the G20 political leaders in international financial negotiations – although experts retained a primary role in diagnosing the crisis and suggesting reform proposals. As such, the conditions for a punctuated type of change were in principle in place; instead, incremental change prevailed.

Why was the reform process incremental although the conditions for more rapid and abrupt transformation appeared to exist? And is there anything specific about financial policy that prevents punctuations from occurring, making this policy field different from those where the existence of punctuations is now well established?[6]

This book answers these questions, investigating the empirical pattern of incremental change in the post-crisis financial regulatory debate. Based on examination of a variety of policy fields within the area of finance broadly defined, the findings of this collaborative project suggest that the specific institutional frictions that characterise global financial governance and the activity of change-agents and veto-players involved in the process of global regulatory change make financial regulation largely immune to the punctuation model of change. Whereas in the standard punctuated model, institutional frictions beget punctuations – they can slow down change but they lead to bigger policy changes than in cases where external inputs would have been introduced more gradually – the combination of institutional frictions with the distinct type of actors involved in the international regulatory process prevents policy punctuations from occurring.

Although we collectively demonstrate that the process of change in international financial rule-making and content, and of the institutions of finance, does not fit with the punctuated model of policy change, we nonetheless argue that the incremental changes here examined do not rule out bigger and deeper transformations. This means that, in finance, paradigm-change is less likely

---

6.   The best-studied example of the combination of incrementalism and occasional punctuations is governmental budgeting (Jones *et al.* 2009). Indeed, the frequency distributions of public budget changes, both in one-country and cross-country studies, suggest that budgeting is highly incremental most of the time, but is occasionally punctuated by very large policy shifts (Baumgartner, Foucault and Francois 2006; Breunig and Koski 2006; John and Margetts 2003; Jones and Baumgartner 2005; Mortensen 2005; True *et al.* 2007).

the result of an exogenous shock than is the case in the area of budgeting (Baumgartner, Foucault and Francois 2006; Breunig and Koski 2006; John and Margetts 2003; Jones and Baumgartner 2005; Mortensen 2005; True *et al.* 2007) or macroeconomics (Hall 1993). In finance, as will be discussed in the Conclusion of this book, paradigm-change is instead associated with incremental, endogenously driven dynamics. In this light, our findings support the body of scholarship that suggests that radical transformations are not solely the result of the orthodox homeostatic or exogenously driven punctured equilibrium model of policy change (Cashore and Howlett 2007; Coleman *et al.* 1996; Howlett 2009; Thelen 2003; Mahoney and Thelen 2010). Radical transformation may also result from the cumulative effects of previous policy changes, thus underscoring the importance of 'process sequencing' (Haydu 1998; Howlett 2009; Kay 2007; Thelen 2003).

The editors and contributors of this volume have set themselves an ambitious goal, that of speaking to scholars interested in the dynamics of policy change at large. We find that the importance of investigating factors at all levels of governance (domestic, interstate and transnational) is of increasing relevance to understanding policy change, especially as the type of fragmented governance encountered in finance against a multitude of actors and vested interests, can arguably be observed in other policy processes. That said, the book is primarily aimed at enriching international political economy (IPE) scholarship. Indeed, one of the motivations of our research project was dissatisfaction with the treatment of the process of change in the existing IPE literature on global financial regulation. Specifically, existing studies offer only partial insights into the question of incremental change and seldom address it directly. Scholars of international financial regulation have focused mostly on the causes of regulatory change rather than what pattern change actually follows. As a result, while important insights have been developed on the actors involved in the politics of reform of international financial rules and on the instruments and resources used in the reform process,[7] we have yet to get a comprehensive picture of why and how change is sometimes quick and at other times slow to materialise, or why, how and when it entails a profound rethink of previous practices or amounts to little more than small adjustments in existing instruments.

This is not to say that existing scholarship is silent on the dynamics of policy change. To the contrary, several scholars have made a number of suggestions that are key to the puzzle explored in our study. For instance, in his work on global finance as a technical system, Porter (2003) has suggested that the regulation of global finance is predisposed towards incremental developmental trajectories because of the legacy of previous technical knowledge and patterns of collaboration. Focusing on governmental policy networks, Baker (2006) has suggested some of the factors that help account for the incremental pattern he detects in the G7 case,

---

7. For instance, as will be discussed at greater length below, important insights have been developed regarding the influence exerted on the process of international financial reform by actors such as governments (Drezner 2007), national regulatory authorities (Singer 2007), international organisations (Abdelal 2007), transgovernmental networks (Baker 2006) and transnational networks of public and/or private sector officials (Porter 2005; Tsingou 2008).

suggesting that incrementalism can be understood in light of prevailing economic ideas and shared understandings, and the routines and procedures that mark G7 activity. In a similar vein, Best (2004) has drawn attention to the incremental nature of the shift from Keynesianism to monetarism by bringing to the surface the legacy of once-dominant ideas, even when new ideas gain currency in academic and public circles. As this brief overview of the arguments on incrementalism reveals, current scholarship acknowledges the need to explain different dynamics of change. But we suggest that some of the explanations advanced to account for the incremental dynamics of change have not been fully explored, nor systematically tested.

Building on these insights, the contributors to this volume share an interest in explaining the incremental pattern of change that has dominated the post-crisis reform agenda. Specifically, we argue that, in order to explain this pattern, we need to complement and expand the conventional focus on the actors involved in the process of regulatory change with a stronger emphasis on the institutional frictions that actors confront.[8] These factors, which are illustrated in the following sections, include: the concentration of financial power in a limited number of states; vested interests in dominant institutional positions; gaps in implementation capacity at the domestic level; and the fragmentation and club-like nature of global financial governance.

This book sets out to make three main contributions to the literature on policy change and global financial governance. First, our study helps determine that an incremental policy-change model best fits with the policy area of international financial regulation. This has implications for the study of change in financial policy and related policy areas (for example, signalling changes in public policy priorities relating to access to credit, financialisation or trade-offs between stability and competitiveness) but also opens up potential comparative research agendas across issue-areas.

Second, we explore the normative dimension associated with the incremental pattern of change. We thus engage with the question of whether incremental changes are simply a cover for pro-status-quo and conservative forces to prevail, a proposition supported by some of the contributions to this volume (in particular, Botzem and Rixen). Indeed, since the publication of Lindblom's article on the politics of 'muddling through' (1959), which addressed the tenets of incrementalism as a mode of policy-making, incrementalism has been accused of being an inherently conservative picture of the policy process. In this book, however, we provide a more nuanced understanding of incrementalism, suggesting that it cannot be always and automatically equated with conservatism. Rather, as some contributions in this volume show (most notably, Baker), in the area of international financial regulation, incrementalism can be a useful political strategy for offsetting conservative forces and may foreshadow more fundamental policy changes.[9]

---

8. As explained in greater detail below, the emphasis on constraining factors and sequencing leads us to engage with the analytic concepts developed within historical institutionalism.

9. Lindblom himself rejected the accusation of conservatism. For a summary of the arguments used by Lindblom *see*, for instance, Rothmayr Allison and Saint-Martin 2011: 3.

Finally, this volume puts forward an important contribution to the study of global financial governance in the aftermath of the global financial crisis by providing a theoretically informed examination of the phenomenon of regulatory change that is meant to build bridges between the study of change in international political economy and in comparative political economy (Farrell and Newman 2011; Fioretos 2011b). Indeed, our explanation of incremental change borrows extensively from the insights developed within the historical institutionalist (HI) tradition on the study of change in domestic settings (as developed, among others, by Pierson 2004; Thelen 1999, 2004; Steinmo, Thelen and Longstreth 1992; Streeck and Thelen 2005). In particular, we build on recent theoretical and empirical studies that have expanded HI's core institutionalist focus with a more clearly agent-centred perspective that takes into consideration the dynamic relationship between actors and the constraints/opportunities of the environment in which they operate (Bell 2011; Mahoney and Thelen 2010).

As explained in some detail in subsequent sections, historical institutionalism (HI) holds valuable substantive insights and analytical tools for theorising how incremental change occurs in international finance and why the international financial system may be more suited to incremental than radical reforms. Although we stress the relevance of HI to our empirical puzzle, it is not the purpose of this book to provide a manifesto for the application of HI to the study of change in global financial governance. Our adoption of HI is more practical than theoretical. We believe that HI provides substantive insights and analytical tools to investigate patterns of institutional, incremental development at the domestic level that can be useful in analysing patterns of institutional development in the international financial system too. Hence, although contributors do not necessarily subscribe to the historical institutionalist label, they share a substantive focus on factors such as power, temporal processes, institutional constraints, and inefficiency – in short, the factors that constitute the core of the HI tradition.

Before proceeding, some clarifications are in order. Firstly, although our interest in incrementalism is accompanied by an emphasis on the constraints that influence the process of change, the role of agency in the reform process is in no way discounted and is a common feature in all chapters. As has long been noted, 'background factors don't do policies. Policymakers do.' (Lundquist, 1980: xiii). Studying actors' preferences, motivations, strategies and ideas is therefore of utmost importance to the puzzle addressed in this study. As such, the chapters in this book explore the constraints associated with two categories of actors: *change-agents* and *veto-players*. Combining the role of actors, which has been widely investigated in existing literature, with the constraints that actors face, we attempt to strike a balance between strategic action and institutional constraints.

Secondly, it is important to clarify what types of change in international finance we analyse. Indeed, one of the most common problems in the study of change is that 'scholars are often insufficiently clear as to exactly what it is that they are studying' (Capano and Howlett 2009: 3–4).[10] That is, significant ambiguity exists on the type and level of change under investigation. In order to sort out this ambiguity, in this study, we reject the distinction according to which incremental change indicates adaptive and reproductive minor change whereas major change indicates disruption of continuity. Rather, we submit, incremental change can be as transformative as major change (*see also* Streek and Thelen 2004). We thus define incrementalism in relation to Peter Hall's (1993: 279) definition of 'normal policy-making,' as a process that adjusts policy without challenging the overall terms of a given policy paradigm – at least in the short run. That is to say, incremental changes preserve some broad continuities with past regulatory policies.

For the purposes of this study, then, incremental changes can be found at different levels – from formal institutions to soft governance arrangements and norms (Abbott and Snidal 2000). In particular, some of the contributors to this study analyse formal institutions and rules (*see* Quaglia in this volume) as well as looser forms of co-operation such as standards and international early-warning systems (*see* Carstensen in this volume). Other contributors focus on either the changes in decision-making practices in financial regulation (Botzem in this volume) or the changes in the prevailing norms that inform international financial regulation and supervision (Baker in this volume). Further, a group of contributions analyses the changes in the distribution of resources (material and immaterial) among different actors and stakeholders participating in international financial policy-making (Pagliari and Young in this volume). Finally, some contributions analyse areas of finance where contentious political factors are most pronounced, whether defined in interstate competitiveness terms or at the domestic level (Rixen and Kjar in this volume).

The remaining part of this introductory chapter is organised as follows. In the next section, we analyse existing literature on the evolution of global financial regulation and how it addresses and/or explains the incremental pattern of change in the post-crisis regulatory-reform process. In Section 3, we develop the analytical tools and concepts that are taken up in the volume's case studies. In particular, we delineate the set of factors shaping the pattern of incremental change in global financial governance. Section 4 explains the relevance of studying the evolution of global financial governance by using the analytical concepts and methods developed within historical institutionalism. Section 5 provides an overview of the book.

---

10. In the public policy literature, the ambiguity that surrounds the study of change is known as the problem of the dependent variable (Capano 2009; Green-Pedersen 2004; Howlett and Cashore 2009).

What do we know thus far? The actors of global financial regulation

The question of who shapes international financial rules and how the process of rule-creation takes place has long interested IPE scholars. Since the pioneering works of Kapstein (1989, 1992) on the negotiations of the Basel accord, scholarship on international finance has made important forays into the political and market pressures that shape international financial rules and harmonisation (Simmons and Elkins 2004; Simmons 2001; Cerny 1994). In particular, scholars have assessed the role played by factors such as the structural power of the United States (Strange 1988), capital mobility (Andrews 1994), domestic social interests (Singer 2007; Seabrooke 2006) and private-sector lobbying (Underhill 1997; Gill 1990), among others. In a review of the post-financial-crisis literature, Helleiner and Pagliari (2011) suggest three distinct explanations for the evolution of international financial regulation, based on the policy arenas that drive the process of rule-creation and change: interstate, domestic, and transnational explanations. Interestingly, and in spite of the significant differences among them, the three explanations share an emphasis on the actors involved in regulatory processes and the resources that they possess to influence them.

For instance, the studies that fall within the first explanation place emphasis on a specific category of actors: leading states or great powers. In this reading, market size and adjustment costs are the crucial resources these actors possess. As Drezner (2007: 28) explains, the logic that unpins interstate explanations is

> market size [which] alters the distribution of payoffs by reducing the rewards of regulatory coordination for large market states and increasing the rewards for small market states. This gives the great powers a bargaining advantage and alters the perception of other actors so as to reinforce the likelihood of regulatory coordination at a great power's status quo ante. Furthermore, market size endows great powers with the option of economic coercion as a way of convincing other actors in the system to change their financial rules in line with those preferred by the great powers. As a result, changes in international financial rules and institutions are closely dependent on the national interests of leading states.

Interstate explanations have several weaknesses, including a limited ability to account for states' interests over time and a neglect of domestic social interests (Büthe and Mattli 2011). For our purposes, it is worth noting that, although interstate explanations do not explicitly address the question of incremental change, they offer some insights in the post-crisis context. For instance, a common theme in the scholarship is that financial regulation will be significantly enhanced when leading states have a common interest in more stringent regulation. Otherwise, leading states act to narrow the scope of regulation (Wood 2005). But the logic that underpins interstate explanations does not help distinguish between the conditions under which the regulation of finance will be modified incrementally or suddenly or be maintained as it is. Additionally, such explanations underplay the role of weaker actors in influencing international regulatory outcomes (Sharman 2006).

Yet it has become important to take the role of such actors into account, especially in the aftermath of the global financial crisis. Following years of preaching to emerging-market countries about internationally recognised standards of financial conduct (Walter 2008), the crisis erupted in the so-called 'sophisticated' financial markets. The reform process has thus far enlarged membership of the financial governance infrastructure to include more emerging-market countries and it is yet possible that some of these countries, such as China, will become more assertive in influencing the international regulatory debate.[11] Furthermore, one of the effects of the crisis has been to rebalance power in favour of emerging markets' financial institutions, many of which, by market capitalisation, now figure among the top twenty world banks – with Chinese banks occupying the three top spots of the ranking in 2009.[12]

The second set of explanations of international financial regulation shift the emphasis to domestic-level actors – be they domestic regulators (Singer 2007) or financial institutions (Busch 2009; Mügge 2006). Domestic actors are deemed able to shape international regulatory outcomes because of the key political resources they possess. Within the domestic explanation of international regulatory outcomes, significant attention is also given to the institutional specificities of national capitalisms (Hall and Soskice 2011). For instance, Hubert Zimmermann (2009) has explained the international regulatory preferences of Germany and the UK in 2008–9 as they relate to the specific characteristics of their national capitalisms – co-ordinated and liberal-market respectively. Similarly, Manuela Moschella (2011b) has explored how, in the immediate aftermath of the global financial crisis, EU international regulatory preferences were significantly shaped by the apparent discrediting of the UK's 'liberal' model of capitalism in favour of the Franco-German 'regulated' model (*see also* Quaglia 2012 and, on pre-crisis coalitions, Quaglia 2010).

Although domestic explanations do not explicitly engage with the question of what causes incremental financial regulatory change, they also contain some important insights. For instance, in his study of domestic regulators, Singer has identified a trade-off between stability and competitiveness in determining more-or-less-international regulatory co-operation across three areas of finance – banking, securities and the insurance sector – suggesting a pattern of international regulatory change that is highly dependent on the preferences of regulators in the leading financial centres. This approach shares many of the drawbacks of interstate explanations while also failing to account for the bargaining and deliberative dynamics that take place at the international level. The same problem affects those explanations that put the emphasis on the characteristics of domestic capitalisms:

---

11. Note, however, that such expectations are relatively contained – *see*, for example, Walter (2009) on this issue. On the increasing dependence of developed countries from emerging markets' finance, *see also* Helleiner and Pagliari 2011: 176.

12. 'Top 20 financial institutions by market capitalization, $bn, 1999–2009', *Financial Times*. http://www.ft.com/intl/cms/7a7a1484-17a3-11de-8c9d-0000779fd2ac.swf. Accessed 13 July 2011.

they are strong in highlighting domestic preferences but do not provide a satisfactory explanation for the process of decision-making at the international level.

This shortcoming is largely addressed by the third set of explanations identified by Helleiner and Pagliari (2011): transnational explanations that explicitly focus on the processes and dynamics that take place in international regulatory fora. This strand of scholarship explains that the evolution of the international financial regulatory regime is heavily influenced by the activities of actors operating across rather than through governments, whether transgovernmental networks that overcome the domestic/international divide (Baker 2006; Porter 2005) or transnational policy communities in which the divide is not solely domestic/international but also public/private (Tsingou 2009) and where specialist expert knowledge prevails (Botzem 2012).

We believe that scholars adopting transnational explanations most clearly address the issue of incremental change. Baker's (2006) and Porter's (2003) insights on incremental evolution in global financial governance as a consequence of technical authority and *esprit de corps* have already been referred to. Likewise, in her account of the influence of private actors after the crisis, Tsingou (2009) attributed the incremental pattern of regulatory reform, in spite of the worst financial upheaval since the 1930s depression, to the enduring power of transnational private interests, because these are deeply engrained in the policy community in charge of the rules of global finance and constrain the spectrum of policy ideas that can be discussed and adopted. There are, nevertheless, two problems with this set of approaches when our focus shifts away from actors and towards understanding the nature of change. The first is that the suggestions about incremental change are spot insights rather than clearly developed hypotheses that could inform a research agenda on the incremental pattern of change. The second is that transnational explanations have primarily focused on the actors involved in the international regulatory process but have paid insufficient attention to the institutional frictions and actor interactions that constrain the activities of the actors analysed.

In what follows, we aim to fill this gap by developing a theoretical framework able to account systematically for the incremental dynamics of change. We take into account the role of agency in the process of change by investigating change-agents and veto-players, but we also endeavour to put greater emphasis on the institutional frictions that, combined with the activity of transgovernmental networks and transnational communities, help explain incrementalism in the international financial regulatory process.

Explaining incremental change in post-crisis financial regulatory reform: redressing the balance between actors and institutions

The theoretical framework suggested here takes as a starting point an agent-centred, constructivist-oriented approach. Since ideas exist in a competitive marketplace in which alternative ideas are always available, actors frame and manipulate ideas to mobilise support (Blyth 2003). In other words, the process of change requires actors to sponsor their ideas and try to persuade other agents to support them (Widmaier, Blyth and Seabrooke 2007; *see also* Chwieroth 2010).

The importance of active policy entrepreneurs and the ideas they support is widely recognised in the literature on the creation of global regulation. As Mattli and Woods (2009: 17) put it, 'public and private entrepreneurs play key roles in mobilising opposition, and ideas may offer the necessary frames for pro-change interests and glue for coalitions'. The role of policy entrepreneurs acquires key importance in the policy area under investigation where the uncertainty associated with financial crises strengthens the importance of actors able to interpret them, diagnose their causes, and propose blueprints for their solutions (Blyth 2002, 2007). In short, economic crises do not speak for themselves (Hay 1996) and their effects do not automatically lead to new policy and ideational consensus (Grabel 2003; Moschella 2010).

As previously discussed, for the purposes of this study, we identify two distinct categories of actors that help explain processes of change in global financial regulation: change-agents and veto-players. The identity of these actors, we submit, can be most diverse: in different times and different circumstances, governments, social interests or transnational technocrats can all be either change-agents or veto-players. Assigning roles is therefore a matter of empirical investigation and is not defined *ex ante* in our theoretical framework.

Whereas change-agents lead the process of change by being explicit advocates of specific changes, or hidden supporters of them, veto-players, in principle, aim to maintain the status quo in order to preserve their privileges and safeguard their interests. In the area of financial reform, several studies have shown how special interests are able to shape rules and institutions in narrow and effectively closed policy communities (Moran 1990; Underhill 1995; Coleman 1996). These actors may sustain the reproduction of existing institutions over time, vetoing or opposing change that affects them. Although veto-players generally oppose change, it is also plausible to think of them as actors expressly promoting change. This happens when veto-players realise that regulatory change is the only way to maintain their privileged positions. For instance, in the context of financial policy, if actors do not adapt to shifting financial innovations and changing economic conditions, the risk of losing their privileged positions is of the highest. Hence, it is possible that 'the very industries that benefited from regulation in the past lobby for change' (Vogel 1996: 13). It is also important to note that, similarly to change-agents, veto-players can be more or less explicit in their strategies.

While we take as a starting point of our analysis the role of agents, as does much of the IPE constructivist scholarship reviewed in the previous section, we complement analysis of the role of the agents with a careful examination of the institutional constraints and opportunities that actors face, including actor interactions.[13] In doing so, we build from important recent attempts to draw attention to an agent-centred model of institutional change (Bell 2011, 2012). That

---

13. Mahoney and Thelen (2010: 31) advance a similar point when they argue that 'the interactions between features of the political context and properties of the institutions themselves [are] critically important in explaining institutional change' and how the type of change actors and the different strategies they adopt are likely to differ in specific institutional settings.

is to say, we acknowledge that agents are the ultimate propellants of change but also that institutional environments shape agents' ability and discretion. Hence, to explain change, 'we need to model agents both as partially constrained by their immediate institutional contexts and also as operating in institutional and structural settings that constantly evolve and potentially open up new opportunities for agents.' (Bell 2011: 898).

In what follows, we therefore concentrate on the dynamic interaction between agents and institutions that helps explain incrementalism in global financial regulatory-reform processes. Since the existing literature on actors involved in international regulatory processes is extensive, as discussed in the previous section, the factors identified below focus on the institutional dimension of the process of change. Nevertheless, as the empirical chapters show, it is the combination of the specific agents involved in global finance and the distinct institutional frictions of global financial regulation that explain the prevalence of incrementalism over punctuations.[14]

The institutional frictions that are relevant to the process of global financial regulatory change are grouped into three blocs, according to the strand of the global finance literature they mainly refer to (Table 1.1).[15] Note, however, that whereas some factors are specific to one of the three political arenas of global financial regulation – interstate, domestic and transnational – other factors do not relate to one single arena. For instance, although we discuss the institutional frictions associated with the presence of vested interests in the section dedicated to the domestic political arena, vested interests can be found at both the intergovernmental and transnational levels. Likewise, the discussion of ideas and routines as institutional frictions is conducted in the section on the transnational arena, although these frictions are present in the intergovernmental and domestic arenas too. In short, the typology proposed below is an analytical tool that assists us in discussing a number of frictions that help account for incremental change in global financial regulation but should not be considered as exclusively assigning a specific friction to any of the three political arenas. Furthermore, the list is neither exhaustive nor exclusive. It is also worth noting that the factors identified below may pertain to one of the stages of the regulatory decision-making process (agenda-setting, negotiations, implementation and enforcement), whereas other factors are present in more than one of the stages. Finally, whereas some constraints are formal, others are more informal.

In what follows, we discuss each of the identified institutional frictions in turn. In examining their characteristics, we also suggest in what ways they are likely to be associated with incremental dynamics of change. That is to say, we provide

---

14. There are studies that attempt to distinguish between the factors that influence the outcome of regulation – i.e., whether public interest or captured regulation prevails (*see* Mattli and Woods 2009, for instance). To our knowledge, however, no similar attempt has been made to systematically analyse and test the conditions that help explain the dynamics of regulation.

15. Note, however, that we also move beyond the scholarship explicitly reviewed in the previous section.

Table 1.1: Institutional frictions and potential paths to incremental change in global financial governance

	Institutional friction	Potential path to incremental change
Interstate dimension	Concentration of financial power	*Change-agents adopt limited reforms to escape veto*
Domestic dimension	Vested interests in dominant institutional position	*Veto-players adapt to new challenges to maintain privileged positions* *Change-actors change slowly to avoid overt opposition*
	Gaps in implementation capacity	*Veto-players lengthen policy implementation* *Change-actors build implementation capacity*
Transnational dimension	Fragmented and club-like global financial governance	*Change-agents seek support across several regulatory bodies* *Veto-players are insulated from public pressures*
	Ideational inertia	*Change-agents road-test new ideas and build institutional support*

some illustrations of how the presence of a specific kind of institutional friction may prevent the emergence of paradigm-change. It is important to note, however, that these suggestions are just illustrative and indicative. As the empirical case studies that follow indicate, and as we discuss in the concluding chapter, there are several pathways to incremental change and, above all, it is the interaction between change-actors and veto-players, on the one hand, and institutions, on the other, that shapes the pattern of regulatory dynamics.

The interstate dimension and processes of incremental change

Although the role of experts and technocrats is crucial in the creation of global financial regulation, the role of governments should not be underestimated (*see* Rixen in this volume). On the one hand, many important decisions are taken through intergovernmental bargaining, in which states attempt to attend to a specific national interest. On the other hand, the implementation of global financial regulation is closely dependent on domestic regulatory regimes, as will be explained at greater length below. Furthermore, since regulatory reform is about more than liberating markets, state actors are a key factor in reforms because they address two things that are more relevant to states than any other actors: 'finding new ways to raise government revenue and designing new mechanisms of policy implementation' (Vogel 1996: 19).

In the interstate arena, the main institutional friction that helps explain the prevalence of incrementalism in the process of global regulatory reform is the concentration of financial power – and associated veto power – in only a few states. For instance, those states with the largest markets occupy a privileged position in global negotiations because they can veto decisions that would damage their financial interests, by threatening to close their markets or to 'go it alone'. As a result, change is often based on the lowest common denominator among state preferences to escape deadlock caused by veto-players (*see also* Quaglia in this volume). That is to say, for regulatory changes to be adopted, change-agents should not support changes that significantly depart from the rules and practices in place in the dominant financial markets. In particular, the transformation of global financial rules would need not to impose significant costs on the most powerful states in the system. This limits the range of reformatory policy options, thus giving rise to incremental patterns of change.

The domestic dimension and processes of incremental change

Within the domestic policy-making arena, two main institutional obstacles to regulatory reform are the presence of vested interests and the lack of implementation capacity. The first is closely related to the concept of institutions adopted in this study: institutions in global financial governance can be conceived as outcomes of political struggles. This means that certain actors are advantaged by existing institutions and have a vested interest in their survival. This is the case of the financial industry in our area of investigation – although the crisis has altered their influence too (Pagliari and Young in this volume). Furthermore, once an institution is in place, actors make greater relation-specific investments, and this develops an interest in preserving current institutions (Pierson 2000a, 2000b, also Gourevitch 1999). For instance, as David Lake (1999: 46) has noted, since private actors 'have grown out of and adapted to the current [global] governance structure', they 'have little interest in seeing it overturned or even significantly modified'. But domestic social actors can also benefit from such arrangements; when the interests of powerful electoral blocks coincide with those of particular financial institutions, enacting reform and changing the status quo can lead to intense political struggles (*see* Kjar in this volume).

Although the actors that benefit from existing institutions prefer the status quo, change is still possible. For instance, actors that benefit from existing institutions may adapt those institutions in order not to lose their comparative advantage. This is particularly the case in a rapidly innovating sector like finance. Indeed, faced with changing economic conditions or with shifting financial innovations, veto-players may realise that their advantage is better preserved by adapting existing rules and institutions than by maintaining the status quo. It is also conceivable that veto-players would accept short-term sacrifices of their interests in order to maintain long-term coalition success (Scharpf 2000: 782). It is within this space that changes may take place in an incremental fashion. Indeed, the logic is that actors with an interest in a specific institution will prefer an incremental adaptation in order to control the process of change. Following this thinking, we can interpret the limited but nevertheless substantive reforms at the European level as a process that addresses some criticisms while deflecting attempts at more radical transformation (*see* Quaglia in this volume).

Next to a process driven by the actors that benefit from existing institutions, disadvantaged actors may also drive the process of change; as Thelen (1999) has noted, losers from an institutional arrangement do not disappear. They also adapt and work to transform this arrangement, including via the formation of coalitions with other actors (Pagliari and Young in this volume). This has important implications for the dynamics of policy change. Indeed, if change-agents occupy a disadvantaged position in the regulatory status quo, they will enact change in slow and incremental steps in order to avoid overt opposition and political blockages by privileged actors. The timing of change is also slowed because agents need to mobilise and nurture political support against entrenched interests. This hypothesis fits with the well established finding in domestic political systems that 'countries with many veto players will engage in only incremental policy changes' (Tsebelis 2000: 464).

The second institutional friction that shapes the pattern of global financial regulatory change relates to organisational and bureaucratic capacity. Indeed, reforms at the international level often depend for their implementation on domestic regulatory authorities and bureaucratic apparatuses. The capabilities and organisation of these regimes therefore provide incentives for and constraints on what governments can put into practice (Raustalia 1997). Furthermore, in the area of finance, the domestic level assumes a key role: many of the global rules of finance are flexible best-practice standards rather than rules *per se* (Tsingou 2008); they are interpreted in regulatory terms and implemented within a domestic setting. The discretion accorded to domestic bureaucratic systems in implementing global financial regulation therefore magnifies the importance of the former and bears important implications for the patterns of policy change in at least two respects. First, veto-players may oppose change at the implementation stage, lobbying domestic regulators for lengthened application of internationally negotiated rules. Second, change-agents need to develop the necessary institutional infrastructure before enacting their preferred policy changes (*see* Baker in this volume).

The transnational dimension and processes of incremental change

Finally, and with particular reference to the transnational dimension of global financial regulation, the institutional frictions that are more likely to shape the pattern of regulatory change in an incremental fashion are the institutional framework and the ideational orientation of global financial governance.[16] The governance framework of global finance is of crucial importance in explaining patterns of change. Two features are of particular relevance: the fragmented nature of the global regulatory regime and the club-like quality of co-operation. The governance of international finance is indeed distributed among multiple transnational public and private international institutions (Porter 2005), in which

---

16. Vogel (1996) adopts a similar distinction between regime organisation and regime orientation, although he refers to domestic regulatory systems.

no single regulatory body clearly dominates. These bodies include the international financial institutions and international groupings of regulators and supervisors, such as the Basel Committee, IOSCO, and the International Association of Insurance Supervisors (IAIS).[17] The governance framework also includes private-sector actors, some of them global representative groupings for banking and other financial industries, others more issue-driven and responsible for standard-setting, such as the IASB. While some of these bodies have distinct competences, they also share responsibilities. This has a number of consequences for the dynamics of regulatory change. Firstly, the development of new policies requires consensus in more than one regulatory body. For instance, the task of developing regulatory standards for systemically important financial institutions (SIFIs) is shared among the FSB and the Basel Committee (which will set additional capital requirements). Under this fragmented institutional framework, change is more likely to be incremental. As a result, change-agents will need to mobilise support in several regulatory bodies, while turf battles and overlapping areas of competence offer veto-players multiple opportunities for influence. A similar institutional patchwork can be observed in the ongoing discussions about resolution regimes (*see* Carstensen in this volume).

Next to the fragmented nature of global financial governance, its club-like quality also affects patterns of regulatory change. Policy networks at the transnational level usually operate through informal and exclusive processes, in which expertise and socialisation are critical resources for influencing regulatory outcomes. These features, we suggest, tilt the balance in favour of incrementalism for at least two reasons.

First, this peculiar structure shields global regulatory debate and decision-making from public scrutiny and pressures (housing finance is a notable exception, as shown by Kjar in this volume). Comparison with other policy fields may help to clarify this point. For instance, Hall's explanation of change in Britain's economic policy-making paradigm emphasises the role played by actors outside the community of policy experts. In his view, paradigm-change was ultimately possible because the contest over policy-choice spilled beyond the boundaries of the Treasury.[18] Similar emphasis on attention paid to an issue by actors outside the community of experts is also present in several studies that have analysed a variety of policy sectors – from nuclear policy (Baumgartner and Jones 1991) to civil rights, environment, energy, transport and foreign trade policies, to provide a few examples (*see* the contributions in Baumgartner *et al.* 2011). In contrast, in the policy field of global financial regulation, the kind of public attention, mobilisation and pressure that these studies identify is most difficult to achieve. As a result, change is 'managed' by a closed policy community that is likely to embark on

---

17. The World Bank, for instance, assists member countries in the design and implementation of policies that strengthen domestic financial systems and helps countries to identify risks in their systems. The Basel Committee, IOSCO and IAIS, in turn, provide specialised knowledge, by setting the standards in the field of banking supervision, securities and insurance supervision respectively.

18. On this point, *see also* Blyth (2013).

small changes whose scope and consequences it can control (*see* Botzem in this volume) and to prefer long timetables for their implementation.

Second, the club-like nature of global finance is a likely source of incrementalism in that policy communities responsible for financial regulation tend to share common mindsets and normative orientations about the proper scope, goals, and instruments of financial regulation; and they are also affected by 'cognitive locks' regarding appropriate courses of action (Blyth 2002).[19] Since these ideas set the parameters of possible and appropriate behaviour, they also constitute a major obstacle to rapid and radical policy changes, especially given the rarity of the moments in which new ideas suddenly displace old ones, leading to abrupt changes in behaviour and policy. Most of the time, policy changes take place within the parameters set by existing ideational frameworks. The 'ideational inertia' is magnified in the presence of well developed agencies and bureaucracies, as is the case in financial regulation. Under these circumstances, 'any efforts to change have to first overcome the power of habitual perceptions, emotions, and practices' (Hopf 2010: 540).

Ideational factors therefore lead to incremental change because new ideas need to be developed and accepted within a policy community. Furthermore, to win the support of 'experts', new ideas also need to be tested against empirical evidence and historical experience (*see* Baker in this volume). This is especially the case in global finance, for which technical knowledge is a key component of governance (Porter 2003). Indeed, the process of change in policy communities made up by experts relies heavily on the process of road-testing of and experimentation with new ideas in the face of empirical anomalies before old ideas are abandoned. The process of change also follows an incremental pattern because policy entrepreneurs have to establish institutional support for ideas in order to translate them into policy action (Widmaier, Blyth and Seabrooke 2007: 754). In global finance, this means that ideas have to gain an institutional presence in the regulatory bodies that drive the process of change. For instance, for the ascendance of ideas about macroprudential regulation, a key factor has been their diffusion from the Bank for International Settlements to other professional ecologies (Baker 2013; Seabrooke and Tsingou 2009). In other words, the development and acceptance of new ideas take place through a drawn-out sequential process (Blyth 2002), in which the stages of collapse and consolidation of ideas are required for an appropriate conceptualisation of change (Legro 2000). Seen from this perspective, even the alleged Bretton Woods 'moment' was not the kind of rapid and radical change that is usually portrayed. Rather, it

---

19. According to Vogel (1996: 20), these beliefs usually reflect 'actors' adherence to broad doctrine, such as economic liberalism; their predisposition toward certain functional tasks [...]; and their commitment to specific policy mechanisms'.

took place well over a decade after the momentous financial crises of the early 1930s. The delay was not just a product of the unique historical circumstances of the era. It took time for old ideas and practices to lose their legitimacy and for new ones to emerge as models for the future (Helleiner 2010: 624).

In conclusion, in this section, we have identified a number of institutional frictions that, when combined with the activity of change-agents and veto-players, help explain the dynamics of change, in this case incrementalism. The institutional frictions identified are those typical of the area of international financial regulation and may help explain the prevalence of incrementalism over the alternative, punctuated model.

By emphasising institutional constraints and frictions, we take inspiration from most of the substantive and analytical features developed by historical institutionalism. While HI has been developed in the subfield of comparative politics to explain the evolution of domestic institutions, we submit that HI has great value for the study of IPE in general and the study of the evolution of global finance in particular (*see also* Fioretos 2011a). In the following section, we explain how HI is relevant to our study and examine its potential contribution to a research agenda relating to global finance, in line with similar efforts to apply HI to explanations of IO behaviour (Moschella 2011a; Rixen, Viola and Zürn forthcoming), tax policies (Rixen 2011) and multilateral co-operation (Fioretos 2011b). We also identify the areas where we move beyond HI or redress it by mixing the insights developed in other theoretical traditions. In particular, we highlight the ways in which HI may usefully complement agent-centred approaches in the explanation of policy changes in global financial regulation.

Historical institutionalism and change in global financial governance

What is the advantage of borrowing from historical institutionalism to explain the empirical puzzle of incremental change in global financial governance? There are at least three main reasons why HI is relevant to the puzzle addressed in this study: the focus of its research agenda, its approach to empirical problems, and its engagement with questions of efficiency and legitimacy, which leads us to reflect on the normative dimension of global financial governance. All three factors helpfully complement agent-centred constructivist scholarship.

First, HI is relevant to our study because of its research agenda. Indeed, the core of HI's research agenda revolves around the question of institutional evolution over time (Pierson 2004; Pierson and Skocpol 2001; Thelen 2004; Sanders 2006). That is to say, 'the substantive profile of historical institutionalism is characterised by attention to large questions with an explicit temporal scope that concern the creation, reproduction, development, and structure of institutions over time' (Fioretos 2011b: 372). As such, the insights developed in HI can help explain the pattern of institutional evolution we observe in global finance. The understanding of institutions in HI is also relevant to our study. In contrast to more rationalist understandings, according to which institutions are exogenous co-ordination mechanisms that generate or sustain equilibria, HI conceives institutions as the legacies of political struggles that emerge from and are embedded in concrete temporal processes (Thelen 1999: 382).[20] That is, institutions emerge from particular historical conflicts and constellations (*see also* Steinmo 1993). In a more expanded version that borrows from sociological institutionalism, institutions are also viewed as a set of shared understandings that affect the way problems are perceived and solutions are sought (as in Katzenstein 1996).[21] From an HI perspective, then, institutions do more than channel policy and structure political conflict: they define preferences.

The conception of institutions that characterises HI heavily informs our analysis. Indeed, the contributions to this volume focus on a variety of institutions – formal institutions and rules (Botzem; Quaglia; Rixen), regimes (Carstensen) and supervisory principles (Baker); and the policy practices and strategies of actors (Pagliari and Young; Kjar) – which are conceived as something more substantial than mere co-ordination mechanisms among the actors involved. From our perspective, the institutions that govern global finance are the result of political struggles and temporal processes that crystallise interests as well as routines and habits. Furthermore, the institutions we study are not external to the actors that seek to change them (or to oppose change). Rather, actors act within institutions, their strategies and motives are shared by institutions, influencing the dynamics of change itself.

An additional practical contribution of HI to our study is its focus on the incremental pattern of change. HI has long been seen to have a bias towards explaining stability rather than change and for privileging structure over agency (*see* the discussion in Crouch and Farell 2004; Katznelson 2003) and indeed, HI's emphasis on path-dependence and mechanisms of reproduction (Pierson 2000a; Mahoney 2000) has led to powerful explanations of institutional stability and persistence.[22] At the risk of simplifying a much more nuanced debate, two mechanisms are usually identified in explaining institutional stability. The first is strictly connected to the distributional outcome of institutions. Since specific institutions benefit some groups more than others, those who are advantaged by the existing institution will struggle to preserve it. The second mechanism, which draws from the economic institutionalist literature (Arthur 1994; David 1985; North 1990), revolves around the notion of increasing returns (Pierson 2000a). Since, in politics, the creation of new institutions requires overcoming barriers to collective action, and is generally characterised by high start-up costs, co-ordination effects, and adaptive expectations, the introduction of new institutions

---

20. For a discussion of each of these three strands in HI *see* Hall and Taylor (1996). Other useful reviews include Lichbach and Zuckerman (2002), Immergut (1998), and Kato (1996).

21. In new institutionalism in sociology, institutions are conceived as 'shared cultural scripts', 'shared cognitions' and 'interpretive frames' of the way the world works (Meyer and Rowen 1991).

22. In the fields of American politics and comparative politics *see*, for example, Pierson (1994), Skocpol (1992), Collier and Collier (1991) and Hall and Soskice (2001); in international relations, *see* Krasner (1988) and Spruyt (1994).

will be most unlikely. In contrast, institutions that succeed in crossing these initial thresholds should be expected to have a good chance of persisting for very long periods of time (Pierson 2000b: 78).

By focusing on the mechanisms of reproduction, HI has long been criticised for not having been conducive to satisfactory explanations of institutional change.[23] However, HI is now a tradition that is able to explain change by identifying several mechanisms that undermine path-dependence processes (Pierson 2004; Thelen 1999, 2004) and by focusing more on the behaviour of political actors that help shape change (*see* Streeck and Thelen 2005; Mahoney and Thelen 2010). In particular, the causes of change have been found in the same mechanisms that ensure institutional reproduction, so that path-dependence contains elements of both continuity and structured change (Thelen 1999: 384). Institutional change is not conceived as a dichotomous variable but as a continuous interaction between continuity and change, which gives rise to an incremental pattern of change (Thelen 1999). Building on these insights, scholars working within the HI tradition have uncovered a variety of forms of incremental change that stand in opposition to exogenously driven changes. These forms include, among others, layering, conversion, drift, and displacement (Streeck and Thelen 2005; Hacker 2004; Mahoney and Thelen 2010).[24] Although incremental, the processes of change identified by HI scholars are regarded as being able to bring about profound transformations (Thelen 2003; Mahoney and Thelen 2010).[25]

The second practical contribution of HI to our work is its approach to theorising change. In particular, we share with HI the methodological approach that begins with the analysis of empirical puzzles that emerge from observed events or comparisons (Thelen 1999: 373). Indeed, most HI studies begin with a question about an empirical puzzle – be it different levels of taxation (Steinmo 1993), or vocational training regimes and party systems across countries (Thelen 2004; Collier and Collier 1991). In a similar vein, we begin with empirical puzzles that emerge from observed events, in our case, the global financial crisis and the ensuing pattern of incremental change in the reform process. Our study, like most HI, gives significant attention to historical contextualisation and temporality, the notion that the timing and sequence of events shape political trajectories by conditioning the interests of and options available to actors in contemporary reform processes (Pierson 2000a, 2004). Temporality and sequence are also key in global financial regulatory processes.[26] Indeed, global financial-governance arrangements

---

23. Bell (2011) offers a comprehensive discussion of some of these criticisms but also shows why these matter for HI less than it sometimes appears by reminding us of the importance of agency in much HI scholarship.

24. For a full discussion of these forms of incremental change *see*, for instance, Mahoney and Thelen 2010: ch. 1.

25. Other examples of small changes leading to change in policy goals include: Coleman *et al.* (1996) on agricultural policy change; Capano (2003) on Italian administrative reform; Posner (2007) on financial integration in the EU; and Moschella (2011a) on IMF surveillance.

26. On global regulation as made up of several stages, *see also* Mattli and Wood 2009 and Abbott and Snidal 2009.

are complex in terms of analytical purchase and implementation capacity. Thus, changing them requires the existence of a number of preconditions. For instance, adopting a macroprudential approach to financial regulation and supervision requires well developed analytical frameworks, expertise, and an organisational infrastructure to analyse the financial system as a whole (*see* Baker in this volume; Moschella 2011a). Likewise, the design of capital controls is influenced by the administrative capacities of different agencies, institutional and legal constraints and other country-specific factors (Ostry *et al.* 2011). The existence of the required knowledge and administrative capacities cannot be assumed; rather, they are more likely to be built over time.

In addition to sequence and temporality, another crucial insight of HI, which fits well with our case, is interaction and interdependence among different institutional subsystems. Indeed, HI conceives of institutions not only in isolation but also as embedded in a wider institutional configuration, whose pieces, which emerged at different times, 'do not necessarily fit together into a coherent, self-reinforcing, let alone functional, whole' (Thelen 1999: 382), but do clash with each other. For instance, Streeck (1997) has shown the ways in which industrial-relations institutions created problems for the stability of other institutions, especially vocational education and social-welfare institutions.

This insight also applies to the area of global finance, where different sectors (banking, securities, insurance) are regulated differently at the global level. Variations affect: (1) the actors involved, from international financial institutions to international groupings of regulators and supervisors; (2) the degree of formal institutional co-operation, from formal treaties to voluntary standards; and (3) the degree of private-sector authority as compared to the public sector (Cutler *et al.* 1999; Graz and Nölke 2008). The governance of global finance is therefore characterised by multiple but closely related regulatory regimes, similar to what Keohane and Victor (2011) call 'regime complexes'. As a result, as in the interdependence among different institutional subsystems identified by HI scholars, change in one area of governance may have implications for another area. Furthermore, changes in the broader institutional configuration (for instance, in terms of new ideas about how to govern financial markets) may well have repercussions on the trajectory of change in individual governance regimes.

Finally, HI contains important insights that can get us to reflect critically on questions of efficiency and legitimacy in global financial governance. Having expressly challenged the functionalist view of institutional development, according to which 'outcome X (an institution, policy, or organisation, for instance) exists because it serves function Y' (Pierson 2000c: 476), one of the key insights of HI scholarship is that the process of adaptation of existing institutions is inefficient because actors work within constraints that are defined by the past. Stickiness, path-dependence and vested interests are the key factors here. A famous instance is that of the QWERTY keyboard, which David (1985) argued illustrated the ways in which a technology that gains an initial advantage over alternatives prevails over time, despite the greater efficiency of alternative technologies. Thus, the outcome is that patterns of adaptation that would ensure greater collective efficiency often do not occur, that positions of privilege and divisions of labour regularly persist though relative balances of power shift, and that institutions frequently outlive their original rationale (Fioretos 2011b: 376).

These insights are particularly crucial for the process of change in global financial governance: as anticipated by HI, interest groups often see great benefits in reproducing existing arrangements rather than changing them; and global financial governance mechanisms may remain little altered despite a new balance of power that in principle can favour emerging markets. In short, HI alerts scholars interested in the politics of global financial regulation to the strength of the forces that oppose change and of the implications of such conservatism for the legitimacy of the global financial system.

In conclusion, HI offers valuable substantive insights and analytical tools to theorise change in global finance and explain why the financial system is more likely to evolve through incremental rather than radical reforms. This is not to suggest that the insights developed within HI scholarship can be uncritically applied to the area of global financial regulation or that HI simply holds the key to the explanation of change in global financial regulation. More narrowly, what we want to suggest is that HI offers the missing element for explanations of change in IPE. Indeed, as previously discussed, the most important and recent studies of policy change in IPE have emphasised the role of actors and their interpretation of reality to account for institutional variation after moments of uncertainty, including wars and economic crises (Widmaier, Blyth and Seabrooke 2007). These studies certainly deserve credit, including for demonstrating the crucial importance of actors and their ideas in an academic field that has long been dominated by materialist explanations. Nevertheless, constructivist accounts of the process of change in the international economy have somehow neglected some of the key institutional factors that interact with agency to bring about change (also Bell 2011). By focusing on this neglected dimension, which stands at the core of HI scholarship, we aim to redress the balance between agency and the institutions within which agents operate. This effort, we submit, helps us provide a thorough explanation of processes of change. Whereas a focus on actors' ideas may well answer the question of *why* change is initiated, the focus on institutional frictions allows us to focus on answering the question of *how* change takes place: whether punctuations or incrementalism prevails. In what follows, we provide a brief overview of how the book elaborates upon these issues and offer a short presentation of our empirical material.

Plan of the book

Incrementalism is a mode of policy change that is well known and often studied in the comparative politics and comparative public policy literature. In the IPE literature on the politics of financial regulation, however, incrementalism is known but under-researched. The book aims to fill this gap by testing and extending the application of insights primarily developed for explaining processes of change at the domestic level. Although the study of IPE will certainly be enriched by the analytical toolkit developed in other academic subfields, it will, we submit, be a two-way process. That is to say, by identifying the specific conditions that make financial regulation incremental, our research project is also able to speak to the broad community of scholars interested in patterns of policy change, providing detailed cases that can open up opportunities for further cross-issue comparative research. The remainder of this chapter provides a preview of the contributions and outlines how the different cases shed light on why incremental change has prevailed in the reform process that followed the global financial crisis. The volume is organised in two parts: the first focuses more on the evolution and reform of the regulatory framework post-crisis while the second is explicit in its emphasis on the actors at the centre of these processes.

The first empirical case is provided by Andrew Baker, who focuses on the development of macroprudential ideas and how this significant ideational change has the potential to bring about more radical policy reform over time. Drawing on policy material and personal interviews pre- and post-crisis, Baker provides an analysis that highlights the dynamics of change across the transnational and domestic levels and explains how ideational coalitions can work to develop ideas into policy, building institutional support and know-how.

Attention then turns to the specifics of the reformed and reforming regulatory landscape. Lucia Quaglia surveys the state of play in financial-services governance in the European Union and examines how the regulation and legislation enacted following the crisis measure up to intentions and the pre-crisis status quo. In her analysis, Quaglia finds institutional innovation and policy impetus but also enduring resistance both by states and private financial actors. As such, across governance levels, she observes that a significant number of veto-players have placed constraints on more comprehensive reform. At the same time, she reminds us that such incrementalism should not be seen as maintenance of the status quo *per se*, as European financial governance has a history of proceeding in small steps.

Moving on to the content of regulatory reform, Martin Carstensen offers an analysis of the nascent regime for bank resolution. By focusing on an area of regulatory concern that was expressly highlighted by the crisis, Carstensen follows the regulatory debate and traces the genealogy of reform ideas and the ideational struggles over how the principle of resolution regimes is to be translated into regulatory mechanics. Carstensen finds that, although resolution as a principle is not fundamentally threatening to pre-crisis global finance, policy implementation can alter how financial crises are funded. As such, Carstensen offers a case where thinking through regulatory dynamics in a manner that seemingly represents little or only incremental change to the operation of finance can lead to significant changes for the governance of finance in the long-run.

The first part closes with a contribution by Thomas Rixen, who examines regulatory reform in relation to offshore financial centres and shadow banking. Rixen focuses on two interlinked cases that attracted a great deal of political attention in the aftermath of the crisis, though assessments of their significance as factors in the crisis remained disputed. Overviewing reforms in these areas, and contrasting these reforms to original intentions, Rixen finds that change can be characterised as mostly symbolic. In explaining this outcome, Rixen points to enduring competitiveness interests of key states and, in particular, their conception of jurisdictional competition. Aside from stressing the importance of the interstate dimension in explaining modest change, Rixen also provides a case where reform fails to keep pace with official pronouncements when those are actually detached from the issues perceived to be at the core of the reform process.

This volume then proceeds with three chapters more explicitly focused on the actors at the centre of the reform. Firstly, Stefano Pagliari and Kevin Young examine how financial institutions, seeing their privileged position in the regulatory framework threatened, have adapted their strategies and formed new advocacy coalitions, thus acting as veto-players in reform. By tying their interests and preferences to the needs of the non-financial private sector, financial institutions have blocked more radical change. Empirically, Pagliari and Young survey the US regulatory and legislative debates about derivatives and, by analysing responses by financial and corporate financial actors, show that adaptability and mobilisation can slow the pace and weaken the content of reform, accounting for incrementalism even in the face of public scrutiny and implementation capacity.

The next chapter, by Sebastian Botzem, shifts attention to the role of experts after the financial crisis, specifically analysing the enduring authority of the IASB. Botzem provides an overview of the key controversies and changes in global accountancy and shows that the IASB chose to undertake institutional reform and modestly change its governance structure and rule-setting procedures, while exhibiting flexible crisis-management in adjusting the content of rules (fair-value accounting) in non-normal times. Botzem shows that veto-players can follow particular tactics to block extensive change. By acting strategically during the crisis, and through the presentation of pre-crisis institutional reform decisions as post-crisis governance overhaul, the IASB managed the pace and content of change and avoided a possible crisis of expertise credibility, maintaining control of the ideational agenda.

The final case moves the focus to the domestic level and housing finance. Examining the US and Danish systems pre- and post-crisis, Iver Kjar explains how actors can use their institutional position at the domestic level to oppose change. Specifically, Kjar takes an everyday IPE approach to highlight the importance of societal interests in lending legitimacy to existing and reforming governance frameworks. Kjar explains that the political power of home-owners as an electoral force has vetoed radical change in housing finance in two seemingly very different financial systems, despite the central role of housing at the onset of the financial crisis. When backed by such societal concerns, the financial institutions that have long benefited from these arrangements are able to maintain a privileged position and withstand calls for more substantial change.

References

Abbott, K. W. and Snidal, D. (2000) 'Hard and soft law in international governance', *International Organization*, 54(3): 421–56.

— (2009) 'The governance triangle: regulatory standards institutions and the shadow of the state', in Mattli, W. and Woods, N. (eds), *The Politics of Global Regulation*, Princeton: Princeton University Press, 44–88.

Abdelal, R. (2007) *Capital Rules: The construction of global finance*, Cambridge, MA: Harvard University Press.

Andrews, D. M. (1994) 'Capital mobility and state autonomy: toward a structural theory of international monetary relations', *International Studies Quarterly*, 38(2): 193–218.

Arthur, B. (1994) *Increasing Returns and Path Dependence in the Economy*, Ann Arbor: University of Michigan Press.

Baker, A. (2006) *The Group of Seven: Finance ministries, central banks and global financial governance*, London: Routledge.

— (2013) 'The new political economy of the macroprudential ideational shift', *New Political Economy* 18(1):112-39.

Bates, R. H. (2000) 'The analytic narrative project', *American Political Science Review*, 94: 696–702.

Baumgartner, F. R., Brouard, S., Green-Pedersen, C., Jones, B. D. and Walgrave, S. (2011) 'The dynamics of policy change in comparative perspective', *Comparative Political Studies*, 44(8): 947–1119.

Baumgartner, F. R., Foucault, M., and Francois, A. (2006) 'Punctuated equilibrium and French budgeting processes', *Journal of European Public Policy*, 13(7): 1082–99.

Baumgartner, F. R. and Jones, B. D. (1993) *Agendas and Instability in American Politics*, Chicago: University of Chicago Press.

— (1991) 'Agenda dynamics and policy subsystems', *Journal of Politics*, 53(4): 1044–75.

Béland, D. and Cox, R. H., (eds) (2011) *Ideas and Politics in Social Science Research*, Oxford: Oxford University Press.

Bell, S. (2011) 'Do we really need a new "constructivist institutionalism" to explain institutional change?', *British Journal of Political Science*, 41: 883–906.

— (2012) 'The power of ideas: the ideational shaping of the structural power of business', *International Studies Quarterly* 56(4): 661-673.

Best, J. (2004) 'Hollowing out Keynesian norms: how the search for a technical fix undermined the Bretton Woods regime', *Review of International Studies*, 30: 383–404.

Blyth, M. (2002) *Great Transformations: Economic ideas and institutional change in the twentieth century*, Cambridge: Cambridge University Press.

— (2003) 'The political power of financial ideas. Transparency, risk, and distribution in global finance', in Kirshner, J. (ed.) *Monetary Orders: Ambiguous economics, ubiquitous politics*, Ithaca: Cornell University Press.

—   (2007) 'Powering, puzzling, or persuading? The mechanisms of building institutional orders', *International Studies Quarterly* 51(4): 761–77.

—   (2013) 'Paradox and change: policy paradigms in two moments of crisis', *Governance: An International Journal of Policy, Administration and Institutions* 26(2):197-215.

Blyth, M., Hodgson, L., Lewis, O. and Steinmo, S. (2011) 'Introduction', Special Issue on the Evolution of Institutions, *Journal of Institutional Economics* 7(3): 299–315.

Breunig, C. and Koski, C. (2006) 'Punctuated equilibria and budgets in the American states', *Policy Studies Journal* 34(3): 363–79.

Botzem, S. (2012) *The Politics of Accounting Regulation. Organizing transnational standard setting in financial reporting*, Cheltenham/Northampton, MA: Edward Elgar.

Busch, A. (2009) *Banking Regulation and Globalization*, Oxford: Oxford University Press.

Büthe, T. and Mattli, W. (2011) *The New Global Rulers: The privatization of regulation in the world economy*, Princeton: Princeton University Press.

Capano, G. (2003) 'Administrative traditions and policy change: when policy paradigms matter, the case of Italian administrative reform during the 1990s', *Public Administration* 81(4): 781–801.

—   (2009) 'Understanding policy change as an epistemological and theoretical problem', *Journal of Comparative Policy Analysis: Research and Practice* 11(1): 7–31.

Capano, G. and Howlett, M. (2009) 'Introduction. The multidimensional world of policy dynamics', in Capano, G. and Howlett, M. (eds) *European and North American Policy Change. Drivers and dynamics*, London: Routledge, 1–12.

Carmassi, J., Gros, D. and Micossi, S. (2009) 'The global financial crisis: causes and cures', *Journal of Common Market Studies*, 47(5): 977–96.

Cashore, B. and Howlett, M. (2007) 'Punctuating which equilibrium? Understanding thermostatic policy dynamics in Pacific Northwest forestry', *American Journal of Political Science*, 51(3): 532–51.

Cerny, P. G. (1994) 'The dynamics of financial globalization: technology, market structure, and policy response', *Policy Sciences*, 27(4): 319–42.

Chwieroth, J. M. (2010) 'How do crises lead to change? Liberalizing capital controls in the early years of new order Indonesia', *World Politics* 62(3): 496–527.

Coleman, W. D. (1996) *Financial Services, Globalisation and Domestic Policy Change*, New York: St Martin's Press.

Coleman, W. D., Skogstad, G. D. and Atkinson, M. (1996) 'Paradigm shifts and policy networks: cumulative change in agriculture', *Journal of Public Policy*, 16(3): 273–302.

Collier, R. B. and Collier, D. (1991) *Shaping the Political Arena: Critical junctures, the labor movement and regime dynamics in Latin America*, Princeton: Princeton University Press.

Crouch, C. and Farrell, H. (2004) 'Breaking the path of institutional development? Alternatives to the new determinism in political economy', *Rationality and Society*, 16(1): 5–43.

Cutler, C. A., Haufler, V. and Porter, T. (eds) (1999) *Private Authority and International Affairs*, Albany: State University of New York Press.

David, P. (1985) 'Clio and the economics of QWERTY', *American Economic Review*, 75: 332–7.

de Laroisière, J. (2009) *The High Level Group on Financial Supervision in the EU*, Brussels, February 25.

Drezner, D. W. (2007) *All Politics Is Global: Explaining international regulatory regimes*, Princeton: Princeton University Press.

Farrell, H. and Newman, A. L. (2010) 'Making global markets: historical institutionalism in international political economy', *Review of International Political Economy*, 17(4): 609–38.

Ferejohn, J. (1991) 'Rationality and interpretation: parliamentary elections in early Stuart England', in Monroe, K. (ed.) *The Economic Approach to Politics*, New York: Harper-Collins, 279–305.

Fioretos, O. (2011a) *Creative Reconstructions: Multilateralism and European varieties of capitalism after 1950*, Ithaca: Cornell University Press.

— (2011b) 'Historical institutionalism in international relations', *International Organization*, 65(2): 367–99.

Gill, S. (1990) *American Hegemony and the Trilateral Commission*, Cambridge: Cambridge University Press.

Green-Pedersen, C. (2004) 'The dependent variable problem within the study of welfare state retrenchment: defining the problem and looking for solutions', *Journal of Comparative Policy Analysis: Research and Practice*, 6(1): 3–14.

Gorton, G. B. (2008) *The Panic of 2007*, NBER Working Paper 14358 (September): Cambridge, MA: National Bureau of Economic Research.

Gourevitch, P. (1999) 'The governance problem in International Relations', in Lake, D. and Powell, R. (eds), *Strategic Choice and International Relations*, Princeton, NJ: Princeton University Press, 137–64.

Grabel, I. (2003) 'Ideology, power, and the rise of independent monetary institutions', in Kirshner, J. (ed.) *Monetary Orders: Ambiguous economics, ubiquitous politics*, Ithaca: Cornell University Press, 25–53.

Graz, J. C. and Nölke, A. (2008) *Transnational Private Governance and Its Limits*, London: Routledge.

Hacker, J. S. (2004) 'Privatizing risk without privatizing the welfare state: the hidden politics of social policy retrenchment in the United States', *American Political Science Review*, 98(2): 243–60.

Haldane, A. G. (2012) 'The dog and the frisbee', speech given at the Federal Reserve Bank of Kansas City's 36th economic policy symposium, 'The Changing Policy Landscape', Jackson Hole, Wyoming, 31 August.

Hall, P. A. (1993) 'Policy paradigms, social learning, and the state: the case of economic policymaking in Britain', *Comparative Politics*, 25(3): 275–96.

— (2010) 'Historical institutionalism in rationalist and sociological perspective', in Mahoney, J. and Thelen, K. (eds) *Explaining Institutional Change: Ambiguity, agency and power*, Cambridge: Cambridge University Press, 204–23.

Hall, P. A. and Soskice, D. (eds) (2001) *Varieties of Capitalism: The institutional foundations of comparative advantage*, Oxford: Oxford University Press.

Hall, P. A. and Taylor, R. C. R. (1996) 'Political science and the three new institutionalisms', *Political Studies*, 44(4): 936–57.

Hay, C. (1996) 'Narrating crisis: the discursive construction of the "winter of discontent"', *Sociology*, 30(2): 253–77.

Haydu, J. (1998) 'Making use of the past: time periods as cases to compare and as sequences of problem solving', *American Journal of Sociology*, 104(2): 339–71.

Heclo, H. (1974) *Modern Social Politics in Britain and Sweden*, New Haven: Yale University Press.

Helleiner, E. (2010) 'A Bretton Woods moment? The 2007–08 financial crisis and the future of Bretton Woods', *International Affairs*, 86(3): 619–36.

Helleiner, E. and Pagliari, S. (2009) 'Crisis and the reform of international financial regulation', in Helleiner, E., Pagliari, S. and Zimmermann, H. (eds) *Global Finance in Crisis: The politics of international regulatory change*, London: Routledge, 1–18.

— (2011) 'The end of an era in international financial regulation? A postcrisis research agenda', *International Organization,* 65(3): 169–200.

Helleiner, E., Pagliari, S. and Zimmermann, H. (eds) (2009) *Global Finance in Crisis: The politics of international regulatory change*, London: Routledge.

Hopf, T. (2010) 'The logic of habit in International Relations', *European Journal of International Relations*, 16(4): 539–61.

Howlett, M. (2009) 'Process sequencing policy dynamics: beyond homeostasis and path dependency', *Journal of Public Policy*, 29(3): 241–62.

Howlett, M. and Cashore, B. (2009) 'The dependent variable problem in the study of policy change: understanding policy change as a methodological problem', *Journal of Comparative Policy Analysis: Research and Practice*, 11(1): 33–46.

Howlett, M. and Migone, A. (2011) 'Charles Lindblom is alive and well and living in punctuated equilibrium land', *Policy and Society*, 30: 53–62.

IMF (2009) *Initial Lessons of the Crisis*, Washington, DC: International Monetary Fund.

Immergut, E. M. (1998) 'The theoretical core of the new institutionalism', *Political Science*, 26(1): 5–34.

Jones, B. D. and Baumgartner, F. R. (2005) *The Politics of Attention: How government prioritizes problems*, Chicago: University of Chicago Press.

Jones, B. D., Baumgartner, F. R., Breunig, C., Wlezien, C., Soroka, S., Foucault, M., Francois, A., Green-Pedersen, C., Koski, C., John, P., Mortensen, P. B., Varone, F. and Walgrave, S. (2009) 'A general empirical law of public budgets: a comparative analysis', *American Journal of Political Science*, 53(4): 855–73.

John, P. and Margetts, H. (2003) 'Policy punctuations in the UK', *Public Administration*, 81(3): 411–32.

Kapstein, E. B. (1989) 'Resolving the regulator's dilemma: international coordination of banking regulation', *International Organization*, 43(2): 323–47.

—— (1994) *Governing the Global Economy: International finance and the state*, Cambridge MA: Harvard University Press.

—— (1992) 'Between power and purpose: central bankers and the politics of regulatory convergence', *International Organization*, 46(1): 265–87.

Kato, J. (1996) 'Review article: institutions and rationality in politics: three varieties of neo-institutionalists', *British Journal of Political Science*, 26: 553–82.

Katznelson, I. (2003) 'Periodization and preferences: reflections on purposive action in comparative historical social science', in Mahoney, J., and Rueschmeyer, D. (eds) *Comparative Historical Analysis in the Social Sciences*, Cambridge: Cambridge University Press, 270–301.

Katzenstein, P. J. (1996) *Cultural Norms and National Security: Police and military in postwar Japan*, Ithaca NY: Cornell University Press.

Kay, A. (2007) 'Tense layering and synthetic policy paradigms: the politics of health insurance in Australia', *Australian Journal of Political Science*, 42(4): 579–91.

Keohane, R. O. and Victor, D. G. (2011) 'The regime complex for climate change', *Perspectives on Politics*, 9(1): 7–23.

Krasner, S. D. (1984) 'Approaches to the state: alternative conceptions and historical dynamics', *Comparative Politics*, 16(2): 223–46.

—— (1988) 'Sovereignty: an institutional perspective', Comparative Political Studies, 21(1): 66–94.

Lake, D. (1999) 'Global governance: a relational contracting approach', in Prakash, A. and Hart, J. A. (eds) *Globalization and Governance*, London and New York: Routledge, 31–53.

Lawson, G. (2006) 'The promise of historical sociology in international relations', *International Studies Review*, 8: 397–423.

Legro, J. W. (2000) 'The transformation of policy ideas', *American Journal of Political Science*, 44(3): 419–32.

Lindblom, C. E. (1959) 'The science of "muddling through" ', *Public Administration Review*, 19: 79–88.

Lichbach, M. I. and Zuckerman, A. S. (eds) (2002) *Comparative Politics: Rationality, culture and structure*, Cambridge: Cambridge University Press.

Lundquist, L. (1980) *The Hare and the Tortoise: Clean air policies in United States and Sweden*, Ann Arbor: University of Michigan Press.

Mahoney, J. (2000) 'Path dependence in historical sociology', *Theory and Society*, 29(4): 507–48.

Mahoney, J. and Thelen, K. (2010) 'A theory of gradual institutional change', in Mahoney, J. and Thelen, K. (eds), *Explaining Institutional Change: Ambiguity, agency, and power*, Cambridge: Cambridge University Press, 1–37.

—— (2010) *Explaining Institutional Change: Ambiguity, agency, and power*, Cambridge: Cambridge University Press.

Mattli, W. and Woods, N. (eds) (2009) *The Politics of Global Regulation*, Princeton: Princeton University Press.

Meyer, J. and Rowan, B. (1991) 'Institutionalized organizations: formal structures as myth and ceremony', *American Journal of Sociology*, 83: 340–63.

Moran, M. (1990) *The Politics of the Financial Services Revolution. The USA, UK and Japan*, Basingstoke: Palgrave Macmillan.

Mortensen, P. (2005) 'Policy punctuations in Danish local budgeting', *Public Administration*, 83(4): 931–59.

Moschella, M. (2010) *Governing Risk: The IMF and global financial crises*, Basingstoke: Palgrave Macmillan.

—— (2011a) 'Lagged learning and the response to equilibrium shock. The global financial crisis and IMF surveillance', *Journal of Public Policy*, 31(2): 1–21.

—— (2011b) 'Searching for a fix for international financial markets: the European Union and domestic political-economy changes', *Journal of Contemporary Economic Studies*, 19(1): 97–112.

Mügge, D. (2006) 'Reordering the marketplace: competition politics in European finance', *Journal of Common Market Studies*, 44(5): 991–1022.

North, D. C. (1990) *Institutions, Institutional Change and Economic Performance*, Cambridge: Cambridge University Press.

Oatley, T. and Nabors, R. (1998) 'Redistributive cooperation: market failure, wealth transfers and the Basle Accord', *International Organization*, 52(1): 35–54.

Obstfeld, M. and Rogoff, K. (2009) *Global Imbalances and the Financial Crisis: Products of Common Causes*. Paper delivered at Federal Reserve Bank of San Francisco Asia Economic Policy Conference, October 18–20. http://elsa.berkeley.edu/~obstfeld/santabarbara.pdf. Accessed 11 February 2013.

Ostry, J. D., Ghosh, A. R., Habermeier, K., Laeven, L., Chamon, M., Qureshi, M. S. and Kokenyne, A. (2011) 'Managing capital inflows: what tools to use?', *IMF Staff Discussion Note SDN/11/06* April 5.

Parker, G. and Barber, T. (2008) 'European call for Bretton Woods II', *Financial Times*, 16 October.

Pierson, P. (1994) *Dismantling the Welfare State: Reagan, Thatcher and the politics of retrenchment*, Cambridge: Cambridge University Press.

—— (2000a) 'Increasing returns, path dependence, and the study of politics', *American Political Science Review*, 94(2): 251–67.

—— (2000b) 'Not just what, but when: timing and sequence in political process', *Studies in American Political Development*, 14(1): 72–92.

—   (2000c) 'The limits of design: explaining institutional origins and change', *Governance*, 13(4): 475–99.

—   (2004) *Politics in Time: History, institutions, and social analysis*, Princeton: Princeton University Press.

Pierson, P. and Skocpol, T. (2001) 'Historical institutionalism in contemporary political science', in Katznelson, I. and Milner, H. V. (eds) *Political Science: State of the Discipline*, New York: Norton, 693–721.

Porter, T. (2003) 'Technical collaboration and political conflict in the emerging regime for international financial regulation', *Review of International Political Economy*, 10(3): 520–51.

—   (2005) *Globalization and Finance*, Cambridge: Polity.

Porter, A., Winnett, R. and Harnden, T. (2009) 'Gordon Brown, G20 summit: Gordon Brown announces "new world order" ', *Daily Telegraph*, 3 April.

Posner, E. (2007) 'Financial transformation in the European Union', in McNamara, K. and Meunier, S. (eds) *Making History: European integration and institutional change at fifty*, Oxford: Oxford University Press, 139–56.

—   (2009) 'Is a European approach to financial regulation emerging from the crisis?', in Helleiner, E., Pagliari, S. and Zimmermann, H. (eds) *Global Finance in Crisis*, London: Routledge, 108–20.

Quaglia, L. (2010) *Governing Financial Services in the European Union*, London: Routledge.

—   (2012) 'The "old" and "new" politics of financial services regulation in the European Union', *New Political Economy* 17(4): 515-535.

Raustalia, K. (1997) 'Domestic institutions and international regulatory cooperation: comparative responses to the convention on biological diversity', *World Politics*, 49(4): 482–509.

Rixen, T. (2011) 'From double tax avoidance to tax competition: explaining the institutional trajectory of international tax governance', *Review of International Political Economy*, 18(2):197–227.

Rixen, T., Viola, L. and Zürn, M. (eds) (forthcoming), *Historical Institutionalism and International Relations*.

Rothmayr Allison, C. and Saint-Martin, D. (2011) 'Half a century of "muddling": are we there yet?', *Policy and Society*, 30: 1–8.

Sanders, E. (2006) 'Historical institutionalism', in Rhodes, R. A. W., Binder, S. A. and Rockman, B. A. (eds) *The Oxford Handbook of Political Institutions*, New York: Oxford University Press, 39–55.

Scharpf, F. W. (2000) 'Institutions in comparative policy research', *Comparative Political Studies*, 33(6/7): 762–90.

Schmidt, V. A. (2009) 'Putting the political back in political economy by bringing the state back in yet again', *World Politics*, 61(3): 516–546.

Seabrooke, L. (2006) *The Social Sources of Financial Power: Domestic legitimacy and international financial orders*, Ithaca, NY: Cornell University Press.

Seabrooke, L. and Tsingou, E. (2009) *Revolving Doors and Linked Ecologies In The World Economy: Policy locations and the practice of international financial reform*, CSGR Working Paper 260/2009 available at http://

www2.warwick.ac.uk/fac/soc/csgr/research/workingpapers/2009/26009. pdf. Accessed 11 February 2013.

Sharman, J. C. (2006) *Havens in a Storm: The struggle for global tax regulation*, Ithaca: Cornell University Press.

Simmons, B. A. (2001) 'The international politics of harmonization: the case of capital market regulation', *International Organization*, 55(3): 589–620.

Simmons, B. A. and Elkins, Z. (2004) 'The globalization of liberalization: policy diffusion in the international political economy', *American Political Science Review*, 98: 171–89.

Singer, D. A. (2007) *Regulating Capital: Setting standards for the international financial system*, Ithaca: Cornell University Press.

— (2009) 'Uncertain leadership: the US regulatory response to the global financial crisis', in Helleiner, E., Pagliari, S. and Zimmermann, H. (eds) *Global Finance in Crisis: The politics of international regulatory change*, London: Routledge, 93–107.

Skocpol, T. (1992) *Protecting Soldiers and Mothers: The political origins of social policy in the United States*, Cambridge: Belknap Press of Harvard University Press.

Spruyt, H. (1994) *The Sovereign State and Its Competitors*, Princeton: Princeton University Press.

Steinmo, S. (1993) *Taxation and Democracy: Swedish, British and American approaches to financing the modern state*, New Haven, CT: Yale University Press.

Steinmo, S., Thelen, K. and Longstreth, F. (eds) (1992) *Structuring Politics: Historical institutionalism in comparative analysis*, Cambridge: Cambridge University Press.

Strange, S. (1988) *States and Markets*, London: Pinter Publishers.

Streeck, W. (1997) 'German capitalism: does it exist? Can it survive?', in Crouch, C. and Streeck, W. (eds) *Political Economy of Modern Capitalism: Mapping convergence and diversity*, Thousand Oaks, CA: Sage, 33–54.

Streeck, W. and Thelen, K. (eds) (2005) *Beyond Continuity: Institutional change in advanced political economies*, Oxford: Oxford University Press.

Thelen, K. (1999) 'Historical institutionalism and comparative politics', *Annual Review of Political Science* 2: 369–404.

— (2003) 'How institutions evolve: insights from comparative historical analysis', in Mahoney, J. and Rueschemeyer, D. (eds) *Comparative Historical Analysis in the Social Sciences*, Cambridge: Cambridge University Press, 208–40.

— (2004) *How Institutions Evolve: The political economy of skills in Germany, Britain, the United States, and Japan*, Cambridge: Cambridge University Press.

True, J., Jones, B. and Baumgartner, F. (2007) 'Punctuated equilibrium theory: explaining stability and change in policymaking', in Sabatier, P. (ed.) *Theories of the Policy Process*, 2nd edition, Boulder, CO: Westview True Press, 155–188.

Truman, E. M. (2009) 'The global financial crisis: lessons learned and challenges for developing countries' (June). http://www.piie.com/publications/papers/paper.cfm?ResearchID=1240. Accessed 8 February 2013.

Tsebelis, G. (2000) 'Veto players and institutional analysis', *Governance: An International Journal of Policy, Administration and Institutions*, 4: 441–74.

Tsingou, E. (2008) 'Transnational private governance and the Basel process: banking regulation, private interests and Basel II', in Graz, J. C. and Nölke, A. (eds) *Transnational Private Governance and its Limits*, London: Routledge, 58–68.

— (2009) 'Regulatory reactions to the global credit crisis: analyzing a policy community under stress', in Helleiner, E., Pagliari, S. and Zimmermann, H. (eds) *Global Finance in Crisis: The politics of international regulatory change*, London: Routledge, 21–36.

Underhill, G. R. D. (1995) 'Keeping governments out of politics: transnational securities markets, regulatory co-operation and political legitimacy', *Review of International Studies* 21 (3): 251–78.

— (1997) 'Private markets and public responsibility in a global system: conflict and cooperation in transnational banking and securities regulation', in Underhill, G. R. D. (ed.) *The New World Order in International Finance*, London: Macmillan, 17–49.

Vogel, S. K. (1996) *Freer Markets, More Rules: Regulatory reform in advanced industrial countries*, Ithaca, NY: Cornell University Press.

Walter, A. (2008) *Governing Finance: East Asia's adoption of international standards*, Ithaca: Cornell University Press.

— (2009) 'Chinese attitudes towards global financial regulatory co-operation: revisionist or status quo?', in Helleiner, E., Pagliari, S. and Zimmermann, H. (eds) *Global Finance in Crisis: The politics of international regulatory change*, London: Routledge, 153–169.

Widmaier, W. W., Blyth, M. and Seabrooke, L. (2007) 'Exogenous shocks or endogenous constructions? The meanings of wars and crises', *International Studies Quarterly*, 51(4): 747–59.

Wood, D. R. (2005) *Governing Global Banking: The Basel Committee and the politics of financial globalisation*, Aldershot, UK: Ashgate.

Zimmermann, H. (2009) 'Varieties of global financial governance? British and German approaches to financial market regulation', in Helleiner, E., Pagliari, S. and Zimmermann, H. (eds) *Global Finance in Crisis*, London: Routledge, 121–36.

chapter two | when new ideas meet existing institutions: why macroprudential regulatory change is a gradual process

Andrew Baker

Introduction

How does ideational change lead to and translate into institutional change? Constructivist scholarship has been very good at identifying how ideational change in periods of crisis can produce institutional transformations (Blyth 2002; Hay 2004; Schmidt 2010; Widmaier, Blyth and Seabrooke 2007). In pointing out that economic ideas can be regarded as prior in accounts of institutional change, constructivist scholarship challenged many of the assumptions of rationalist political science (Blyth 2002). However, constructivism has been less good at examining how ideational change translates into institutional change and how that process is itself mediated by an existing institutional environment (Bell 2011), giving rise to different dynamics of change (*see* Moshella and Tsingou's introductory chapter in this volume). This chapter suggests that the rise to prominence of macroprudential ideas in the field of financial regulation provides a good live laboratory for examining some of these issues and considering how ideational change translates into institutional change.

Macroprudential ideas rose to prominence in a period of little over six months in international regulatory networks and with central banks, following the financial crash of 2008. They moved from their previously marginalised position to the very centre of the policy agenda and have become the principal regulatory ideational frame to emerge from the financial crash. Macroprudential regulation (MPR) is a system-wide, top-down approach to regulation and financial stability that seeks to 'curb the credit cycle' through regulatory interventions that impose constraints on private institutions. The thinking behind macroprudential regulation contrasts quite starkly with the pre-crash, bottom-up approach of exclusively microprudential regulation, based on simplified versions of efficient-market theories. In particular, it provides a rationale and systematic intellectual case for a far more interventionist stance by regulators. In this respect, the move towards macroprudential regulation is a significant intellectual shift but one that has not been translated into major policy innovations or a radically different regulatory regime. Rapid and quite radical intellectual change is yet to be accompanied by significant institutional and policy change. In its contribution to this volume's explanations of incrementalism in the post-crisis financial reform process, this chapter sets out to examine the reasons for this and to identify why macroprudential regulatory change is proceeding only slowly, seemingly following an incremental and gradual dynamic.

What I propose in this chapter is similar to Stephen Bell's recent call to achieve an appropriate synthesis between modern constructivism and agent-centred historical institutionalism (Bell 2011) but with a different emphasis. While I agree with Bell that the achievement of some sort of synthesis between constructivist approaches and agent-sensitive historical institutionalism is desirable, my concerns are somewhat different from his; Bell focuses on how institutions behave and in unearthing the dynamics of how they change. My interest and focus in this chapter is on ideational change as a significant social and political phenomenon in its own right, one that has significant political, institutional and regulatory implications. Economic ideas as systems of thought and policy programmes have a capacity to transform institutional and social relationships. Understanding how, why and in what circumstances this happens requires that we examine how new ideas interact with existing institutional settings and interest-based politics as configured by these institutional settings.

In this respect, the regulation of financial markets and banking systems requires practitioners to have views about how financial markets function, what characteristics they display and even normative beliefs about the social worth and value of market activities. Modern financial systems are complex interconnected systems and designing appropriate regulatory practice requires regulators and policy-makers to have mental maps of and certain ideas about how these systems operate. This includes regulators taking positions on the efficiency and effectiveness of these systems and the legitimate scope of their own role in relation to those systems. The ideas that policy-makers have about the systems and entities they are supposed to be regulating are therefore integral to informing and defining the scope of their regulatory responses. However, new or changing ideas and policy programmes do not appear on a blank canvas but rather interact with existing institutional contexts. By focusing on the emerging macroprudential regulatory regime, the aim here is to illuminate how macroprudential ideas are subject to a process of institutional mediation, interaction, absorption and contestation, which affects the content of macroprudential policy programmes and regulatory practice. These interactions will ultimately determine the character of any post-financial-crash regulatory transformation; this chapter seeks to identify patterns in these interactions and what they are likely to mean for the significance of the macroprudential ideational shift in regulatory beliefs (Baker 2013a).

In the next section of the chapter, I make the case for an ideational-institutionalist synthesis. The third section of the chapter introduces macroprudential ideas and charts the process through which they rose to prominence after 2008. The fourth section examines how macroprudential ideas constitute an incomplete and evolving frame and shows that macroprudential knowledge-development is a protracted process. Finally, the interactions between change-agents and veto-players over questions of macroprudential policy-development are placed in an institutional context, with a particular focus on the Basel III agreement. It is argued that macroprudential policy-development is assuming many of the characteristics of a process historical institutionalists refer to as 'layering', which is lengthening the time taken to develop macroprudential policy and also diluting its substantive content in the short term.

An ideational-institutionalist synthesis

The constructivist case, particularly agency-based economic constructivism, identifies ideational change as a driver for institutional change. Constructivist scholarship has shown that during periods of financial crisis and economic distress, existing economic assumptions and ideas can be challenged by a rival series of causal claims about how the economy actually functions and the appropriate role of regulation and public policy (Widmaier, Blyth and Seabrooke 2007; Blyth 2002). When material interest and probability calculations become difficult, due to the uncertainty engendered by economic and financial distress, agents have recourse to economic ideas to enable them to navigate the economic uncertainty facing them, by providing an interpretative frame that helps them to understand their relationship to unfolding economic problems. Consequently, Mark Blyth claims that economic ideas perform a number of discrete sequential roles during periods of crisis, including: diagnosis and interpretation; making coalition-building and collective action possible; allocating blame and discrediting existing institutions; providing institutional blueprints for the construction of new institutions; and generating expectations and conventions that stabilise newly created institutions (Blyth 2002: 35–45). Ideational change is certainly an empirically identifiable phenomenon in periods of financial and economic distress (Blyth 2002; Hall 1993; Oliver and Pemberton 2004). In this respect, ideas and ideational change matter because human beings are an inherently reflective species, continuously interpreting and reinterpreting the world and events around them, and this process is intensified and becomes more critical during periods of economic distress, when seemingly established economic relationships and conventions break down. Crucially, changes in economic ideas challenge existing assumptions about how the world is constituted and create a rationale for a changed role for policy and for public interventions in markets, which in turn requires institutional change. Ideational change also matters because ideas frame the way key policy-makers look at the world, shaping their priorities, their sense of their own role and their understanding of what is possible, appropriate and desirable.

Constructivist scholarship has illuminated the process through which ideational change occurs, by highlighting the role of norm entrepreneurs who engage in 'persuasive struggles', making legitimacy claims and appeals to mass publics (Widmaier Blyth and Seabrooke 2007); however, constructivist literature has rather neglected how new ideas interact with existing institutional contexts (Bell 2011). Further, insufficient attention has been paid to what happens to ideas when they interact with, and are absorbed by, existing institutions. In particular, the outcome and consequences of those interactions and how they affect wider institutional and social relationships, and the implications of and for, actual policy programmes that newly salient ideas give rise to have all been neglected in existing constructivist studies.

Recognising this, Stephen Bell alleges that 'constructivists have ended up with a form of analysis which relegates institutions to a vague or almost meaningless role' (Bell 2011: 890). Bell points out that institutions are 'inherited sets of rules and duties that need to be navigated and negotiated', as well as interpreted, and that 'ideas need institutional support to be effective', which will enable them to become 'embedded in a historical context' (Bell 2011: 891). These are useful insights when it comes to considering and appreciating both the process through which macroprudential ideas about financial regulation rose from their previously marginalised position to prominence, following the financial crash of 2008, and the progression they are likely to make in terms of evolving into a fully fledged policy programme (Baker 2013a). Moreover, as Bell notes, institutional environments shape actors' interpretations, motivations, loyalties, preferences and incentives. In this respect, an array of institutions – national central banks, the Financial Stability Board (FSB), the International Monetary Fund (IMF), the Bank for International Settlements (BIS), the Basel Committee on Banking Supervision (BCBS), national legislatures and finance ministries – are all playing a crucial role in determining the trajectory and evolution of macroprudential regulation. Furthermore, these institutions and their personnel are likely to have vested interests associated with and motivated by their institutional affiliation, which in turn will affect how they come to understand and interpret particular versions of macroprudential thinking. In this sense, research into the progress and significance of macroprudential ideas needs to pay attention to institutional locations and cultures, so as to illuminate the motivations of and influences on the agents engaged in debates about appropriate macroprudential policy and practice.

For Bell, what is required is an appreciation of and an analytical framework for illuminating the continuous interaction between agents, ideas and institutions (Bell 2011). Such an approach involves acknowledging that institutional environments produce real (although always interpreted) costs and benefits for agents, by shaping their interpretations and the resources and opportunities open to them. This notion of dialectical interaction involves accepting and investigating how ideas shape institutions but also that existing institutions will shape how ideas are absorbed and interpreted, in a process of 'mutual shaping' (Bell 2011: 894). In this sense, ideas, by establishing meaning and understanding, provide the basis for meaningful action in political and institutional life. At the same time, the very agents who act as the carriers of ideas will have varying degrees of constrained discretion and space, within particular institutional contexts at particular points in time, to act and to change institutional contexts. This degree of constrained discretion needs to be explained and examined, in an approach that seeks to illuminate the dialectical interaction between agents and institutions. Explaining this further, Bell points out that institutional life is not about dull conformity (Bell 2011: 894), rather the ambiguities of rule and institutional interpretation (Mahoney and Thelen 2010) open up space for agents to be creative, or to exercise agency, rather than simply being constrained by their institutional environment. Finally, agent strategies, decisions and courses of action are based on institutionally specific assessments of resources and capabilities, as actors seek to exploit their institutional positions and deploy resources so as to win battles and reshape institutional environments.

The macroprudential ideational shift as radical intellectual change

The basic premise of this chapter is that the macroprudential ideational shift that followed the financial crash of 2008 was a relatively radical intellectual change, at least when compared to the previous intellectual orthodoxy based on the efficient-market thesis, which informed pre-crash regulatory practice in international networks and most advanced countries. However, relatively radical intellectual change has not translated into dramatic regulatory and institutional change and the process of building effective functioning macroprudential regulatory regimes appears to be proceeding slowly and in a gradual fashion. The rest of the chapter sets out to explain this, beginning with an account of the intellectually radical nature of the macroprudential ideational shift (Baker 2013a).

While macroprudential ideas are not entirely new, macroprudential policies remain largely untested and systematic, detailed macroprudential analysis remains in its infancy. Nevertheless, constituent macroprudential concepts do have an intellectual history. For example, the idea that financial markets can be procyclical owes much to the insights of Hyman Minsky, while the notion that financial markets can be characterised by herding and tunnelling dynamics was something recognised long ago by John Maynard Keynes, as was the notion of a fallacy of composition, which also plays an important role in macroprudential thinking.[1] However, while the term macroprudential was first used in the documentation of the Basel Committee for Banking Supervision in 1979, it was not until in the early 2000s, following the Asian financial crisis, that staff at the Bank for International Settlements (BIS) began to develop a macroprudential research agenda and flesh out what a macroprudential policy regime might look like. These ideas remained unpopular with leading central banks in the first half of the decade and received little practical support, or take-up. For example, in several well documented exchanges at the Jackson Hole Conference of the Kansas City Federal Reserve in 2003, and at later meetings of central bankers at the BIS headquarters in Basel, Alan Greenspan was notoriously dismissive of the macroprudential analysis and arguments of two BIS officials, Claudio Borio and William White, who were warning of the dangers of an inflating financial boom. Other central bankers at these meetings largely agreed with Greenspan (Balizil and Schiessl 2009). As Claudio Borio of the BIS has pointed out, 'a decade ago the term macroprudential was barely used and there was little appetite amongst policy makers and regulators to even engage with the concept, let alone strengthen macroprudential regulation' (Borio 2009: 32). Today, however, Borio has observed that 'we're all macroprudentialists now' (Borio 2009) and according to Borio it was 'the recent financial crisis that gave it (MPR) an extraordinary boost' (Borio 2009: 32). Macroprudential ideas have moved from relative obscurity, largely confined to enclaves of the BIS, to the centre of the policy agenda, dominating and driving the post-crisis financial reform debate, particularly in the international community of central bankers.

---

1. Note that this chapter does not intend to get involved in a sustained discussion of the intellectual genealogy of macroprudential regulation; this is partially covered in Baker 2013a.

Macroprudential regulation involves a focus on the financial system as a whole, so as to limit the costs of financial distress in terms of macroeconomic output. This is accompanied by an acceptance that an institution can take actions that are individually rational but which in aggregate generate undesirable outcomes for the system as a whole (Crockett 2000). Financial risk is thus viewed as being endogenous to the system as a whole. Four constituent concepts provide the intellectual underpinning for MPR. First is the notion of a fallacy of composition (Borio 2011), or the idea that it is aggregate or collective systemic outcomes that matter more than individual incentives and courses of action. Second, within the macroprudential frame, financial markets are seen to be procyclical, with market prices inherently predisposed to extreme movements and volatility (Borio, Furfine and Lowe 2001; Borio and White 2004; White 2006; BIS 2006). Third, market participants are prone to 'herding', adopting behaviour close to the overall mean, as they suspend their own judgement due to observation of and deferral to the judgement and behaviour of others. A fourth and final macroprudential concept relates to the linkages and externalities that proliferate in complex systems. As complexity and interconnections increase, evident in shadow banking and financial innovation for example, externalities proliferate, meaning that relatively small, unexpected events can generate increasingly costly explosions and systemic instability and fragility (Haldane 2010; Alessandri and Haldane 2009; Taleb and Blyth 2011; Haldane and May 2011). Moreover, a branch of literature points out that the excessive complexity such interconnections engender often exceeds human cognitive capacity, making risk incalculable (Best 2010; Haldane 2010; Turner 2011; Blyth 2011). Analysis of this kind provides a powerful rationale for moving the perimeter of regulation to cover shadow banking; and also for modularising or separating financial activities, through Glass-Steagall type legislation and for taxing or even prohibiting certain financial activities and transactions, because their social costs in terms of lost output can exceed any economic value they generate (Haldane 2010; Turner 2011; Tucker 2010).

This type of macroprudential thinking is very different from the pre-crisis conventional regulatory wisdom, which, in the words of one regulator, was based on a simplified version of the efficient-markets hypothesis and had become part of a wider 'institutional DNA' (Turner 2011: 29). The pre-crisis consensus saw market completion and mathematical sophistication as the key to effective risk-management, while financial innovation evident in 'the originate to distribute' model, was seen as a way of diversifying and diffusing risk, increasing the stability and robustness of the financial system as a whole. Consequently, greater transparency, more disclosure and more effective risk-management by financial firms based on market prices became the cornerstones of the regulation of efficient markets. The Basel II agreement, for example, established a reliance on internal risk-management systems based on the state-of-the-art, value-at-risk (VaR) models of big banks. Supervisors engaged in assessments of these models, effectively asking institutions and their managers what they did, resulting in a focus on process or IT capacity, rather than results or risk capacity (Tsingou 2008; Warwick Commission 2009).

During 2008, as we moved towards the height of the crisis, the efficient-markets orthodoxy and a 'do little' position remained ascendant in technocratic networks. Indeed, the initial, centrepiece international policy document of the crisis, a report by the Financial Stability Forum (FSF 2008), which set out an agenda for responding to early liquidity problems and stress in securities and derivatives markets, reiterated 'the familiar trilogy' (Eatwell 2009). The core message in this report was that greater transparency, more disclosure and more effective risk-management by banks and investment funds were the best market-enhancing light-touch response (FSF 2008). The inadequacy of this thinking became clear when the sheer number of financial institutions requiring public financial support following the collapse of Lehman Brothers in the autumn of 2008 meant that financial distress took on a systemic quality. The extreme downward movement in a number of interrelated asset classes could not be explained by the efficient-markets approach. From this perspective, systematic mistakes by markets (as the sum of individual rational decisions), as opposed to isolated random ones, could not happen, at least when adequate information was available, because optimising agents would drive prices into equilibrium. In contrast, the macroprudential approach, emphasising the importance of systemic thinking and highlighting the procyclical and unstable tendencies of financial markets, provided a ready-made conceptual apparatus for explaining the events of autumn 2008. This conceptual approach also criticised the dominance of the existing orthodoxy and its overreliance on VaR models, asserting that such an approach was a cause of the crisis, which had further 'hard-wired' procyclicality into the financial system (FSA 2009). In this context, the existing orthodoxy became part of the problem, and had to be replaced with new thinking.

As Claudio Borio, a macroprudential pioneer at the BIS, has pointed out, macroprudential ideas had been 'evolving quietly in the background, known only amongst a small but growing inner circle of cognoscenti' (Borio 2011: 1). Macroprudential ideas consequently had a prior intellectual and institutional presence, particularly at the BIS, which meant that advocates of macroprudential thinking were well positioned and already had a presence in the established financial technocratic research and report-writing machinery that politicians called upon to provide them with diagnoses, answers and proposals following the financial crash of 2008. As Walter Mattli and Ngaire Woods have pointed out, 'successful [regulatory] change is made more likely where new ideas provide a way to regulate that both offers a common ground to a coalition of entrepreneurs pressing for change and fits well with not-discredited existing institutions' (Mattli and Woods 2009: 4–5). Macroprudential proposals had not discredited institutional and individual backers that were already linked into key policy-making networks in the form of Borio's inner circle of cognoscenti. Proposals in the field of financial governance, as Tony Porter has observed, are more likely to become influential if they have been grounded in prior research and technical reports and have an institutional presence (Porter 2003). In this respect, following the financial implosion of 2008, macroprudential advocates were not starting from scratch. Individuals such as Borio and White were already recognised and positioned within key policy networks, with a track record of advancing macroprudential ideas for nearly a decade. The macroprudential perspective therefore enjoyed an advantage in terms of institutional access and a body of existing work that outlined the inadequacies of the efficient-markets orthodoxy and was well positioned to fill the vacuum left by the apparent collapse of efficient-market thinking.

The rise to prominence of macroprudential ideas was the result of a proactive promotional strategy by a relatively small number of key macroprudential norm entrepreneurs (Finnemore and Sikkink 1998), who engaged in a public process of diagnosis, persuasion and prescription. In the UK, economists John Eatwell, Charles Goodhart and Avinash Persaud converted Adair Turner, the new head regulator of the FSA, to the macroprudential cause, in briefings during the summer of 2008. Turner became one of the most forceful and eloquent advocates of the macroprudential position and began to make the macroprudential case at meetings of the FSF in Basel.[2] As the FSF prepared reports for G20 meetings, macroprudential references and thinking also began to find their way into G20 communiqués, albeit somewhat cryptically under the heading 'mitigating procyclicality', with support expressed for counter-cyclical capital buffers for the first time in the Horsham communiqué of 2009 (G20 2009). William White, formerly a prominent macroprudential pioneer at the BIS, had by then retired but was advising and briefing the German G20 team, and also briefing Canadian officials using the frame of MPR analysis (Balizil and Schiessel 2009). The increased access to the levers of national state policy-making that macroprudential advocates enjoyed in Eurozone states, the UK and Canada enabled the basics of a macroprudential consensus to be built through the G20 and the FSB. By the summer of 2009, the new FSB was calling on the BCBS to commence work on counter-cyclical capital buffers, and it was agreed that a new Basel III agreement, with a macroprudential component, would be negotiated.

In the UK, the FSA's principal document, *The Turner Review*, diagnosed and set out an action plan for responding to the crisis, within a macroprudential frame (FSA 2009). Persaud and Goodhart also teamed up with Andrew Crockett, former BIS Director-General and long-time advocate of MPR, to publish the Geneva Report into the crisis in July 2009, which again made the case for MPR (Brunnemier *et al.* 2009). Through his participation in the UN's Stiglitz Commission, Persaud also ensured MPR featured in their recommendations (UN 2009). The De Larosière report produced by the EU also identified the need for a macroprudential approach (de Larosière 2009). G30 reports produced by a combination of public- and private-sector officials similarly endorsed and explored MPR (G30 2009, 2010). Naturally, as a concept that originated with and had been pioneered by BIS staff, BIS staff continued to promote and applaud the emerging Basel consensus in favour of MPR, publishing their own reports and papers and further elaborating the case for MPR (Borio 2009; Borio, Tasharev and Tsatsronis 2009), with the BIS even laying claim to be the principal institutional owner and intellectual driver of the concept (Clement 2010; Galati and Moessner 2011).

---

2. Information revealed to author in private conversations.

With so many expert reports advocating MPR and a macroprudential philosophy, an irresistible momentum in favour of a macroprudential approach to regulation was built and diffused throughout the key policy-locations in the international financial architecture. A new consensus based on the macroprudential analytical frame took hold, shaping the policy priorities of major central banks including the Federal Reserve, the European Central Bank and the Bank of England, with all three pledging to set up new policy committees and arm them with some macroprudential responsibilities (Bernanke 2011; Constancio 2011; Tucker 2011). Following the financial crash of 2008, therefore, MPR became established as a normative and political priority amongst the leaders and ministers of the G20 and also became diffused and established in the work programmes of the more technical committees of the BCBS, the FSB, the BIS, national central banks and even public private policy communities comprising major industry representatives, such as the G30. The research machinery of the global financial architecture has partly been reoriented and reconfigured as a consequence of this process, focusing on future macroprudential knowledge-generation.

Macroprudential ideas consider financial instability to be endogenous and endemic to the system. Taken together, MPR's constituent concepts potentially create the case for a far more extensive series of public interventions in financial markets. They involve a normative stance that regulation should be driven by a desire to ensure that the costs to society as a whole are less than the private costs incurred by private-sector institutions (Persaud 2009; Alessandri and Haldane 2009; Turner 2011). As I have argued elsewhere, the emergence of macroprudential ideas does resemble what Peter Hall has called third-order change, according to Hall's three criteria for such a form of change (Baker 2013a, 2013b). First, there is a new macroprudential policy discourse and lexicon (a new gestalt), second there is a change in the hierarchy of goals behind policy (from micro to macro) (Hall 1993: 279) and third, a change in causal assumptions or accounts of how the world facing policy-makers actually works (Hall 1993: 280).

Intellectually, therefore, the macroprudential shift is quite radical and took place in a period of approximately six months, following the height of the financial crisis in 2008. The consequence of this ideational shift is that policy-makers' cognitive filters have switched to a different setting. Policy-makers are now using various combinations of the four key constituent concepts – fallacy of composition, procyclicality, herding, and complex externalities – to inform and guide regulatory initiatives and practice. A whole range of policy proposals that were previously out of reach can now be placed on the table and seriously discussed. These include: counter-cyclical capital requirements; dynamic loan-loss provisioning; counter-cyclical liquidity requirements; administrative caps on aggregate lending; reserve requirements; limits on leverage in asset purchases; loan-to-value ratios for mortgages; loan-to-income ratios; minimum margins on secured lending; transaction taxes; constraints on currency mismatches; capital controls; and host-country regulation (Elliot 2011). The macroprudential shift therefore represents a potential trajectory change in financial regulation. After three decades of entrusting more and more autonomy to private actors to price and manage their own risk, that trajectory is, potentially at least, reversed. Macroprudential concepts potentially empower regulators by providing them with the intellectual equipment to set limits to market activities, reducing the scale and restricting the scope of financial transacting (Turner 2011). Political contests played out over time will determine if this results in a reformulation of the powers, strategies and hierarchies of the regulatory state, extending beyond audit and surveillance (Moran 2003) towards much more interventionist forms of command regulation and system-wide counter-cyclical management. The evidence of macroprudential progress, thus far, suggests that intellectual radicalism has not yet translated into dramatic policy change, as the process of building functioning macroprudential policies proceeds slowly. The reasons for this slow pace of change will be explored further in the rest of this chapter.

Macroprudential ideas as an incomplete and evolving frame

Macroprudential policy is a new ideology and a big idea. That befits what is, without question, a big crisis. There are a great many unanswered questions before this ideology can be put into practice. These questions will shape the intellectual and public policy debate over the next several decades, just as the great depression shaped the macroeconomic policy debate from the 1940s to the early 1970s (Haldane 2009: 1).

The macroprudential case is a good illustration of how new ideas, which may rise to prominence in a relatively short period of time following a period of financial distress, do not automatically translate into dramatic institutional and policy change. The rest of this chapter outlines two sets of reasons for this. The first lies in the very nature and form of the ideational shift towards macroprudential thinking that followed the financial crash of 2008. This process had two remarkable features. The first was that it unfolded in a relatively short time, between six and twelve months. By the second half of 2009, MPR had been established as a policy priority in regulatory networks through the spate of activity described in the previous section. The second remarkable feature was the relatively few functioning examples of macroprudential policy instruments and the relative lack of experimentation with macroprudential-style policies. The Spanish example of counter-cyclical capital buffers or dynamic provisioning and the Canadian use of leverage limits were outliers in developed-country financial systems, although a number of Asian systems sought to constrain lending and investment activities using macroprudential-type financial stability justifications, without actually naming them as such (Borio 2011). Policy experimentation allows knowledge to be built and developed on how to operate and implement a new policy approach, before an old approach is formally denounced and jettisoned, and prior to the wholesale adoption and endorsement of the objectives, assumptions and discourse of the new approach. In the macroprudential case, such a process of experimentation did not transpire, largely due to the dramatic events of 2008, which meant the old efficient-markets perspective all but collapsed and an alternative intellectual frame came to prominence in a short period of time. Consequently, discourse, objectives and assumptions shifted in a macroprudential direction before a concrete, practical macroprudential policy programme had been fully worked out, let alone experimented with.

One of the consequences of the macroprudential ideational shift therefore, both in its dramatic nature and the lack of prior experimentation, is that as, Andrew Haldane of the Bank of England's new Financial Policy Committee outlines in the quotation above, many questions relating to macroprudential regime-construction remain to be answered. Accordingly, Bank of England officials have noted, 'the state of macroprudential policy resembles the state of monetary policy just after the second world war, with patchy data, incomplete theory and negligible experience, meaning that MPR will be conducted by trial and error' (Aikman, Haldane, and Nelson 2011). Macroprudential policy authorities, as Haldane acknowledges will not be able to draw on decades of research and experience, 'the authorities will be sailing largely in uncharted waters in a new boat, with a new crew' (Jones 2011). Crucially, as the editors of this volume observe in their introduction, 'when technical knowledge on specific regulatory issues is not well developed, or when organisational capacity to implement a specific regulatory decision is poor or absent, regulatory reform is likely to follow a slow, gradual process precisely because time is needed to develop the relevant knowledge and organisational capacities' (Moschella and Tsingou in this volume). As the quotations from Bank of England officials illustrate, this is precisely the situation that applies to the development of macroprudential policy. Macroprudential policy is so new, and experience with it is so limited, that we have entered a very fluid phase of policy experimentation based on trial and error.

Regulators, both international and domestic, are devoting a great deal of energy and effort to addressing the questions alluded to by Haldane. An extraordinary amount of macroprudential analysis is underway in the regulatory policy community, as various technical reports seek to define the legitimate parameters and content of macroprudential policy, and construct notions of international 'best practice'. For example, a recent joint FSB, IMF and BIS report (2011) references two specialist conferences and cites 21 different reports and research papers with a macroprudential theme, produced by three organisations, in 2010–11 alone, illustrating the extent to which macroprudential analysis has become a growth industry and a mainstay of the post-crash global financial architecture. The relative newness of macroprudential ideas and the novelty of macroprudential policy mean that a technical process of experimentation, puzzling and refinement is giving the development of the macroprudential ideational frame an evolutionary dynamic. In this respect, ideas, as Martin Carstensen has pointed out, have a micro structure and evolve incrementally, even in supposed periods of stability or stasis (Carstensen 2011; Carstensen this volume).

The FSB/ IMF/ BIS report to G20 leaders (FSB/IMF/BIS 2011) on macroprudential policy, described systemic-risk identification as a 'nascent field, that requires fundamental applied research, so as to inform the collection of analysis and data, to fill data gaps and to lead to the development of better models'. Furthermore, newly introduced tools, the report suggests, will need to be tried out in different circumstances and their performance evaluated against expectations, as macroprudential institutions are still being introduced nationally and there is no experience of the performance of these institutions to guide their design. The report is clear in stating that, 'there is no widely agreed and comprehensive theoretical framework for the optimal choice and calibration of macroprudential tools. It is still too early to provide a definite assessment of the set of macroprudential tools that will prove most useful further down the road, in part because financial innovation and change within the financial system will give rise to new risks in due course' (FSB/IMF/BIS 2011: 9–10). The most controversial aspect of this report was the explicit statement that capital controls are not *per se* macroprudential instruments, as they typically have macroeconomic objectives (FSB/ IMF/ BIS 2011: 12). This is despite the fact that one of the FSB's own members, the Banco Central da Brasil, used macroprudential reasoning to justify the use of capital controls in 2010 (Banco Central da Brasil 2010). The macroprudential ideational frame is therefore subject to a process of contestation as regards what can legitimately be included under the macroprudential umbrella. The fact that macroprudential analysis and knowledge remains in its infancy has also been highlighted by the Institute of International Finance (IIF), a group comprising many of the world's leading banks and financial institutions which lobbies and produces reports on international financial governance questions. An IIF report published in 2011 argued that macroprudential policy should be developed in a measured and cautious fashion because 'the science in this area is still at an earlier stage'. 'Using capital as an instrument of macrostabilization is unprecedented and untested. Authorities should therefore exercise great caution before going down this route' (IIF 2011: 22).

Ultimately, macroprudential policy development has been informed by its character as an almost exclusively technocratic project, which initially took the form of an 'insider's coup d'état', primarily driven forward by technocrats whose aim is to achieve technocratic mastery of financial markets, by 'rethinking' and 'mapping' the financial network (Erturk *et al.* 2011).[3] By their nature, technocrats like to proceed cautiously on the basis of data sets and empirical evidence, which take time to accumulate. Consequently, the task of filling macroprudential regulators' empty policy arsenal is proceeding gradually, as evidence, data and rationales are compiled and tested, as the reports mentioned above illustrate. This itself is a slow, gradual process but it also illuminates how the character of the macroprudential project has been shaped by the fact that the rise to prominence of macroprudential ideas was the result of their prior institutional grounding in technocratic networks, while its principal protagonists and architects have also been insider technocrats. Ideas, their character and how they progress are therefore informed by their institutional inception. As we shall now see, those ideas and the outcomes they have given rise to were also shaped by a process of institutional mediation and incorporation.

---

3. This is not to say that macroprudential policy does not have normative implications but these have not always been explicitly acknowledged by technocrats.

Veto-players, change-agents and transnational institutional settings

A further reason for the slow incremental pace of macroprudential policy and institutional development is the extent to which macroprudential regulation is politically contested by change-agents and veto-players; and most especially how interactions between change-agents and veto-players are shaped by the existing institutional contexts in which policy-formation takes place. In their introductory contribution, the editors raise the issue of the number of actors involved in the regulatory process and the distribution of power among them. For the editors, regulatory sectors with numerous veto-players are more likely to follow slow dynamics of change (*see* Moschella and Tsingou in this volume), as 'countries (or institutional systems of policy formation) with many veto players will engage in only incremental policy changes' (Tsebelis 2000: 264). Ultimately, because the quantitative settings of macroprudential policy instruments and the institutional arrangements for macroprudential decision-making have implications for the day-to-day investment strategies and market operations of a variety of market actors, the private sector finds it far easier to identify where their material interests lie in relation to these issues, than over the macroprudential philosophies and concepts that rapidly rose to prominence during 2009. Likewise, because developing a macroprudential policy regime involves creating new policy institutions, entailing a partial reconfiguration of existing institutional arrangements, through the incorporation of new institutions into existing decision-making processes, existing institutional actors – legislators, political parties, other agencies and bureaucracies – are likely to take a closer interest and develop stronger positions on macroprudential institutional questions, as they seek to protect their own turf and status. The result is a contested, contingent and even controversial sphere of macroprudential policy development, which is likely to lead to political compromises and is liable to dilute macroprudential policy content, slowing the process of macroprudential reform. Understanding how this process unfolds requires a full appreciation of the institutional venues and contexts in which macroprudential policy-formulation takes place. Only then can the process of institutional incorporation, which shapes the development and evolution of ideas and policy programmes, be illuminated. The best example of this process to date has been evident in the Basel III agreement negotiated in 2010, which revised the Basel II agreement and established a new framework of principles for international banking regulation.

The Basel III agreement

Historical institutionalism provides a tool kit for making sense of and understanding the dynamics that produced the Basel III agreement. The Basel III agreement closely resembles what Mahoney and Thelen refer to as 'layering'. Layering occurs when new rules are attached to existing ones, involving amendments, revisions and additions to existing rules (Mahoney and Thelen 2010: 16). Layering typically involves change-agents working within the existing system by adding new rules on top of or alongside existing ones. A process of layering also involves specific roles for change-agents and veto-players, which can be applied to the case of the Basel III agreement. Veto-players in a situation of layering are able to preserve old rules but are unable to prevent the addition of new rules. Change-agents in a situation of layering perform the role of 'subversives', working against the system from within it ('termites in the basement'), appearing supportive of existing arrangements but promoting new rules on the edge of old ones, as new institutional arrangements are grafted on to old ones (Mahoney and Thelen 2010: 26). This clearly fits with the pattern of macroprudential norm-entrepreneurs exercising an 'insiders' coup d'état' but it is even more evident in the patterns of politics surrounding the Basel III agreement. For example, microprudential risk-management through VaR models revolving around price signals have not been jettisoned in Basel III; rather, they are now overlain by macroprudential instruments such as counter-cyclical capital buffers. Thus, in accordance with a pattern of layering, new rules have been added to existing ones. Basel III revises and adds to Basel II. Existing rules such as the required ratio of equity capital to risk-weighted assets have been adjusted upwards from 2 per cent to 7 per cent, fitting with the pattern of layering, but they also entail substantive (albeit minimal) changes in risk weights.

There are four reasons why this pattern of layering resulted in the case of Basel III. First, there is the issue of capacity. Change agents seeking to give Basel III a macroprudential quality – largely national regulators and officials at the BIS – were in no position to persuade the industry to abandon VaR risk modelling, even if they wanted to. A re-writing of the fundamental microprudential elements of Basel III was never really on the agenda and some surveillance of the risk-management strategies of banks will continue. Once macroprudential ideational change had been instigated, however, neither were industry and other potential opponents in a position to stop regulators from writing some countercyclical capital element into Basel III, at least on a point of principle. The strategies and resources open to both change-agents and veto-players in the context of the post-crisis regulatory-reform agenda were therefore most likely to produce a form of layering.

A second reason relates to the internal constitution of macroprudential ideas and how their internal component parts relate to microprudential ideas (Carstensen 2011). Notably, while the macroprudential perspective is the antithesis of the efficient-markets perspective, microprudential is not an antonym of macroprudential. Microprudential supervision and regulation can be a constituent part of a macroprudential regime but it is the adequacy of microprudential approaches that is disputed by the macroprudential perspective. Consequently, macroprudential approaches overlay microprudential approaches rather than replacing them in their entirety. The co-existence of an internal-ratings approach with macroprudential policy instruments is therefore entirely compatible with the claims and internal constitution of macroprudential ideas; the addition of new rules to old practices that is characteristic of layering was therefore a likely outcome.

A third reason is the lobbying capacity of large banks, stemming from first-mover advantage and the personal connections leading personnel from the IIF have with members of the Basel Committee (Lall 2012; *see also* Pagliari and

Young in this volume for an analysis of lobbying strategies in the aftermath of the crisis). Initial empirical evidence reveals that industry lobbies, particularly the IIF, have been successful in watering down the provisions of Basel III, especially during 2010, and direct participants in the Basel process have confirmed the role of industry lobbying in producing a much more restricted Basel III than originally envisaged (Lall 2012; Turner 2011). In particular, the institutional form of the Basel Committee meant that industry figures enjoyed access to key committee members and were also best informed about Basel Committee proposals (Lall 2012). The institutional filter of the Basel Committee has always been more open to industry groups such as the IIF than other potential interests, such as the World Council of Credit Unions (WCCU), who found that their submissions calling for less reliance on internal-ratings models made no headway because the Basel Committee only received them twelve months after the decision to preserve Basel II's internal-ratings approach had already been made (Lall 2012: 25). Lall has consequently argued that the Basel Committee's opaque institutional context has provided large global banks with first-mover advantages of access in successive regulatory processes. In the case of Basel III this has resulted in proposals on higher minimum capital ratios, the international leverage ratio, minimum liquidity ratio, and capital surcharge on systemically important institutions all being diluted.

Fourthly, inter-jurisdictional conflict meant that while US, UK and Swiss representatives argued for a much higher equity–capital ratio (Hanson, Kashyap and Stein 2011), EU regulators wanted lower requirements, fearing this would disadvantage their ailing banks. An inter-state, or inter-jurisdictional contest in which actors seek to gain competitive advantage for their own financial sectors has therefore further diluted Basel III, and may in turn create further opportunities for market-players to engage in regulatory arbitrage (Mügge and Stellinga 2010; Helleiner 2012; for an analysis of the importance of jurisdictional competition in a different area of the post-crisis reform agenda *see* Rixen in this volume).

The historical institutionalist characterisation of 'layering' and the role of 'insider subversives' in promoting change can also shed light on the strategies of macroprudential norm entrepreneurs. In the macroprudential case, some of the technocrats connected to the central banking community, who without doubt have a significant amount to gain from an expansive macroprudential agenda, which would expand the powers and resources open to their own institutions, have been somewhat frustrated by the minimal nature of Basel III. One of the features of 'subversives' as change-agents identified by Mahoney and Thelen is that subversives often bide their time, disguising the true extent of their preferences, waiting for the moment at which they can actively advance their preferences and content themselves with a short term strategy of minimal layering (Mahoney and Thelen 2010: 26–27). In the case of UK representatives (Turner 2011), the justification for a more expansive stance on capital ratios in Basel III drew on macroprudential arguments that capital requirements needed to be set far above any reasonable estimate of the losses likely to be incurred by an individual bank, because what mattered was the macro-systemic stability of credit supply and not just the risk of individual failure (Turner 2011; Miles, Yang and Marcheggiano 2011). In this regard, while there is clearly an institutional motivation and incentive for Bank of England staff to make such an argument, there is also evidence that Bank of England officials have promoted these ideas, due to what Finnemore and Sikkink refer to as 'ideational commitment', when norm-entrepreneurs promote ideas because they genuinely believe in them (Finnemore and Sikkink 1998: 898).

Such a recognition once again demonstrates the importance of an analytical approach that seeks to establish a dialectical synthesis between institutional and ideational factors. From a macroprudential perspective, Bank of England officials have argued that, in an ideal world, Basel III capital ratios would be 15–20 per cent of risk-weighted assets (Miles, Yang and Marcheggiano 2011; Turner 2011). This objective is, however, viewed as a long-term one because, while higher equity ratios would not in the long run carry an economic penalty, a starting point of sub-optimally high leverage means that higher equity ratios could slow recovery from a crisis-induced recession (Turner 2011). This argument was accepted by more ambitious macroprudentialists, such as Adair Turner and the BIS macroeconomic assessment group, whose analysis informed the Basel III design. The position of macroprudential change-agents, therefore, is that Basel III is a step in the right direction but that the system remains more vulnerable to instability than is ideal and that the long-term answer must be to move towards the 15–20 per cent level (Turner 2011; Miles, Yang and Marcheggiano 2011). For many macroprudentialists therefore, Basel III remains unfinished business and in its current form is only a temporary best-fit solution.

In this particular instance, while the private sector was not in a position to veto an increase in equity ratios, they did play a *de facto* veto role, minimising and diluting requirements, through an implicit threat that higher ratios would lead to a shrinking of balance sheets, causing a new credit crunch (Hanson, Kashyap and Stein 2011: 24). As a consequence of these arguments, Basel III is to have a slow phase in with many new requirements not becoming effective until January 2019. The veto powers of private actors, while not enough to prevent a rule change, did dilute Basel III, producing only a minimal layering effect relative to Basel II; but from a macroprudential perspective, Basel III is an imperfect, unfinished and temporary solution that will require future revision. These layering dynamics mean that the construction of MPR is proceeding in an incremental and gradual fashion but is very much viewed as a long-term project by its advocates.

The language surrounding the major macroprudential component of Basel III, a country-by-country counter-cyclical capital buffer of between 0 and 2.5 per cent, is also deliberately ambiguous. The relevant passage reads: 'For any given country, this (counter-cyclical capital) buffer will only be in effect when there is excess credit growth that is resulting in a system wide build up of risk'. In other words, a failure to deploy a counter-cyclical capital buffer can be justified if system-wide credit growth is not deemed excessive. How judgements about excess credit growth will be detected and communicated is obviously a domestic matter, one that will be determined by the power, discretion and capacity of key agencies to make certain calls, insulated from countervailing political pressures. In other words, the language used by Basel III encourages what Mahoney and

Thelen refer to as 'drift', when a gap opens up between rules and enforcement, allowing for diverse outcomes and different interpretations (Mahoney and Thelen 2010: 21). The capacity to implement counter-cyclical capital buffers will depend on the configuration of institutional arrangements in domestic settings. The wording of the key passages in Basel III effectively empowers potential national veto-players to block counter-cyclical policy efforts. Again, such a pattern places a potential brake on the implementation of macroprudential policy, restricting the process in substantive terms. Counter-cyclicality is of course, politically treacherous, because the macroprudential agenda's great economic strength, tempering the extremes of credit cycles through counter-cyclical management, is also its great political weakness. In an economic downturn, immediately following a crisis, when the political will for more regulation is precisely at its greatest, the macroprudential perspective advocates a more generous approach to regulatory and capital requirements; but then it favours tightening these requirements during a growth phase, precisely when the political appetite for such requirements may have dissipated, as the memory of the crisis has faded. This leaves macroprudential regulators with a tricky political conundrum to solve: how to arm themselves with sufficient institutional autonomy, policy-making capability and discretion to neutralise procyclical political pressures. Answers to this question will materialise from the interaction of policy-makers' ongoing learning in an era of macroprudential experimentation and the institutional mediation of interest-based politics between change-agents and veto-players.

Conclusion

In this chapter, I have made the case for an approach to regulatory change that seeks to achieve a synthesis between constructivist and institutionalist approaches, based on an examination of the rise to prominence of macroprudential ideas following the financial crash of 2008. Such a synthesised approach, sensitive to how new ideas interact with existing institutional contexts, helps to shed light on the dominant dynamics that have characterised actual macroprudential policy-development and resulted in the gradual and incremental nature of this process to date. The ideas that regulators have about markets and how they function determine the range of policy instruments that are open to them. In this sense, ideas can provide a rationale for the creation of new institutions and the empowerment of these institutions, with a range of policy tools that can change relations between state regulators and private market-actors. What happens to ideas and the form policy programmes actually take, however, cannot be read off ideational developments alone. Rather, ideas interact with existing institutions and a subsequent process of institutional incorporation results. In the case of the macroprudential ideational shift that emerged after the financial crash of 2008, the philosophical acceptance of macroprudential concepts and objectives happened in a short period in the first half of 2009. There had been little previous policy experimentation with macroprudential policy instruments and therefore this process of experimentation and more detailed knowledge-construction is currently underway. Because macroprudential ideas were initially promoted by insider technocrats in existing regulatory networks, the process of macroprudential policy-development is proceeding slowly, precisely because the very carriers of these concepts operate on the basis of data sets and are reluctant to take much action without detailed research and evidence. Further, the institutional settings for developing macroprudential policy, notably both the Basel Committee and the FSB (at the international level) and central banks (at the national level), have cast technocratic regulators in the role of macroprudential change-agents. As change-agents, these actors have been constrained by both private industry lobbies and national legislatures acting as veto-players. This chapter has argued that the result of the interactions between change-agents and veto-players, in institutional settings such as the Basel Committee, is a form of policy-development displaying the characteristics of a form of 'layering', in which new rules and practices are grafted on to and overlay existing rules and practices. Evidence of a form of layering was identified in the case of the Basel III agreement. Crucially, the change-agents who promote layering are typically insider subversives and play a long and patient game. There is certainly evidence of this in relation to technocratic macroprudential norm-entrepreneurs, who seem certain to progressively push for an expansion of the requirements of the Basel III agreement over the long term. This chapter has therefore argued that the series of dynamics and interactions we are currently witnessing between emerging macroprudential ideas and existing institutional contexts are slowing the pace of macroprudential regulatory change, as well as diluting its substantive content, in such a way that macroprudential policy development has assumed the status of a long-term project that is, for the time being, proceeding in only an incremental and gradual fashion.

References

Aikman, D., Haldane, A. and Nelson, B. (2011) 'Curbing the credit cycle', *Vox*. http://voxeu.org/index.php?q=node/6231. Accessed 12 May 2011.

Alessandri, P. and Haldane, A. (2009) 'Banking on the state', Bank of England Discussion Paper.

Baker, A. (2013a) 'The new political economy of the macroprudential ideational shift', *New Political Economy*, 18(1): 112-139.

—— (2013b) 'The gradual transformation? The incremental dynamics of macroprudential regulation', *Regulation & Governance*, DOI:10.1111/rego.12022.

Balizil, B. and Schiessl, M. (2009) 'The man nobody wanted to hear: global banking economist warned of coming crisis', *Spiegel online*, 07/08. http://www.spiegel.de/international/business/0,1518,635051,00.html. Accessed 11 February 2013.

Banco Centro do Brasil (2010) 'CMN and BC adopt measures of macroprudential nature'. http://www.bcb.gov.br/textonoticia.asp?codigo=2823&idpai=NEWS. Accessed February 11, 2013.

Bank for International Settlements (2006) *76th Annual Report*, Basel: Bank for International Settlements, June.

Bell, S. (2011) 'Do we need a new "constructivist institutionalism" to explain institutional change?', *British Journal of Political Science* 41: 883–906.

Bernanke, B. (2011) 'Implementing a macroprudential approach to supervision and regulation', 47th Annual Conference on Bank Structure and Competition, Chicago, Illinois, May 5.

Best, J. (2010) 'The limits of financial risk management: or, what we didn't learn from the Asian crisis', *New Political Economy*, 15(1): 29–49.

Blyth, M. (2002) *Great Transformations: Economic ideas and institutional change in the twenty first century,* Cambridge: Cambridge University Press.

Borio, C. (2009) 'Implementing the macroprudential approach to financial regulation and supervision', Banque de France, *Financial Stability Review,* No.13, September.

—— (2011) 'Implementing a macroprudential framework: blending boldness and realism', *Capitalism and Society,* 6(1): 1–23.

Borio, C., Furfine, C. and Lowe, P. (2001) 'Procyclicality of the financial system and financial stability issues and policy options', *BIS Papers* No.1, March: 1–57.

Borio, C., Tarashev, N. and Tsatsaronis, K. (2009) 'Allocating system wide tail risk to individual institutions', BIS mimeo.

Borio, C. and White, W. (2004) 'Whither monetary and financial stability: the implications for evolving policy regimes', BIS working paper 147, Basel: Bank for International Settlements.

Brunnemier, M., Crockett, A., Goodhart, C., Persaud, A. and Shin, H. (2009) *The Fundamental Principles of Financial Regulation*, Geneva Report on the World Economy 11, Geneva: International Centre for Monetary and Banking Studies, London: Centre for Economic Policy Research.

Carstensen, M. (2011) 'Ideas are not as stable as political scientists want them to be: a theory of incremental ideational change', *Political Studies*, 59(3): 596–615.

Clement, P. (2010) 'The term "macroprudential": origins and evolution', *BIS Quarterly Review* March: 59–67.

Constancio, V. (2011) 'Macroprudential policy: strengthening the foundations, enhancing the toolkit and taking action', First Conference of the Macroprudential Research Network (MaRs), Frankfurt, 5 October.

Crockett, A. (2000) 'Marrying the micro and macroprudential dimensions of financial stability', *BIS speeches*, 21 September.

de Larosière Group (2009) *Report of the High Level Group on Financial Supervision in the EU,* Brussels.

Eatwell, J. (2009) 'Practical proposals for regulatory reform', in Subacchi, P. and Monsarrat, A. (eds) *New Ideas for the London Summit: Recommendations to the G20 leaders,* London: Royal Institute for International Affairs, Chatham: The Atlantic Council, 11–15.

Elliot, D. (2011) 'Choosing among macroprudential tools', The Brookings Institute. http://www.brookings.edu/~/media/Files/rc/papers/2011/0607_macroprudential_tools_elliott/0607_macroprudential_tools_elliott.pdf. Accessed 11 February 2013.

Erturk, I., Froud, J., Leaver, A., Moran, M. and Williams, K. (2011) 'Haldane's gambit: political arithmetic and/or a new metaphor', CRESC Working Paper 097, http://www.cresc.ac.uk/sites/default/files/wp%2097.pdf. Accessed 11 February 2013.

Finnemore, M. and Sikkink, K. (1998) 'International norm dynamics and political change', *International Organization* 52(4): 887–917.

FSA (2009) 'The Turner review', FSA: London.

FSB/IMF/BIS (2011) 'Macroprudential policy tools and frameworks', *Progress Report to G20*, 27 October. http://www.financialstabilityboard.org/publications/r_1103.pdf. Accessed 11 February 2013.

FSF (2008) 'Report of the financial stability forum on enhancing market and institutional resilience', 7 April. http://www.financialstabilityboard.org/publications/r_0804.pdf. Accessed 11 February 2013.

G30 (2009) *Financial Reform: A framework for financial stability,* Washington DC: Group of Thirty.

— (2010) *Enhancing Financial Stability and Resilience: Macroprudential policy, tools and systems for the future,* Washington DC: Group of Thirty.

Galati, G. and Moessner, R. 'Macroprudential policy – a literature review', BIS Working Papers No. 337. http://www.bis.org/publ/work337.pdf. Accessed 12 February 2013.

Hanson, S., Kahyap, A. and Stein, J. (2011) 'A macroprudential approach to financial regulation', *Journal of Economic Perspectives*, 1: 1–26.

Haldane, A. (2009) 'Small lessons from a big crisis', Remarks at the Federal Reserve Bank of Chicago, 45th Annual Conference, 'Reforming Financial Regulation', 8 May 2009.

— (2010) 'The $100 billion question', Bank of England Discussion Paper, originally presented at the Institute of Regulation & Risk, Hong Kong, March 2010.

Haldane, A. and May, R. (2011) 'Systemic risk in banking ecosystems', *Nature*, 469: 351–5.

Hall, P. (1993) 'Policy paradigm, social learning and the state: the case of economic policymaking in Britain', *Comparative Politics*, 25(3): 275–96.

Hanson, S. G., Kashyap, A. K. and Stein, J. C. (2011) 'A macroprudential approach to financial regulation', *Journal of Economic Perspectives*, 25(1): 3–28.

Hay, C. (2004) 'Ideas, institutions and interests in the comparative political economy of great transformations', *Review of International Political Economy*, 11(1): 204–26.

Helleiner, E. (2012) 'The limits of incrementalism: the G20, FSB and the international regulatory agenda', *Journal of Globalization and Development*, 2(2): 1–19.

IIF (2011) 'Macroprudential oversight: an industry perspective', Submission to the International Authorities. http://www.iif.com/regulatory/article+971.php. Accessed 11 February 2013.

Jones, C. (2011) 'The third arm: macroprudential policy', *Financial Times,* 22 September.

Lall, R. (2012) 'From failure to failure: the politics of international banking regulation', *Review of International Political Economy*, 19(4): 609–38.

Mahoney, J. and Thelen, K. (2010) 'A theory of gradual institutional change', in Mahoney J. and Thelen, K. (eds) *Explaining Institutional Change: Ambiguity, agency and power in historical institutionalism,* Cambridge: Cambridge University Press, 1–37.

Mattli, W. and Woods, N. (2009) 'In whose benefit? Explaining regulatory change in global politics', in Mattli, W. and Woods, N. (eds) *The Politics of Global Regulation,* Princeton NJ: Princeton University Press, 1–43.

Miles, D. Yang, J. and Marcheggiano, G. (2011) 'Optimal bank capital', External MPC Unity, Discussion Paper, No. 31, January 2011.

Moran, P. (2003) *The British Regulatory State: High Modernism and Hyper Innovation*, Oxford: Oxford University Press.

Mügge, D. and Stellinga, B. (2010) 'Absent alternatives and insider interests in postcrisis financial reform', *Der Moderne Staat: Zeitschrift für Public Policy, Recht und Management*, 3(2): 321–8.

Oliver, M. and Pemberton, H. (2004) 'Learning and change in 20th century British economic policy', *Governance*, 17(3): 415–441.

Persaud, A. (2009) 'Macroprudential regulation: fixing fundamental market and regulatory failures', Crisis Response (Note number 6), The World Bank Group, Financial and Private Sector Development, July.

Porter, T. (2003) 'Technical collaboration and political conflict in the emerging regime for international financial regulation', *Review of International Political Economy*, 10(3): 520–51.

Schmidt, V. A. (2009) 'Taking ideas and discourse seriously: explaining change through discursive institutionalism as the fourth new institutionalism', *European Political Science Review*, 2(1): 1–25.

Taleb, N. and Blyth, M. (2011) 'The black swan of Cairo: how suppressing volatility makes the world less predictable and more dangerous', *Foreign Affairs*, 90(3): 33–9.

Tseblis, G. (2000) 'Veto players and institutional analysis', *Governance*, 4: 441–74.

Tsingou, E. (2008) 'Transnational private governance and the Basel Process: banking regulation and supervision, private interests and Basel II', in Graz, J. C. and Nölke, A. (eds) *Transnational Private Governance and Its Limits,* London: Routledge: 58–68.

Tucker, P. (2010) 'Remarks to the Institute of International Bankers, annual breakfast for regulatory dialogue', Washington DC, 11 October.

—   (2011) Discussion of Lord Turner's lecture, 'Reforming finance: are we being radical enough?', Clare Distinguished Lecture in Economics and Public Policy, Cambridge, 18 February.

Turner, A. (2011) 'Reforming finance: are we being radical enough?', Clare Distinguished Lecture in Economics and Public Policy, Cambridge, 18 February.

UN (2009) *Report of the Commission of Experts of the United Nations General Assembly on Reforms of the International Financial and Monetary System*, September 2009. http://www.un.org/ga/econcrisissummit/docs/FinalReport_CoE.pdf. Accessed 12 February 2013.

Warwick Commission (2009) 'The Warwick Commission on international financial reform: in praise of unlevel playing fields', December, Coventry: University of Warwick.

White, W. (2009) 'Modern macroeconomics is on the wrong track', *Finance and Development* December: 15–18.

—   (2006) 'Procyclicality in the financial system: do we need a new macrofinancial stabilisation framework?', BIS Working Paper, no.193, January.

Widmaier, W., Blyth, M. and Seabrooke, L. (2007) 'Exogenous shocks or endogenous constructions? The meanings of wars and crises', *International Studies Quarterly*, 51: 747–59.

chapter three	financial services governance in the European Union after the global financial crisis: incremental changes or path-breaking reform?[1]

Lucia Quaglia

Introduction

In the Introduction to this volume, the editors note that 'Since the onset of the global financial crisis, "change" has been the catchword in the international regulatory debate'. It has also been the catchword in the regulatory debate in the European Union (EU). EU rules are important because, to a large extent, they provide the framework for national regulatory changes in the member states. Moreover, the EU is one of the largest jurisdictions worldwide, it is increasingly active in shaping global financial rules in international fora and it is one of the main interlocutors of the US in the policy debate on this subject (Posner 2009).This chapter examines the regulatory changes enacted by the EU after the global financial crisis. Section Two outlines the main pieces of legislation adopted or proposed by the EU after the crisis, arguing that those changes were mostly incremental, even though the whole of the reform is greater than the sum of its parts. The next section evaluates a variety of explanations articulated in the Introduction to this volume located at the interstate, domestic, and transnational levels, arguing that the former has the greatest explanatory power.

The reform of financial services governance in the EU after the crisis

A host of new regulatory initiatives were undertaken by the EU in the aftermath of the global financial crisis, besides the short-term crisis-management measures adopted in the midst of the credit crunch (Quaglia *et al.* 2009). Those EU actions that did not result in 'hard' legislative measures, such as recommendations on managers' remuneration (CEC 2009), are not examined here because they are not legally binding. This section first examines the changes in governance arrangements (that is, the reform of the institutional framework for regulation and supervision); it then examines the legislative changes undertaken. For each legislative measure discussed, the main change-agents and veto-players are highlighted. 'Whereas

1. Financial support from the European Research Council (204398 FINGOVEU) and the British Academy and Leverhume Trust (SG120191) is gratefully acknowledged. This paper was written while I was a visiting fellow, first at the Max Planck Institute in Cologne and then at the European University Institute in Florence. I wish to thank the participants of Copenhagen workshop and in particular the discussant, Kevin Young, for perceptive comments on an earlier draft.

change-agents lead the process of change by being explicit advocates of specific changes or hidden supporters, veto-players, in principle, aim at maintaining the status quo' (Moschella and Tsingou in this volume).

The reform of the institutional framework for regulation and supervision in the EU

The global financial crisis triggered the reform of the EU framework for financial regulation and supervision. In 2009, a group of high-level practitioners and financial experts, chaired by the former governor of the Banque de France, Jacques de Larosière, produced a report on the issue, which was named after the chair of the group. Building on the de Larosière report (2009), in September 2009, the Commission put forward a series of legislative proposals for the reform of the micro- and macro-prudential frameworks for financial supervision in the EU (for the development of macroprudential ideas internationally *see* Baker in this volume). The Commission's proposals were eventually agreed by the Council and European Parliament in the autumn of 2010 and were implemented in early 2011.

The main institutional innovations were the establishment of the European Systemic Risk Board, its chair to be elected by and from the members of the General Council of the European Central Bank (ECB) and in charge of monitoring macroprudential risk; and the transformation of the so-called level-three Lamfalussy committees into independent authorities with legal personality, an increased budget and enhanced powers. The newly created bodies, namely the European Banking Authority, the European Insurance and Occupational Pension Authority, and the European Securities Markets Authority, were charged with the tasks of co-ordinating the application of supervisory standards and promoting stronger co-operation between national supervisors.[2] Nonetheless, the new agencies have limited competence and their effective ability to regulate the financial sector remains to be seen.

In the negotiations for these institutional reforms, disagreements broke out in the Council and between the Council and the European Parliament (EP) concerning the powers of the newly created bodies, as well as the role of the EP in the proposed architecture. The main veto-players, at least for certain aspects of this institutional reform, were the UK, Ireland and Luxembourg, which were reluctant to transfer powers away from national supervisors to bodies outside their borders (Buckley and Howarth 2010). Moreover, the UK government was reluctant to grant decision-making powers to EU-level bodies while public funds to tackle banking crises came from national budgets (*European Voice*, 4 March 2009). To this effect, Gordon Brown, then British Prime Minister, secured a guarantee that the new supervisory system would not include powers to force national governments to bail

---

2. There was also a directive amending the existing directives in the banking, securities and insurance sectors and a Council decision entrusting the ECB with specific tasks in the functioning of the ESRB.

out banks. The UK also stressed that the EU's supervisory architecture should fit in with global arrangements and should support the development of 'open, global markets' (Darling 2009). That said, a number of member states, particularly those with large financial centres, namely the UK, France and Germany, favoured the limited-reform approach and were hesitant about transferring substantive power to the EU level (Buckley and Howarth 2010). This led to a significant reduction in the scope of the Commission proposals during the negotiations in the Council.

By contrast, the EP was an agent of change, arguing that the Commission's proposals did not go far enough, and was adamant about safeguarding the powers of the European Supervisory Authorities (ESAs). However, the MEPs also had a vested interest in enhancing the oversight role of the EP in the new architecture. Hence, the EP called for the strengthening of the financial and human resources available to the ESAs. It also called for the presidency of the ESRB to be given to the president of the ECB, so as to augment the authority of this newly created body. MEPs inserted provisions to enable the ESRB to communicate rapidly and clearly. They defended the powers of ESAs to take decisions that are directly applicable to individual financial institutions in cases of manifest breach or non-application of law, and where there is disagreement between national authorities. The EP was keen for the ESA to be able temporarily to prohibit or restrict harmful financial activities or products already covered by specific financial legislation or in emergency situations (*Financial Times*, 14 July 2010). On all these issues, the EP was successful in getting what it wanted.

The revision of capital requirements for banks and investment firms

The main changes in banking legislation concerned rules on capital requirements. Prior to the crisis, international capital requirements were set by the Basel II accord, agreed by the Basel Committee on Banking Supervision (BCBS) in 2004 (BCBS 2004). In the EU, the main elements of the Basel II accord had been incorporated into the Capital Requirements Directive (CRD) III[3] in 2006. Various revisions of the CRD were carried out in parallel to the international debate on this issue taking place in the BCBS. The revisions of the CRD in 2009 and 2010 set higher capital requirements on the trading book and re-securitisations; imposed stronger disclosure requirements for securitisation exposures; and required banks to have sound remuneration practices that did not encourage or reward excessive risk-taking. The scope of these changes, however, remained quite limited, because a comprehensive revision of the Basel II accord was pending.

---

3. The first CRD was issued in 1993, incorporating the Basel I accord into EU legislation; in 1998, the CRD II incorporated the amendments of the Basel I accord; and in 2006 the CRD III incorporated the Basel II accord into EU legislation. Actually, what is generally referred to as CRD III, includes two directives: Directive 2006/48/EC relating to the taking up and pursuit of the business of credit institutions and Directive 2006/49/EC on the capital adequacy of investment firms and credit institutions.

The Basel III accord was eventually signed by the BCBS in December 2010 (BCBS 2010a: 8). Afterwards, it had to be transposed into EU (and national) law in order to become legally binding. The Basel III accord applies to 'internationally active banks', whereas EU legislation applies to all banks (more than 8000) as well as investment firms in the EU. In July 2011, the Commission adopted a legislative package designed to replace the CRD III with a directive that governs the access to deposit-taking activities (CEC 2011a) and a regulation that establishes prudential requirements for credit institutions (Commission 2011b) – this package is often referred to as the CRD IV. After its approval, the proposed directive will have to be transposed by the member states in a way suitable to their own national environment. It contains rules concerning the taking-up and pursuit of the business of banks, the conditions for freedom of establishment and the freedom to provide services and the definition of competent authorities. The directive also incorporates two elements of the Basel III accord, namely, the introduction of two capital buffers on top of the minimum capital requirements: a capital conservation buffer identical for all banks in the EU and a counter-cyclical capital buffer to be determined at national level.

The proposed EU regulation contains prudential requirements for credit institutions and investment firms. It covers the definition of capital, whereby the proposal increases the amount of own funds that banks need to hold as well as the quality of those funds; it introduces a liquidity coverage ratio – the exact composition and calibration of which will be determined after an observation and review period in 2015 – and it proposes a leverage ratio subject to supervisory review. The proposal also set higher capital requirements for over-the counter (OTC) derivatives that are not cleared through central counterparties (CCPs). The use of a regulation that, once approved, is directly applicable without the need for national transposition is designed to ensure the creation of a single rule-book in the EU. The regulation eliminates one key source of national divergence. For example, in the CRD III, more than one hundred national discretions (differences in national legislation transposing the EU directive) remained.

In the negotiations on Basel III first, and the CRD IV later, there was a divide between the US and the UK on the one side, acting as agents of change, and continental European countries, which behaved as a veto-players of a sort (interviews; *Financial Times*, 15 February 2011). The US and the UK wanted a stricter definition of capital, to be limited to ordinary shares; higher capital requirements, including capital buffers; a leverage ratio; liquidity rules; and a short transition period. Continental countries, in particular France and Germany, wanted a broader definition of capital, including hybrids and silent participations, and lower capital requirements, arguing that 'traditional' (continental) banks engaged in less risky trade finance/financial activities. They opposed the leverage ratio, asked for a modification of certain aspects of the liquidity rules and wanted a longer transition period (interviews, *Financial Times*, 15 February 2011).

Continental policy-makers were worried about the effect on the real economy of the stricter rules on banks' capital advocated by Anglo-Saxon regulators. They were also eager to set in place capital rules that would not disrupt the business model of their banks and banking system (Buckley, Howarth and Quaglia 2012).[4] In the downloading of Basel III rules, several issues controversially settled (or papered over) in the BCBS were reopened in EU negotiations. Some member states, most notably the UK (*Financial Times*, 21 July 2011), but also international bodies, such as the International Monetary Fund (IMF) (2011), complained that the drafted EU capital rules, then under discussion, diverged significantly from the content of Basel III. Tighter capital rules were hampered by disagreement amongst the main member states, which was rooted in the different configurations of their national financial industries and of the link between the banking sector and the real economy.

The new regulation on credit-rating agencies

Credit-rating agencies (CRAs) were considered amongst the main culprits of the crisis for failing to rate financial products properly (Brunnermeier *et al.* 2009). They substantially over-rated many complex securities created through the financial activity of securitisation and were slow in revising their ratings once market conditions deteriorated. Prior to the crisis, CRAs were regulated internationally by a voluntary Code of Conduct Fundamentals, issued by the International Organisation of Securities Commissions (IOSCO) in 2004 (IOSCO 2004) and revised in the wake of the crisis (IOSCO 2008).

The French presidency of the EU in the second semester of 2008 implicitly made EU legislation on CRAs one of its priorities. The European Council called for a legislative proposal to strengthen the rules on credit-rating agencies and their supervision at EU level in October 2008 (European Council 2008). France and Germany were the main sponsors of the new rules on CRAs; hence, they acted as agents of change. The UK did not oppose the new legislation but was critical of certain aspects of it, such as the treatment of CRAs headquartered in third-country jurisdictions and the power of the European Securities Markets Authority (ESMA) in authorising CRAs. Influential MEPs supported the regulation of CRAs in the EU. The Commission, which, prior to the crisis had ruled out the possibility of regulating CRAs, came forward with a legislative proposal in record time. The (revised) IOSCO Code provided the benchmark for the Commission's draft regulation on CRAs. However, the Commission argued that the IOSCO rules needed to be made more concrete and be backed by enforcement.

CRAs initially opposed the idea of EU rules on rating – they had a clear vested interest in doing so, preserving the 'soft' (that is, not legally binding) rules to which they were subjected. Subsequently, they adapted their lobbying strategies, focusing on the amendment of the most onerous parts of the proposed legislation, such as the requirements that regulators should gather information about the model used by CRAs, the quality of people employed, and so on. This criticism was also

---

4. For example, the definition of capital proposed by the BCBS was not suitable for German or French mutual banks.

shared by countries that have traditionally been in favour of light-touch, principle-based regulation, as evidenced by the response to the Commission's consultation of the British Treasury, the Swedish Finance Ministry and the Finnish Finance Ministry as well as that of the main CRAs, namely, Standard & Poor's, Moody's, Fitch and AM Best.

The Regulation on CRAs was agreed relatively quickly by the EU, in less than a year. According to the new rules, all CRAs whose ratings are used in the EU need to apply for registration in the EU and have to comply with rules designed to prevent conflicts of interest in the rating process and to ensure the quality of the rating methodology and the ratings. CRAs operating in non-EU jurisdictions can issue ratings to be used in the EU, provided that their countries of origin have a regulatory framework recognised as equivalent to the one put in place by the EU, or that such ratings are endorsed by an EU-registered CRA (Council of Ministers and European Parliament 2009).

In June 2010, the Commission proposed an amendment of the Regulation on CRAs adopted in 2009. Since ratings issued by a CRA can be used by financial institutions throughout the EU, the Commission proposed a more centralised system for supervision of CRAs, whereby the newly created European Securities and Markets Authority was entrusted with exclusive supervisory powers over CRAs registered in the EU, including European subsidiaries of US-headquartered CRAs, such as Fitch, Moody and Standard & Poor. Despite the opposition of the British authorities, the ESMA was given powers to request information, to launch investigations, and to perform on-site inspections. The amended regulation was adopted by the Council and the EP in May 2011 (Council and EP 2011). In the summer of 2011, the downgrading of government bonds in the countries directly hit by the sovereign-debt crisis by the (mainly US-headquartered) CRAs gave new momentum to the debate on the creation of the European rating agency, a proposal that was put forward by the EP (2011), which, in this case, was trying to act as an agent of change.

The new directive on alternative investment fund managers (AIFMs)

Prior to the financial crisis, in policy discussions in international fora, two different approaches could be detected concerning the regulation of hedge funds: one in favour of regulation, sponsored by Germany and France, and one resisting regulation, championed by the US and the UK (Fioretos 2010). During preparations for the April 2009 G20 summit, the split over how to regulate hedge funds re-emerged. Several European countries, led by France and Germany – as suggested by Sarkozy's and Merkel's joint letter (2009) – with the support of Italy, pushed for a tougher regulatory regime for hedge funds and wanted the funds to be overseen similarly to banks. Hence, they were acting as agents of change. By contrast, the US and UK authorities acted as veto-players, favouring more disclosure over more regulation (*Wall Street Journal,* 14 March 2009), with limited changes to the status quo. The G20 agreed '...to extend regulation and oversight to all systemically important financial institutions, instruments and markets. This will include, for the first time, systemically important hedge funds' (G20 2009). This was seen as a victory for the continental call for the regulation of hedge funds. However, as it is often the case in financial regulation, the devil was in the details and a heated struggle ensued in the EU on how to translate the G20 commitments into legally binding legislation.

In June 2009, the European Commission presented its proposal for the draft directive on AIFMs, which included managers of hedge funds, private equities funds and real-estate funds, hence covering quite a broad range of financial entities. It is noteworthy that, prior to the crisis, the Commission had acted as a veto-player, ruling out the need for hedge-fund regulation in the EU (Moschella 2011). Reportedly, the first draft of the Commission's proposal was informed by the regulatory preferences expressed by France and Germany (Quaglia 2011). The UK and the hedge-fund industry had to fight a rear-guard action in order to have the initial proposal substantially amended and were in part successful in doing so during the Swedish presidency[5] of the EU in the second semester of 2009.

The hedge-fund industry in the EU is mainly based in London; thus, in this case, there was a substantial overlap between the vested interests of the industry directly affected by the new rules and the UK. Unlike CRAs, hedge funds were slow in adapting their lobbying strategies to a changed policy context. Actually, that new legislation was proposed by the EU came as a surprise to them. During the consultation phase, they had opposed the prospect of EU rules on hedge funds and proposed instead some 'soft' (industry-led) rules in an attempt to stave off legislation. Once the directive was proposed by the Commission, AIFMs initially reacted as a bunch of 'frightened sparrows' (cited in Woll 2012). Afterward, they adjusted their lobbying strategy, focusing their criticisms on certain provisions of the draft directive and mobilising in full the British authorities. In the EP, the socialists were also agents of change, calling for hedge-fund regulation before and after the financial crisis. The US weighed in on the EU debate on issues related to the equivalence provisions for hedge funds headquartered outside the EU.

An agreement between the Council of Ministers and the EP was eventually reached in late October 2010 and the directive is due to come into force in 2013. It introduces a legally binding authorisation and supervisory regime for all AIFMs in the EU, irrespective of the legal domicile of the alternative investment funds managed. Hence, AIFMs will be subject to authorisation from the competent authority of the home member state and to reporting requirements concerning systemically important data to supervisors. The directive sets up a European passport for AIFMs. Hence, an AIFM authorised in its home member state will be entitled to market its funds to professional investors in other member states, which will not be permitted to impose additional requirements (Council of Ministers and European Parliament 2011).

---

5. Sweden has a significant private equity industry; hence, it was seen as having a vested interest in the revision of the text of the directive.

The new European market infrastructure regulation

Prior to the global financial crisis, a large number of derivatives were traded over the counter, not through stock exchanges, and were not cleared through central counterparties (CCPs). Derivative trading on stock exchanges increases transparency and central counterparties reduce counterparty risk (i.e., the risk of default by one party to the contract), so that the default of one market participant would not cause the collapse of other market players, thereby putting the entire financial system at risk. In September 2009, the G20 Pittsburgh Summit agreed that 'all standard OTC derivative contracts should be traded on exchanges or electronic trading platforms, where appropriate, and cleared through central counterparties by end-2012 at the latest'. Furthermore, they acknowledged that 'OTC derivative contracts should be reported to trade repositories and that non-centrally cleared contracts should be subject to higher capital requirements' (G20 2009).

Afterwards, the Commission issued a series of communications on this matter. Commissioner Barnier also stressed the importance of EU–US convergence on the regulation of derivatives markets. In September 2010, the European Commission proposed a regulation on OTC derivatives, CCPs and trade repositories. It envisaged reporting obligations for OTC derivatives to trade repositories; clearing obligations for standardised OTC derivatives through CCPs; and common rules for CCPs and trade repositories. The European Securities and Markets Authority (ESMA) would be responsible for the surveillance of trade repositories and for granting and withdrawing their registration. In order to be registered, trade repositories must be established in the EU. However, a trade repository established in a third country can be recognised by ESMA if it meets a number of requirements designed to establish that such trade repository is subject to equivalent rules and appropriate surveillance in that third country. Interestingly, the regulation also foresees the need to conclude an international agreement to that effect and stipulates that, if such an agreement is not in place, a trade repository established in the third country would not be recognised by ESMA. CCPs in third countries would be able to operate in the EU subject to an equivalence clause (CEC 2010).

Prior to the crisis, the UK and the US had opposed any regulation of derivatives markets (Helleiner and Pagliari 2010), acting as veto-players. After the crisis, however, they became agents of change. The US set in place a new regime for OTCs before the EU did and followed the EU debate closely. In the EU, the main agents of change were the Commission, with support from Germany and France (*European Voice,* 10 June 2010). The British government was broadly in favour but opposed some elements of the proposed legislation, such as certain powers given to ESMA. Yet, with reference the scope of the new legislation, the UK acted as an agent of change in an attempt to expand the scope of the proposed rules substantially. The initial Commission proposal only covered the OTC market but, in a hearing before the EP, Patrick Pearson, head of the financial markets infrastructure unit at the Commission, argued for the scope to be extended to all derivatives. In the Council of Ministers, the UK argued in favour of expanding the scope of new market infrastructure legislation to include exchange-traded derivatives, not just OTC ones (*Financial Times* 13 May 2011: 20; 4 October 2011). The UK, supported by the Nordic member states, also called for open-access provisions, whereby exchanges would have to allow clients to access any CCP, while clearing-houses would be obliged to accept any trade executed at other venues. Germany resisted this extension of scope (Buckley *et al.* 2012).

The scope of the regulation and access provisions had implications for competition between exchanges and clearing firms across the EU, as well as outside it. Germany's Deutsche Börse, which is a major player in trading and clearing derivatives, operates a 'vertical silos' structure, like that of the Polish stock exchange and unlike other exchanges in Europe, such as the London Stock Exchange (LSE). In a vertical structure, the stock exchange incorporates trading and post-trading services of clearing and settlement. The Deutsche Börse has most to lose from open-access provisions because this change would split its vertical model. Not surprisingly, German and Polish policy-makers opposed open access, arguing that the extension of the scope was not in line with G20 commitments. They also saw it as an attack on the business model of their national stock exchanges (*Risk Magazine*, 29 September 2011). UK policy-makers, supported by the Dutch and Scandinavians, were in favour of open access, arguing that it would allow independent CCPs to compete with CCPs that are tied to an exchange. The LSE could gain market-share from any breaking up of the vertical silos model, even though the British authorities claimed that they advocated open access with a view to closing potential loopholes in the legislation and ensuring end-user choice (*Financial Times,* 4 October 2011).

The Parliament and the Council agreed on their negotiating positions in July 2011 and October 2011, respectively. Subsequently, a trialogue between the Council, the Parliament and the Commission took place. The final (Level 1) text of the regulation was agreed in March 2012. ESMA is in the process of drafting Level 2 rules that support the Level 1 regulation. The proposal eventually approved limits the European Markets Infrastructure Regulation (EMIR) scope to OTC derivatives. It covers all segments of the OTC derivatives market (interest rate, credit, equity, foreign exchange and commodities) and there are some exemptions from clearing and reporting requirements for non-financial firms. An article on the access of CCPs to venues of executions was included in the final draft, giving access rights of CCPs to transactions traded on a venue of execution. However, this provision does not imply the implementation of interoperability arrangements between those CCPs.[6]

---

6.   http://europa.eu/rapid/pressReleasesAction.do?reference=MEMO/12/232&format=HTML&age
     d=0&language=EN&guiLanguage=en

Interstate, domestic, and transnational explanations for incremental changes

All in all, the reforms introduced by the EU after the crisis were mostly incremental. On the one hand, it is true that the new rules either regulate activities or financial institutions that were previously unregulated in the EU and its member states (CRAs), or at the EU level (AIFMs), or at the national, EU and international levels (OTCDs). In other instances, they impose heavier, more prescriptive and more burdensome requirements on financial entities that were already regulated prior to the crisis, as in the case of higher capital requirements for banks and new liquidity management rules (Basel III).

On the other hand, in several instances, the content of the rules initially proposed was watered down during the negotiations, as in the case of the AIFM directive. Some watering down also took place when the EU decided to incorporate the revised international standards on capital requirements into EU legislation. Moreover, several key controversial issues, such as the problem of financial institutions that are too big to fail,[7] were not addressed. For these reasons, taken individually, the measures adopted by the EU are incremental changes rather than path-breaking reforms, especially given the fact that they were the response to the most severe financial crisis since the 1930s. What accounts for this? The introduction to this volume puts forward a series of explanations that can be applied to the empirical records (*see* Moschella and Tsingou's Introduction in this volume).

If one takes an *interstate perspective*, the different preferences amongst the main member states limited the scope of change. 'Financial regulation will be significantly enhanced when leading states have a common interest in more stringent regulation' (Moschella and Tsingou in this volume), but this was not the case in the EU. As is common in EU negotiations, legislative outcomes were often the result of compromises and trade-offs amongst the member states gathered in the Council and of arm-twisting between the Council and the Parliament. Hence, the new rules were often based on the lowest common denominator, to placate veto-players and avoid deadlock.

By and large, the new or revised rules as well as the reshaped institutional framework were actively sponsored, or at least strongly supported, by France, Germany, Italy, Spain and the EP (especially the socialist groups). They were the main agents of change and were the members of what Quaglia (2010a, 2010b) identified as the 'market-shaping' coalition that was active in the making of EU financial regulation well before the financial crisis. The proposed EU measures were seen as necessary to safeguard financial stability and protect investors. Some of the proposed rules, such as those concerning AIFMs, CRAs and OTCDs, also embodied the deeply ingrained dislike in these European countries of 'casino capitalism' (Strange 1997), which was seen as serving the fortunes of the City of London.

---

7.   Shortly before the Bank of England took over banking supervision, Governor Mervyn King controversially called for the breaking up of the big banks. He also remarked that '[...]if a bank is too big to fail [...] it is simply too big.' (*The Guardian*, 17 June 2009).

The new rules, or at least certain aspects of them, were generally resisted by the UK, Ireland, Luxembourg and a variable mix of Nordic countries, which acted as veto-players, depending on the specific legislative measures under discussion. These were the main members of what Quaglia (2010a, 2010b) identified as the 'market-making' coalition, which, prior to the financial crisis called for a market-friendly approach to financial regulation in the EU. It is, however, noteworthy that, as substantiated in the following discussion of the domestic politics perspective, continental countries were particularly keen to set in place stricter rules concerning financial services that were not of major direct concern to their financial systems, such as AIFMs and OTCDs.

A somewhat special case was the revision of the Basel II accord, which resulted in the Basel III accord as well as the parallel revisions of the CRD. Despite the fact that banking regulation and integration is fairly advanced in Europe (the first banking directive dates back to 1977), the EU was deeply divided in the negotiations on the Basel III accord. The UK favoured strict new rules on capital requirements, whereas France, Germany and Italy called for 'softer' rules and a longer transition period. This had much to do with domestic political-economy considerations related to the existing low level of banks' capital and the bank–industry links in continental European countries, as argued by domestic-level explanations. Eventually, the outcome was still based on a compromise between the different preferences of the main member states.

In the case of capital requirements, the UK was the main agent of change in the EU debate as well as in the international debate in the BCBS, where the US was its main ally. The UK was also an agent of change in trying to expand the scope of EMIR. This suggests that the role of different countries as either agents of change or veto-players was not a given. It very much depended on the legislative measures under discussion and the implications of those measures for national financial systems. For example, most of the AIFMs in Europe are based in the UK. By contrast, France has a thriving sector of managed funds, which were already regulated in the EU and were potentially in competition with hedge funds (Woll 2012). This distinctive feature of the French financial system contributed to the eagerness of the French authorities to regulate AIFMs in the EU. The British attempt to expand the scope of EMIR has much to do with the competition between the LSE and the Deutsche Börse. All this suggests that policy-makers were not only worried about setting in place rules for a safer, more stable financial system. They were also playing the competition game, trying to set in place EU rules that were most advantageous for their national financial industry.

Taking a *domestic perspective*, vested interests were weakened in the aftermath of the crisis but afterwards managed to regain a dominant institutional position (*see* Pagliari and Young in this volume). Powerful players in the financial industry were keen to limit the scope of the reforms (and of the adjustment costs related to it). The market-players primarily affected by the new or revised rules, such as CRAs and AIFMs, initially resisted the proposed rules. Subsequently, they engaged in intense lobbying with a view to having the proposed rules amended, on the grounds that they would be over-prescriptive and costly to implement, creating potential regulatory arbitrage *vis-à-vis* countries outside the EU. This argument was also used by banks that lobbied on certain aspects of the Basel III accord and the CRD IV.

In general, the financial industry found a sympathetic interlocutor in the British authorities. The concern about international 'regulatory arbitrage' has traditionally been at the forefront of British policy-makers' minds, given the fact that London is a leading financial centre which hosts many non-British-owned financial institutions and successfully competes with other financial centres worldwide to attract business (interviews, London, May 2007; July 2008). Moreover, AIFMs and CRAs were mostly based in the UK.

However, on regulation that was of substantial direct relevance to the banking system, first and foremost the Basel III accord and the CRD, domestic banks got a sympathetic reception from their own national authorities throughout the EU. In part as a result of the state-led recapitalisation in the wake of the crisis, the main British banks were relatively well capitalised when the Accord was negotiated, hence they were likely to have few problems in meeting the new capital requirements set by the Basel III accord. By contrast, the banks in many continental European countries were under-capitalised for a variety of reasons: because there had been less state-led recapitalisation in the midst of the crisis and other institutional features in place prior to the crisis (for the case of the public banks in Germany, *see* Hardie and Howarth 2009).

Further, the impact of stricter capital requirements on lending to small and medium enterprises was a major concern for continental European countries, which have a bank-based financial system, where banks provide funding to the real economy. This was less of a concern for the Anglo-Saxon countries, which rely more on financial markets for corporate finance (Buckley, Howarth and Quaglia 2012). In the literature, the international regulatory preferences of countries such as Germany and the UK are often related to the specific characteristics of their national capitalisms – co-ordinated and liberal-market respectively (*see* Moschella and Tsingou in this volume).

Beside taking a domestic perspective or an interstate perspective, one could consider the *transnational dimension* of financial-services regulation. Financial services are borderless activities, which are mostly regulated and supervised at the national level, though there are attempts to co-ordinate internationally, in particular to prevent regulatory arbitrage. For example, the issue of 'equivalence' of third-country legislation to the newly introduced EU rules was very contentious during the negotiations of several pieces of EU legislation. With reference to CRAs and AIFMs, many policy-makers felt that a mechanism was needed to recognise third-country regulation as 'equivalent' to the EU. The British authorities were generally the most vocal, because of the international status of the City of London and the large number of foreign (non-EU) players operating therein. By contrast, French policy-makers expressed some concerns about non-EU AIFMs entering the single market using the 'Trojan horse' of the passport for AIFMs (*Financial Times*, 27 April 2009). The regulation of OTCDs also posed problems of recognition of third-country legislation and access to sensitive data by foreign regulators, which is why EU legislation went as far as contemplating an international agreement on trade repositories.

Internationally, the EU and the main member states often played an important role in the debate on reforming financial regulation. Hence the agents most keen to reform financial services regulation were active in the EU as well as in international fora. During the French presidency of the EU in the second semester of 2008, Nicolas Sarkozy argued that the G8 should be enlarged to include emerging economic powers such as Brazil, China, India, Mexico, and South Africa (Sarkozy 2008). In October 2008, the French President, accompanied by Commission President José Manuel Barroso, held a meeting with President George W. Bush, paving the way for the first summit of G20 leaders in Washington, DC in November 2008 (Hodson 2010). Since then, G20 Summits have been held in London and Pittsburgh in 2009, and in Toronto and Seoul in 2010. With the backing of the EU, the G20 has *de facto* replaced the G7 and G8 as the most important forum for international economic and financial co-operation.

At the international level, the EU appeared less divided than in the pre-crisis period, not least because it tried to agree a 'common language' before the main G20 summits. Before the crisis, the competition between the market-making and the market-shaping camps also played out internationally. Indeed, two different approaches could be detected in international fora: one in favour of extending the perimeter of regulation to hedge funds, rating agencies, tax havens and so on, sponsored by Germany and France, and one resisting regulation, championed by the US and the UK (Helleiner and Pagliari 2010). At the most important G20 summits in the wake of the crisis, the Anglo-Saxon countries switched their position to favour extending regulation (Hodson 2010, *see also* Hodson 2011).

In the BCBS, the EU was represented by the European Commission, which, however, had observer status, like the ECB, without voting power. The central banks and the supervisory authorities of the G20 members, including nine EU member states, were full members of the Committee. Hence, the national authorities, as opposed to the EU authorities (namely, the Commission), were in the driving seat in the negotiations in Basel. An EU position, as such, was absent, despite attempts by the Commission to co-ordinate the positions of the European members of the Committee (confidential interviews, June–July 2011). The balance of power shifted, however, once it was time to incorporate the Basel III accord into the CRD IV, which was officially proposed by the Commission after several rounds of consultation with the national authorities and industry.

The other transnational mechanism for change was ideational politics. The global financial crisis undermined some of the key assumptions of the market-making regulatory approach in the EU (Quaglia 2012) as elsewhere (*see* Baker in this volume, Helleiner and Pagliari 2010). It was policy-learning that largely contradicted the policy-learning of the late 1990s and early 2000s, which had hailed the British model as a successful one for the EU in the struggle over the global competition for financial services (Mügge 2010; Posner and Véron 2010). Prior to the global financial crisis, British policy-makers and their regulatory philosophy had been very influential in shaping the EU's regulation of financial services. Their model was, however, perceived as discredited by the global financial crisis (Baker 2010; Helleiner and Pagliari 2010).

After the crisis, even in the UK, the stronghold of the market-making coalition, alternative views about financial services regulation began to emerge, at least in some quarters. As the Turner Review acknowledged (FSA 2009: 38–9), the global financial crisis robustly challenged on 'both theoretical and empirical grounds' the existing 'regulatory philosophy' and the 'intellectual assumptions' of 'efficient', 'rational' and 'self-correcting markets' on which it was based. In his oral evidence before the Treasury Committee, Lord Turner spoke of 'an intellectual failure' of the international regulatory community in respect of the global set of rules in place (House of Commons 2010). Andy Haldane, Executive Director at the Bank of England, authored some imaginative papers demonstrating the very limited contribution of the financial sector to the real economy in the UK (a similar view being echoed by Lord Turner)[8] and arguing that over time, the banks, have come to 'bank on' the state, with the state providing financial assistance to the banks in case of trouble (Alessandri and Haldane 2009).

The main supporters of the market-making regulatory approach, notably UK policy-makers, did not completely abandon it, but advocated it less forcefully, and some policy-makers within the market-making coalition began to question it. One of the most notable 'conversions' was that of the Commission, which switched to a market-shaping approach. In 2009, the appointment of a new (French) Commissioner for the Internal Market, Michel Barnier, was seen as a victory for the French government. He was seen by some (mainly British) policy-makers as 'suspicious of the free market' (*The Economist*, 2 December 2009). With reference to the proposed revision of the Markets in Financial Instruments directive, the Commissioner argued that the 'objective is to ensure... a stronger regulatory framework ... greater market transparency... as well as more protection for investors'.[9] On the related OTC regulation, the Commissioner argued that there has been 'a paradigm shift away from the traditional view that derivatives are financial instruments for professional use and thus require only light-handed regulation'.[10]

In the wake of the crisis and with plenty of political opportunism, policy-makers of the market-shaping coalition forcefully reiterated their 'anti-free-market' and 'anti-Anglo-American' rhetoric, feeling at least partly vindicated by the global financial crisis. The then French President, Nicholas Sarkozy, remarked that 'The idea of the all-powerful market that must not be constrained by any rules, by any political intervention, was mad. [....] Self-regulation as a way of solving all problems is finished. Laissez-faire is finished. The all-powerful market that always knows best is finished' (Sarkozy 2008). Similarly, the German Finance

---

8. Lord Turner in an interview for *Prospect Magazine* in August 2009 warned that a 'swollen' finan-cial sector paying excessive salaries had grown too big for society (*Financial Times*, 27 August 2009).

9. http://ec.europa.eu/unitedkingdom/press/press_releases/2010/10123_en.htm. Accessed February 2011.

10. http://europa.eu/rapid/pressReleasesAction.do?reference=IP/09/1546&format=HTML&aged=0 &language=EN&guiLanguage=en

Minister, Peer Steinbruck argued that 'the free-market-above-all attitude and the argument used by "laissez-faire" purveyors was as simple as it was dangerous and [German recommendations for more regulation] elicited mockery at best or were seen as a typical example of Germans' penchant for over-regulation'.[11] The Italian Finance Minister, Giulio Tremonti, before the crisis erupted in full force, called for more regulation and state interference, in his book *Hope and Fear*, arguing against 'the dictatorship of the market' (*Financial Times*, 23 June 2008). Hence, new ideas about financial regulation were road-tested and gradually percolated into the revision of financial services regulation, with the building-up of institutional support for a less market-friendly approach. Moreover, in the wake of the crisis, public attention, mobilisation and pressure on issues related to financial regulation increased and change was no longer 'managed' by a closed policy community of experts, as it had been in the pre-crisis period (Moschella and Tsingou in this volume).

Amongst the three explanations examined, the first one, interstate bargaining, seems to have the greatest explanatory power in the EU and the transnational dimension the lowest. Despite the fact that the EU is in several respects a polity in the making, EU legislation is still produced through intergovernmental negotiations, as well as negotiations between the Council and the EP. Hence, legislative output is generally a compromise between the preferences of the member states. However, these preferences are largely rooted in the domestic political economy of national financial systems. Consequently, there is a strong link between the explanations located at the EU level and the domestic level.

Conclusion

This chapter has examined the reform of financial-services governance in the EU with a view to answering the questions set out in the Introduction to this volume: was regulatory change in the EU incremental and, if so, why? It is argued that the main agent of change in reforming EU financial regulation was the Commission, which is the only body that can officially propose legislation in the EU. Of course, the Commission did so after consulting the member states informally and after holding open public consultations. In certain cases the Commission was spurred to act by other agents of change, such as the EP in the case of CRAs, and the market-shaping member states in the case of AIFMs. The main veto-player was the financial industry, which was most affected by the regulatory changes. After an initial setback in the aftermath of the crisis, the financial industry regained a prominent institutional position (on the excessive influence of the financial industry, *see* Mügge 2011). Some member states, first and foremost the UK, were sympathetic to some concerns of the industry and were worried about potential regulatory arbitrage with jurisdictions outside the EU. It should, however, be noted that for Basel III, the main veto-players opposing stricter rules were continental countries and their banks, and not the Anglo-Saxon countries.

---

11. EU observer, 26 September 2008, http://euobserver.com/9/26814

Despite the fact that, as noted in the Introduction to this volume, the conditions for a punctuated type of change were, in principle, in place, incremental changes prevailed in the EU regulatory reform that followed the crisis, due to several veto-players and entrenched interests mentioned above. However, much of EU history has been driven by small changes that cumulatively foster big changes, as pointed out by Posner (2007) with reference to financial regulation after Economic and Monetary Union (EMU). This observation raises the question of whether post-crisis incremental change is likely to persist or whether there is the potential for it to evolve into something bigger. Arguably, the sum of these incremental changes amounts to a substantial reform, albeit perhaps not the 'radical transformations' mentioned by the editors in the introductory chapter. 'Incrementalism need not be equated with conservatism' (Moschella and Tsingou in this volume). The effects of the new pieces of legislation will very much depend on how these are implemented by member states. In the case of the ESAs, their influence in the governance of financial services in the EU will depend on how they use their newly acquired power and build up (or don't) their credibility in the market.

References

Alessandri, P. and Haldane, A. G. (2009) *Banking on the State,* Paper delivered at the Federal Reserve Bank of Chicago Twelfth Annual International Banking Conference on 'The international financial crisis: have the rules of finance changed?', Chicago, 25 September.

Baker, A. (2010) 'Restraining regulatory capture? Anglo-American crisis politics and trajectories of change in global financial governance', *International Affairs*, 86(3): 647–63.

Basel Committee on Banking Supervision (2004) *Basel II: International Convergence of Capital Measurement and Capital Standards: a Revised Framework,* Basel.

— (2010a) *Basel III: A Global Regulatory Framework for More Resilient Banks and Banking Systems,* Basel.

— (2010b) *Basel III: International framework for Liquidity Risk Measurement, Standards and Monitoring,* Basel.

Brunnermeier, M. *et al.* (2009) 'The fundamental principles of financial regulation', *Geneva Reports on the World Economy*, 11.

Buckley, J. and Howarth, D. (2010) 'Internal market gesture politics? Explaining the EU's response to the financial crisis', *Journal of Common Market Studies Annual Review*, 48(s1): 123–43.

Buckley, J., Howarth, D. and Quaglia, L. (2012) 'Internal market: the ongoing struggle to "protect" Europe from its money men', *Journal of Common Market Studies,* Annual Review, 48(s1): 119–141.

Commission of the European Communities (2009) *Recommendations on Remuneration Policies in the Financial Services Sector 2009/384/EC,* 30 April 2009.

— (2010) *Proposal for a Regulation of the European Parliament and of the Council on OTC Derivatives, Central Counterparties and Trade Repositories 2010/484/5/EC,* 15 September 2010.

— (2011a) *Proposal for a Directive on the Access to the Activity of Credit Institutions and the Prudential Supervision of Credit Institutions and Investment Firms 2011/453/EC,* 20 July 2011.

— (2011b) *Proposal for A Regulation on Prudential Requirements for Credit Institutions and Investment Firms 2011/452/EC,* 20 July 2011.

Council of Ministers and European Parliament (2009) *Regulation (EC) No. 1060/2009 of 16 September 2009 on Credit Rating Agencies,* 17 November.

— (2011) *Regulation (EU) No. 513/2011* of 11 May 2011 amending Regulation (EC) No. 1060/2009 on Credit Rating Agencies, 11 May.

Darling, A. (2009) Letter to Miroslav Kalousek, Czech Finance Minister, 3 March.

de Larosière Group (2009) *The High Level Group on Financial Supervision in the EU.* Brussels, 25 February.

EurActive (2010) *EU Cuts Deal to Set Up Banking Watchdogs.* http://www.euractiv. com/euro-finance/eu-cuts-deal-set-banking-watchdo-news-497410. Accessed 11 February 2013.

European Council (2008) *Brussels European Council 15/16 October 2008 Presidency Conclusion,* Brussels, 16 October.

European Parliament (EP) (2011) *Beefing Up Credit Rating Agency Rules,* 8 June.

Federal Chancellery (2009) *Chair's Summary of the Berlin G20 Preparatory Summit,* 22 April.

Financial Services Authority (FSA) (2009) *The Turner Review: A regulatory response to the global banking crisis,* March.

Fioretos, O. (2010) 'Capitalist diversity and the international regulation of hedge funds', *Review of International Political Economy,* 17(4): 696–23.

G20 (2009a) *The Leaders' Statement,* Pittsburgh Summit, Pittsburgh, 25 September.

Hardie, I. and Howarth, D. (2009) 'Die Krise but not la crise? The financial crisis and the transformation of German and French banking systems', *Journal of Common Market Studies,* 47(5): 1017–1039.

Helleiner, E. (2010) 'A Bretton Woods moment? The 2007–2008 crisis and the future of global finance', *International Affairs,* 86(3): 619–36.

Helleiner, E. and Pagliari, S. (2010) 'The end of self-regulation? Hedge funds and derivatives in global financial governance' in Helleiner, E., S. Pagliari and H. Zimmerman (eds), *Global Finance in Crisis,* London: Routledge: 74–90.

Hodson, D. (2010) *The Paradox of EMU's External Representation: The case of the G20 and the IMF,* Conference paper. EUSA Conference, Boston, 3–5 March 2010.

— (2011) *Governing the Euro Area in Good Times and Bad,* Oxford: Oxford University Press.

House of Commons (2010) *Financial Regulation,* Oral evidence before the Treasury Committee, 23 November.

Howarth, D. and Quaglia, L. (2013) 'Banking on stability: the political economy of new capital requirements in the European Union', *Journal of European Integration,* 35(3): 333-346.

International Monetary Fund (2011) United Kingdom: Staff Report for the 2011 Article IV Consultation—Supplementary Information, July, IMF Country Report, No. 11/220, Supplementary Report.

International Organisation of Securities Commissions (2004) *Code Of Conduct Fundamentals For Credit Rating Agencies,* December, Madrid.

— (2008) *Code Of Conduct Fundamentals For Credit Rating Agencies,* May, Madrid.

— (2009) *Hedge Funds Oversight,* Madrid.

Moschella. M. (2011) 'Getting hedge funds regulation into the EU agenda: the constraints of agenda dynamics', *Journal of European Integration,* 33(3): 252–66.

Mügge, D. (2010) *Widen the Market, Narrow the Competition: Banker interests and the making of a European capital market,* Colchester: ECPR Press.
—   (2011) 'Limits of legitimacy and the primacy of politics in financial governance' *Review of International Political Economy,* 18(1): 52–74.
Pagliari, S. and Young, K. *The Wall Street-Main Street nexus in financial regulation: business coalitions inside and outside the financial sector in the regulation of OTC derivatives,* in this volume, pp. 95–123.
Posner, E. (2007) 'Financial transformation in the European Union', in McNamara, K. and Meunier, S. (eds) *Making History: European integration and institutional change at fifty,* Oxford: Oxford University Press, 139–56.
—   (2009) 'Making rules for global finance: transatlantic regulatory cooperation at the turn of the millennium', *International Organization,* 63: 665–99.
Posner, E. and Véron, N. (2010) 'The EU and financial regulation: power without purpose?', *Journal of European Public Policy,* 17(3): 400–15.
Quaglia, L. (2010a) *Governing Financial Services in the European Union,* London: Routledge.
—   (2010b) 'Completing the single market in financial services: the politics of competing advocacy coalitions', *Journal of European Public Policy,* 17(7): 1007–22.
—   (2011) 'The 'old' and 'new' political economy of hedge funds regulation in the European Union', *West European Politics,* 34(4): 665–82.
—   (2012) 'The "old" and "new" politics of financial services regulation in the European Union', *New Political Economy,* 17(4): 515–35.
Quaglia, L. *et al.* (2009) 'The financial turmoil and EU policy cooperation 2007–8', *Journal of Common Market Studies Annual Review,* 47(1): 1–25.
Sarkozy, N. (2008) 'The international financial crisis', speech by the President of the Republic (excerpts), Paris, 25 September.
Sarkozy, N. and Merkel, A. (2009) 'Letter to Mirek Topolanek, Prime Minister of the Czech Republic and Jose Manuel Barroso, President of the European Commission in preparation for the G-20 Summit', 16 March.
Strange, S. (1997) *Casino Capitalism,* Manchester: Manchester University Press.
Woll, C. (2012) 'The defense of economic interests in the European Union: the case of hedge fund regulation', in Mayntz, R. (ed.) *Institutional Change in Financial Regulation,* Frankfurt a.M.: Campus.

chapter four | global in life, still national in death? special bank resolution regimes after the crisis

Martin B. Carstensen

Introduction

One of the most costly lessons of the recent financial crisis in Europe and the US has been how important an effective framework for resolving financial institutions is. From the dramatic and catastrophic bankruptcy of Lehman Brothers, which left markets and regulators in that famous state of panic, to the inefficient break-up of the Benelux-based Fortis group, in which national prerogatives took the front seat at the expense of co-operation, or the choice of the Icelandic state only to provide help to depositors domiciled in Iceland, leaving UK and Dutch depositors uncompensated, the lesson was heeded that a fundamentally stable international financial system is premised on states building efficient national resolution regimes that are then more or less harmonised through international regulation. This is especially clear in the case of large international banks, which benefit from a global marketplace in which to offer their services but still come home to the national regulator to die. As famously pointed out by Bank of England Governor, Mervyn King (2009), global banks are global in life, but national in death. To close down banks more effectively – both banks that work across borders and banks that are more nationally oriented – a popular argument in the post-crisis debate has been to set up special bank resolution regimes, that is, a set of policies that give the authorities enhanced powers to prevent, intervene and resolve ailing financial institutions. The idea is controversial, because authorities potentially gain increased power over financial institutions and because moving these regimes to an international level naturally leads to a pooling of national sovereignty.

Similarly to the other case studies in this volume, this chapter asks if the institutional changes in integration and harmonisation of bank resolution regimes in the wake of the crisis are of an incremental nature or best characterised as a punctuated equilibrium. The short version of the answer is that, following the definition of incremental change presented in the Introduction to this volume – as significant changes that adjust policy without challenging the overall terms of a given policy paradigm – we may speak of significant yet incremental change. Thus, a near consensus has been established between international organisations and the big industry players as represented by the Institute of International Finance (IIF), that regulators should be granted the necessary instruments and tools to resolve distressed financial institutions. However, the more ambitious goal of establishing cross-border resolution regimes – where, for example, resolution funds are shared between different states and depositors and creditors and shareholders are treated equally and not discriminated against along national lines – is close to being reached only in the European case. Work on a banking union – which would include common resolution funding and a set of resolution tools – became a centrepiece of European Union (EU) crisis-management. The international policy elites – comprising both public and private actors – generally agree that an internationalised system is preferable but national authorities and financial industries, who would have to pay for such a regime, are reluctant to give up national sovereignty.

Though, as argued by Moschella and Tsingou in the introductory chapter, favourable conditions for large and punctuated types of changes in financial regulation were generally present following the crisis, cross-border resolution and internationalised resolution frameworks were two of the areas where an outcome of no change was a more realistic prospect than of big change. Since the aim of creating a cross-border resolution regime is to further financial integration, it naturally entails a loss of national sovereignty, something which, unsurprisingly, governments have been reluctant to support. The outcome of international regulatory efforts so far could serve to remind us of Germain's (2009) words that 'to date no financial crisis has ever been *resolved* at the international level' (680, emphasis in original); and it seems unlikely that this will change any time soon. Thus, though the idea of special bank resolution regimes is increasingly being implemented in national legislation, it remains to be seen if it will have a real impact on cross-border resolution.

To explain why the idea of special bank resolution regimes has been central to post-crisis debates, it is helpful to place it within the theoretical argument about the role of dynamic interaction between change-agents and veto-players presented in the introductory chapter. As noted by Moschella and Tsingou, change-agents generally lead the process of change as explicit advocates of specific changes or as hidden supporters; veto-players aim to maintain the status quo in order to preserve their privileges and safeguard their interests. In such a perspective, incremental change may easily constitute the most ambitious possible aim, a political victory in its own right. If we look for veto-players in relation to regulation on bank resolution, national authorities of countries with big financial industries, such as the American, British, Dutch or German, have been central to the process. The American authorities have opted out of anything more demanding than Memoranda of Understanding – i.e., bilateral agreements – because they see no interest in losing sovereignty by moving bank resolution to a truly global level. Following their participation in and support of the Euro, central players such as the Dutch and German authorities do feel an interest in moving important parts of bank resolution to the European level, to sever the bond between sovereigns and big lenders, but they are reluctant to support the all-out universal approach of the EU Commission, for fear of having to pick up the cheque for the resolution of southern European banks without getting a corresponding influence over their national economies.

On the other side, we find change-agents, most importantly the big financial institutions (as represented by the IIF) and international organisations like the Financial Stability Board (FSB), the Basel Committee on Banking Supervision

(BCBS), the International Monetary Fund (IMF), and the EU Commission. Though the two sets of actors share the argument that the solution to the problem of bank resolution is more financial integration rather than less, they do so for different reasons. The big financial institutions see a clear interest in upholding their pre-crisis freedom of manoeuvre, which enabled them to expand their business across borders. Though at this point it seems unrealistic to imagine a fully harmonised international system for bank resolution, it is in the interest of the IIF to support such efforts as an alternative to more structural reforms, for example the break-up of financial concerns. Or in the words of Moschella and Tsingou, the big financial players have realised that regulatory change is the only way to maintain their privileged position, and they are opting for an ambitious but not structural approach. On the other hand, arguing for further financial integration almost seems to be in the DNA of the international organisations and bureaucracies, not least for the ones which, following the implementation of an international approach, would enjoy greater influence on bank resolution, the EU Commission being a key example. The financial industry and international organisations have thus joined forces in trying to convince the national authorities of the necessity of moving resolution to an international level.

The aim of this chapter is to analyse the post-crisis debate on international integration and harmonisation of special bank resolution regimes, to determine if we are witnessing a significant shift in policies and ideas about how to resolve financial institutions – more specifically, whether regulatory debates and policy initiatives in the wake of the crisis have brought regulation closer to the universal or territorial model (*see* section 2 below) – and to offer a first, tentative explanation for these developments. The chapter is structured as follows. The next section presents the metric that will be used to determine the direction and magnitude of change introduced by new resolution policies, namely the two contrasting ideal-types of 'universality' and 'territoriality'. In the two subsequent sections, the global and European debates respectively are analysed to show how the idea of an internationalised resolution regime has gathered great support among international policy elites but still remains to be institutionalised. The fourth section explains why reform efforts are stalling and points to the reluctance of national authorities to give up sovereignty as a primary explanatory factor.

How to measure change in special resolution regimes

How could one imagine that ideas and institutions in the area of bank resolution could change in the wake of the crisis? Or put differently, what are the parameters of realistic change? As argued by Kudrna (2012: 11), there are two principled ways of closing the regulatory gap between transnational banks and national resolution regimes, namely either to integrate the regime at an international level, which provides the largest possible jurisdiction to match the operations of international banking groups, or, alternatively, to shift resolution back to the national level, requiring cross-border banks to reorganise as a string of operationally independent national subsidiaries. Following this we can suggest three degrees and forms of potential post-crisis change: full integration and harmonisation of bank resolution regimes, called a universal approach; an intermediate approach of integration and harmonisation, called a modified universal approach; and finally less integration, that is, shifting resolution to a national level, called a territorial approach (*see* Claessens *et al.* 2010; BCBS 2010: 17; Schoenmaker 2011). Naturally, in practice none of these models is currently found in its pure form, though financial regulation has, for the last twenty years or so, moved from a territorial approach towards a universalist approach, ending up with a modified universalist approach. Thus, the post-crisis setup could, in principle, move in any of the three directions.

To begin with the territorial approach, although few and far between, some have argued that the best response to the crisis would be to re-embed cross-border banks in national resolution regimes. Thus, for example, Pomerleano (2009) proposes 'that large, internationally active financial institutions – that are too big to fail or too interconnected to fail – should be reduced to holding companies of national operations that are organised as stand-alone units in the respective countries'. This would constitute a stand-alone subsidiary model, in which each subsidiary is also functionally independent, with the aim of making financial institutions less complex and more resolvable under local laws. From the perspective of the banks, this also has as an unfortunate consequence that the benefits from group structures in terms of cost-efficiency and economies of scale and scope are lost. On a more concrete level, the approach could, for example, mean that limitations were imposed on intra-group transactions, to prevent contagion and protect creditors of a given legal entity (Claessens *et al.* 2010: 87). Such a structure would reduce the risks to financial stability by creating domestic financial institutions subject to local jurisdictions in the respective markets; but it would also mostly give up on internationalisation and globalisation, posing a threat to further financial integration (Claessens *et al.* 2010: 91). This was generally the approach taken by the UK Financial Services Authority (FSA) at the onset of the post-crisis debate (FSA 2009; *see also* Kudrna 2012) as well as by the Warwick Commission (2009: ch. 8; *see also* Rodrik 2009). Interestingly, this approach to bank resolution has been more practised than preached, since few elite actors explicitly support its arguments. However, national authorities have, in the majority of cases, approached concrete instances of resolution from a territorial perspective.

As a contrast, we find the universal approach. Here cross-border banks are structured as branches in each country subject to a single common process for resolution, and all creditors of the same class, wherever located, are treated equally. The authorities would follow the so-called 'universality principle': 'This means that countries would recognise the extra-territorial effect of proceedings initiated abroad. Depositor preferences and ring-fencing assets would be ruled out' (Claessens *et al.* 2010: 85). The home-country supervisor organises the resolution and bears the costs, if not an agreement has been reached to pool resources and establish an international resolution fund to avoid the 'too big to save' problem. In all likelihood, it would also be necessary to create an international financial supervision authority, a lender of last-resort liquidity facility as well as an international deposit insurance and recapitalisation fund (Claessens *et al.* 2010:

91). The central difference from the territorial approach is that creditors and depositors are not discriminated against along national lines but rather treated equally as creditors and depositors with equal rights and interests in the resolution process. Thus, and importantly, significant national sovereignty is given up to gain increased financial integration. The universal approach has been proffered by a number of influential actors and international organisations, notably the European Commission, the IMF, the FSB, the BCBS and the industry organ, the IIF. It is also supported by academics like Goodhart and Schoenmaker (2009), Claessens *et al.* (2010), Freixas (2012) and Dewatripont and Freixas (2012). On the other hand, political actors from leading Western economies have remained sceptical of the idea of giving up sovereignty over the regulation of their own financial industries.

Finally, as a mix between the two ideal-types, we find 'modified universalism'. In this pragmatic model, focus is more on close co-operation between different authorities and the sharing of information (for example, through 'memoranda of understanding') as an alternative to the formalised burden-sharing of universalism: 'Modified universalism would give host countries the right, but not the obligation, to bring local resolutions against local parts of a SIFI (Systemically Important Financial Institution) while the home country addresses the overall resolution of the SIFI. One key condition is equitable treatment of a bank's creditors at all its entities and abroad' (Claessens *et al.* 2010: 88–9). For the modified universal model to be effective, harmonisation of, for example, resolution tools and triggers among the relevant countries would be necessary, to avoid conflicts during a crisis. The three models are compared in Table 4.1.

Table 4.1: Overview of ideal types of cross-border resolution

	Universalism	**Territoriality**	**Modified universalism**
Legal and other rules governing distribution	All assets globally are shared among creditors according to priorities of home country.	Assets can be ring-fenced so that they are first available for resolution of local claims, with any excess remitted to other jurisdictions.	Host country can decide to ring-fence but can also choose to co-operate, including remitting assets to home country.
Control of the resolution process	Home country controls resolution of SIFI and entities (branches and (most) subsidiaries).	Home country controls only the resolution of parent and domestic branches and subsidiaries. Host country mandated to pursue local resolutions.	Home country controls resolution of SIFI and all its branches. Host country can decide to co-operate as regards subsidiaries.
Legal/judicial and other processes	Local rules are consistent with universalism (e.g., no deposit preferences, laws allow other jurisdictions to pursue resolution).	Legal rules can vary, but may create inequalities of treatment between domestic and foreign creditors.	Some convergence in rules and processes (otherwise limited scope for co-operation).

Adapted from Claessens *et al.* (2010: 84).

The global debate on bank resolution

Resolution regimes are not easy to agree on, because their implementation changes the distribution of costs and rewards from resolving a financial institution. Of course, substantial burden-sharing between industry and the state is even more difficult to agree on in times of crisis, where actors are under severe economic and political pressure that make short-term solutions an enticing choice. Therefore, it comes as no big surprise that most of the actual initiatives to create special bank resolution regimes have occurred at the national level, with less energy spent on solving the problem of cross-border bank resolution.[1] According to the BCBS (2011), these and other national initiatives demonstrate a clear post-crisis trend towards the introduction of special resolution regimes. According to the committee, a number of gaps in national resolution toolkits remain, notably, a lack of certain essential powers, including powers to terminate unnecessary contracts, continue needed contracts, sell assets and transfer liabilities. Another important question – which cannot be answered unilaterally within the national models of bank resolution – is how to build a strong international framework for the resolution of cross-border banks and banks too big to dismantle within a single polity.

The onset of the financial crisis has brought the issue of crisis management and insolvency to the very top of the European and international financial regulatory agenda (Attinger 2011: 36–44). On a global level, the debate on how to resolve ailing banks has taken place at G20 summits, the first of which was held in November 2008 (G20 2008; *see also* Helleiner and Pagliari 2010). Through a number of reports by the FSB together with the BCBS (2010) on the 'too-big-to-fail' problematic and resolution of cross-border banks, the issue of bank resolution in time came to occupy a prominent position in the regulatory debate.

Debate has focused on creating compatible domestic and international policy frameworks for systemically important financial institutions, setting a new international standard for resolution regimes, including requirements for cross-border co-operation and recovery and resolution planning (FSB 2012). To address the too-big-to-fail issue, the G20 at the meeting in Seoul in 2010 asked the FSB to set out key attributes of effective resolution regimes, which were subsequently endorsed by the G20 at the Cannes Summit in November 2011. In its work, the FSB has focused on converging and strengthening national resolution regimes, cross-border co-operation arrangements in the form of bilateral or multilateral-institution-specific co-operation agreements, improving resolution planning by firms and authorities and implementing measures to remove obstacles to resolution (FSB 2011a).

---

1. Notably, a range of new special bank resolution regimes have, in a number of instances, been implemented in national financial regulation, e.g., in the US, UK, Germany and Denmark (*see* Attinger 2011; Avgouleas 2009; Brierley 2009; Carstensen forthcoming; FDIC 2011; Mayes 2009).

More concretely the FSB has – among other things – proposed:

- A set of common standards to be adopted into national resolution regimes to enable authorities to resolve failing financial firms in an orderly manner, notably transfer powers from an ailing institution to a viable institution (under extreme circumstances also with temporary public ownership).

- Replacement of management.

- The power to establish a bridge bank.

- Bail-in within resolution (write-down or conversion into equity of unsecured and uninsured creditor claims).

These powers were complemented by safeguards such as respect for creditor hierarchy and the principle that no creditor should be worse off using the resolution tools than in normal liquidation; as well as principles for funding of firms in resolution that stipulated privately financed deposit insurance or resolution funds and, if necessary, *ex-post* recovery from the industry of the costs of providing temporary financing to facilitate the resolution of the firm (FSB 2011b).

There were also requirements for resolvability assessments and for recovery and resolution planning for global SIFIs – including mutual recognition of or support for foreign resolution measures – and for the development of institution-specific cross-border co-operation agreements and information-sharing to enable home and host authorities of global SIFIs to be better prepared for dealing with crises (FSB 2011b and 2011c; *see* Avgouleas *et al.* (2013) on crisis preparation using 'living wills').

Representing the international financial industry, and primarily the big banks, the IIF has been clear in its support of the FSB's principles for resolution regimes as a viable global standard (IIF 2012). However, the IIF does not find that the principles are comprehensive *enough* to tackle the issue of cross-border resolution, the main problem being that they leave too much discretion for the authorities in triggering resolution and distributing losses and gains in resolution as well as incentives for them to ring-fence assets to satisfy national interests. The IIF has, through a number of reports (IIF 2010, 2011, 2012), sought to further the international integration of resolution regimes by pushing three main principles of post-crisis resolution reform:

- predictability in resolution means and equal and effective investor and creditor protection (IIF 2012);

- avoidance of any policies that require firms to adopt particular structures (IIF 2011); and

- increased international regulatory integration (IIF 2010).

Regarding the latter, the IIF has consistently advocated a global approach in which avoiding ring-fencing of assets and discrimination of investors along national lines is a top priority. According to the IIF,

The absence of an international framework for dealing with cross-border failures is partly responsible for the emergence of inward-looking 'self-sufficiency' approaches to regulation and supervision based on ring-fencing of national entities, creating a serious risk of fragmentation of the global economy (IIF 2010: 11).

In explaining what is meant by 'self-sufficiency', the IIF points to the Turner Review's (2009) willingness to 'use its powers to require international banks to operate as subsidiaries in the UK, to increase capital requirements on local subsidiaries, and to impose other restrictions on business operation' (IIF 2010: 34). According to the IIF, such forced requirements would forego the significant value of letting companies organise as they believe best matches their economic interest and thus more broadly dampen economic performance and growth.

Focusing on the alleged efficiency losses from a less integrated and more fragmented financial system, the IIF has argued that the crisis gave rise to the possibility of closing the gap between globally functioning financial companies and nationally minded regulatory authorities, in order to sustain economic growth. This should be done through the harmonisation of resolution tools such as bail-in of subordinated debt or unsecured senior debt, contingent capital (popularly called CoCos) and bridge banks, all preferably funded through an *ex-post* arrangement, that is, one in which the industry commits to provide funding after the event. However, the IIF (2010) does not support requiring financial institutions to draw up 'living wills' – since it 'is both misjudged in conception...and wasteful of valuable resources' (IIF 2010: 20) – or requiring a restructuring of organisational structure to enable more efficient resolution.

The EU debate on banking resolution

The recommendations by the FSB – and the call from G20 leaders to review resolution regimes in light of the crisis – formed the background for the EU Commission's June 2012 directive proposal on a framework for the recovery and resolution of financial institutions (European Commission 2012a). The proposal – which was for a long time stalled for fear that some of its more controversial parts would destabilise financial markets – is planned to be a substantive step in the direction of a 'banking union', which will expectedly include the creation of an integrated resolution regime, a single European supervisory authority with ultimate decision-making powers in relation to systemic and cross-border banks and a single European deposit insurance. The current proposal seeks to establish an EU framework for bank recovery and resolution by harmonising the crisis-management tools of the member states. In the Commission proposal these are divided into three powers (European Commission 2012a; *see* European Commission 2012b for a simple overview).

The main points of the proposal are:

A *prevention power*, by which banks are required to draw up recovery plans setting out arrangements to enable a bank to take early action to restore its long-term viability and authorities are tasked to prepare resolution plans for when banks are no longer viable. Authorities are also able to ensure resolvability by requiring banks to change legal or operational structures to ensure they can be resolved with the available tools. This should not dictate how a group operates internally (separated subsidiaries, integrated liquidity and risk management, and so on) but aims to ensure that the legal structure does not constitute an obstacle to resolvability.

An *early intervention power*, which enables authorities to put the measures described in the recovery plans into action; to draw up an action programme and a timetable for its implementation as well as to appoint a special manager for a limited period.

Harmonised *resolution powers*, which provide a Europe-wide common toolbox for resolution, including the following main resolution tools: the sale of business tool, enabling the authorities to sell all or part of an ailing bank to another bank; the bridge bank tool, through which the authorities may identify good assets and separate them into a new bank (bridge bank), with the aim of selling the business to the private sector when market conditions are appropriate; the asset-separation tool, whereby the bad assets of the bank are put into an asset-management vehicle (the tool may only be used in conjunction with other tools to prevent an ailing bank receiving support without undergoing restructuring); and the bail-in tool which – to buy time and preserve value by recapitalising and subsequently dismantling an ailing institution as a 'going concern' or continue vital functions – wipes out shareholders and recapitalises the bank, writing down or converting into equity the claims of unsecured creditors. To make the bail-in tool credible, the directive proposal requires a sufficient amount of liabilities subject to write-down to provide necessary bail-in capacity, suggesting that ten per cent of total liabilities could represent a viable threshold but leaving it up to national authorities to determine the exact percentage.

The issue of further financial integration through the strengthening of cross-border resolution also takes up a substantial part of the Commission's proposal. The Commission proposes that resolution colleges are established, with the participation of the European Banking Authority, to function as a foundation for increasingly integrated EU-level oversight of cross-border entities. Essentially, these measures are aimed at co-ordination and information-sharing rather than what the Commission believes is necessary in the long run, namely, a 'banking union'.

One of the most controversial subjects in the proposal is funding of the resolution powers. To avoid the state and taxpayers being forced to provide resolution funding, supplementary funding will be provided by national resolution funds, which will raise contributions from banks proportional to their liabilities and risk profiles reaching 1 per cent of covered deposits in ten years (representing, as of March 2012, around €80 billion for the EU as a whole and €65 billion for the

Euro area). Falling short of a common European resolution fund, the proposal does open up the possibility that resolution funds collected in one state – amounting to a maximum of half of the funds that a national financing arrangement has available at the moment – be used for resolution in another member state. If the *ex-ante* funds are insufficient to deal with the resolution of an institution, further contributions will be raised *ex-post*. Where indispensable, borrowing facilities from the central bank will also be a funding possibility.

Though the EU resolution regime is, in principle, constructed to avoid future crises, it has come to play an important role in the struggle to save the Euro, specifically in demonstrating commitment to the common currency by building a 'banking union'. Thus, at the June 2012 Council meeting, a potentially important step in the direction of a more full-fledged banking union was taken when it was decided to establish common European banking supervision, with a special eye to cross-border banks and the banks that receive loans through the European Financial Stability Facility. A number of important further steps in that direction were also taken – an integrated system for the supervision of cross-border banks a single deposit-guarantee scheme and an EU resolution fund – which all point in the direction of setting up a European banking union, at least in the long term. It should be noted, though, that in an optimistic estimation from the Commission, full implementation of a banking union is not expected until 2014.

What kind of change and why?

What kind of ideational and institutional change, then, has followed in the wake of the financial crisis in the area of special resolution regimes? In a national context, ideas not seriously dealt with before the crisis have now certainly risen to prominence and are being implemented in national legislation, forming an international trend towards the introduction of special resolution regimes (BCBS 2011). Most of the ideas now being discussed and implemented were around before the crisis hit. Thus, though these ideas are not new, they have been moved to the top of the policy agenda and are being implemented in the new national resolution regimes; this makes special resolution regimes a significant development in post-crisis financial regulation. Another important question is whether the resolution tools will actually be put to use in this crisis or a future one, that is, whether European or national authorities will be willing to resolve a major financial institution in trouble and, if so, the extent to which the new resolution tools will be effective in a crisis situation of great complexity. Ideational consensus has arisen and institutions are being led to some harmonisation of resolution tools but if we are to talk of significant change these ideas and institutions need to matter in practice: and, clearly, it is far too early to say if they will.

At the international level, as should be clear from the above analysis, ideas about building a special resolution regime have moved to the top of the agenda in international regulatory reform. As was the case in national reforms, the idea of an international cross-border resolution regime existed well before the crisis but it took the financial crisis for the ideas to gain political traction. Which ideas, then, are being considered: the universal, modified universal or territorial approach? On the global level – as represented primarily by the FSB – regulatory reform has, with the focus on harmonisation, co-operation and information-sharing, been framed within a modified universal approach. Lacking more formal power, the FSB has provided a number of suggestions on how to harmonise national resolution regimes, enhance cross-border co-operation and improve contingency planning in cross-border financial institutions. The financial industry – as represented by the IIF – was quick to realise that to avoid the worst outcome – for example, regulators going for a break-up of financial institutions that are 'too big to fail' and 'rolling back' financial globalisation by turning cross-border financial institutions into holding companies organised as stand-alone units in the respective countries – accepting bail-ins and other resolution tools was a necessary sacrifice. Thus, over the last couple of years, the IIF has become a staunch supporter of an ambitious universal approach to bank resolution. Or to put it in the words of the Introduction to this volume, the IIF has adapted to new challenges to maintain a privileged position. Despite a committed financial industry, though, on a global level policies are – as could be expected considering the national sovereignty at stake – very far from reaching a fully integrated level.

On a European level, things look very different. After having postponed the EU resolution policy out of fear of negative market reactions, the plan to recapitalise Spanish banks finally brought the question of a credible European resolution regime to the forefront of crisis-management. After demands primarily from Germany that influence and control should follow the liability of granting loans to ailing banks, talk of an actual banking union reached the top of the Commission's agenda, with a common European financial supervisor as the first concrete result. Broad agreement exists that a universal model for resolving ailing financial institutions is necessary, to sever the connection between sovereigns and their lenders – and make the threat of resolving too-big-to-fail financial institutions credible – but disagreement over how the system should be arranged persists. An institutional setting is currently in the making for the ideas to translate into policy action but we do not yet know if and how that will happen. Thus, at this point, we only see the contours of a European institutional platform (*see also* Quaglia in this volume for an analysis of how this relates to the broader European-level reform agenda).

Though post-crisis bank resolution regimes are only just emerging, making it impossible to finally determine whether we will end up with fundamental or incremental change, it is possible to identify some of the most important change-agents behind these reform efforts. International organisations and forums like the G20, the Basel Committee and FSB have obviously been instrumental in putting the question of special resolution regimes on the international agenda; but the reforms being implemented are generally decided on a national level and so much of the explaining could probably be done within the domestic dimension, with reference to national change-agents. This also applies in the case of the EU. Though the Commission has been an enthusiastic supporter of a universal European resolution regime – leading to finalisation of an inner market for financial services – the funds necessary to build such a system, as well as the national sovereignty that must necessarily be given up, come from the member states. Among these, net contributors such as Germany and the Netherlands have, unsurprisingly, been most sceptical about effectively mutualising the debt of French, Spanish or Italian lenders through a banking union.

As argued above, pre-crisis bank resolution regimes were largely national in scope and so the move from co-ordination between national systems to a universal system will be lead by states. Considering that international post-crisis regulatory efforts are probably more likely to lead to fragmentation than the strong international standards necessary for a move to a universal resolution regime (Helleiner and Pagliari 2011), reluctance among net contributors – with Germany standing prominent among these – goes a long way to explain the foot-dragging. It is not so much German financial market-size *per se* that explains the central position of Germany in building a European resolution regime (or 'banking union') as it is the importance of the German state and financial industry standing behind and guaranteeing the financial viability of the European banking sector and thus taking on an indirect responsibility for ailing banks in other countries. And it is the risks associated with *de facto* pooling of European sovereign debt without a fiscal union to control member-state spending and budgets that makes both the Bundesbank and German business interests and politicians wary. Thus, the building of a pan-European bank resolution regime depends to a large degree on Germany's perception of its national interest.

The problem of resolving cross-border banks is nicely analysed by Schoenmaker (2009, 2011) as a 'financial trilemma', where the three objectives of financial stability, financial integration and national financial policies cannot simultaneously be met. One of these objectives has to give, otherwise the result will be, as has so far been the case, financial instability. To obtain financial stability, either regulators roll back financial integration, for example through ring-fencing assets by requiring cross-border banks to be organised as a string of subsidiaries abroad, or they build further financial integration by establishing burden-sharing at an international level, meaning, in the European context, a move away from national resolution to an EU-based 'banking union' integrating resolution funds, financial supervision and deposit insurance at the European level. To do so, however, national policy-makers will have to give up a significant amount of national sovereignty, focus less on their immediate national interest and be willing to use taxpayers' money to bail out banks from other member states, which is politically sensitive, to say the least. Moreover, the current economic and financial environment has obviously not been conducive to further financial integration. Quite to the contrary, countries in crisis have scrambled to save as many assets as possible for their own economies and recent reports indicate that banking across borders is fizzling (*The Economist* 2012). The short answer to why a common European resolution regime has taken so long to agree on is thus quite simple: setting up a common European supervisor, deposit-guarantee and resolution fund requires giving up important powers over national financial sectors as well as 'strong' economies (like the German) underwriting the private debt of lenders in 'weak' economies such as those of Spain or Italy.

Conclusion

As should be clear from the analysis set out above, several years into the crisis a lot has been done, leading to the implementation of new resolution tools and – on an ideational level – the development of concrete policy ideas about how to avoid taxpayers having to foot the bill for the errors of bank managers. Most of the ideas were also around before the crisis – and in that sense they are not new – but it has not been possible before now to get them on the agenda and implemented. Most of the concrete changes are found at the national level, where an increased harmonisation of resolution tools and triggers has occurred but, even here, the question still remains whether these tools will actually be put to use in any future crisis. One problem is that the tools might not be enough, even if they were consistently put to use. Take as an example the hotly debated bail-in tool, which is supposed to recapitalise the balance sheet of an ailing financial institution without any injection of external capital. As argued by Attinger (2011: 39) the bail-ins

> allow for the recapitalization of the balance sheet without any injection of external capital. The assumption is that after brushing up the balance sheet, new investors will be found more easily, as the bank looks far healthier, and, in fact, is healthier, as its liabilities will have been considerably reduced. However, it is far from guaranteed that the market will react positively and that investors are willing to inject fresh money into the credit institution concerned.

This is just one example; the general point is that we know relatively little about how these tools work in practice, especially during a full-blown crisis in all of its complexity. When the Danish authorities for the first time in modern European history used a bail-in tool to make creditors pay for the resolution of Amagerbanken and, later, Fjordbank Mors, they experienced the problem of being shut out of international money markets, which put severe pressure on the Danish financial sector. Since then, the Danish resolution regime has *de facto* been taken out of use (Carstensen forthcoming). In the Danish case, we are talking about relatively small banks in a relatively small and home-market-oriented financial sector. Making creditors pay for resolution would be much more difficult when shutting down a company the size of Lehman Brothers or AIG in the middle of an enormously complex global crisis.

Building effective resolution regimes at both the national and international levels is indeed an ambitious endeavour and, in time, it might very well turn out that reform efforts were in vain. For now, though, the incremental changes implemented so far are useful for change-agents and veto-players alike, although for different reasons. The change-agents of the big financial institutions seem mostly focused on maintaining their relatively privileged position, whereas the change-agents of international organisations seek to enhance their position in the landscape of international financial regulation. At the same time, on an interstate level, the actors who sit on the money – the national authorities – stall the process in an effort to avoid expenses from bank resolution. Indeed, post-crisis reform of special bank resolution regimes lends credibility to the assertion that, for actors advantaged by existing institutional arrangements and with no interest in altering the previous pattern of resource distribution, it is easy to see the political value of incremental change.

References

Attinger, B. J. (2011) 'Crisis management and bank resolution: quo vadis, Europe?', *Legal Working Paper Series no. 13*, December 2011, European Central Bank.

Avgouleas, E. (2009) 'Banking supervision and the special resolution regime of the Banking Act 2009: the unfinished reform', *Capital Market Law Journal*, 4(2): 201–35.

Avgouleas, E., Goodhart, C. and Schoenmaker, D. (2013) 'Bank recovery and resolution plans (living wills) as the catalyst of global financial reform', *Journal of Financial Stability*, 9(2): 210–218.

Basel Committee on Banking Supervision (2010) *Report and Recommendations of the Cross-Border Bank Resolution Group*, March 2010, Basel: Bank for International Settlements.

— (2011) *Resolution Policies and Frameworks – Progress so far*, July 2011, Basel: Bank for International Settlements.

Brierley, P. (2009) 'The UK Special Resolution Regime for failing banks in an international context', *Financial Stability Paper no. 5*–July 2009, London: Bank of England.

Carstensen, M. B. (forthcoming) 'Projecting from a fiction: the case of financial crisis in Denmark', *New Political Economy*.

Claessens, S., Herring, R. J., Schoenmaker, D. and Summe, K.A. (2010) *A Safer World Financial System: Improving the resolution of systemic institutions, Geneva Reports on the World Economy 12*, International Center for Monetary and Banking Studies.

Dewatripont, M. and Freixas, X. (2012) 'Bank resolution: lessons from the crisis', in Dewatripont, M. and Freixas, X. (eds) *The Crisis Aftermath: New regulatory paradigms*, Center for Economic Policy Research: 105–43.

The Economist (2012) 'The retreat from everywhere', April 21 2012, http://www.economist.com/node/21553015. Accessed 11 June 2012.

European Commission (2012a) *Proposal for a Directive of the European Parliament and of the Council Establishing a Framework For the Recovery and Resolution of Credit Institutions and Investment Firms*. http://ec.europa.eu/internal_market/bank/docs/crisis-management/2012_eu_framework/COM_2012_280_en.pdf. Accessed 12 February 2013.

— (2012b) 'New crisis management measures to avoid future bank bail-outs', press release, Brussels, 6 June 2012.

Federal Deposit Insurance Corporation (2011), 'The orderly liquidation of Lehman Brothers Holding Inc. under the Dodd-Frank Act', *FDIC Quarterly* (5) 2: 1–19.

Financial Services Authority (2009) *The Turner Review: A regulatory response to the global banking crisis*, London: FSA.

Financial Stability Board (2011a) *Effective Resolution of Systemically Important Financial Institutions: Recommendations and timelines*, Basel: Financial Stability Board.

— (2011b) *Key Attributes of Effective Resolution Regimes for Financial Institutions*, October 2011, Basel: Financial Stability Board.

— (2011c) *Policy Measures to Address Systemically Important Financial Institutions*, 4 November 2011, Basel: Financial Stability Board.

— (2012) *Extending the G-SIFI Framework to Domestic Systemically Important Banks: Progress report to G-20 Ministers and Governors*, Basel: Financial Stability Board.

Freixas, X. (2012) 'Towards a new framework for bank resolution', *voxEU*, 1 September 2012. http://www.voxeu.org/article/towards-new-framework-bank-resolution. Accessed 5 October 2012.

G20 (2008) *Declaration, Summit on Financial Markets and the Global World Economy*, November 2008, Washington. http://www.g20.org/images/stories/docs/eng/washington.pdf. Accessed on 19 June 2012.

Germain, R. (2009) 'Financial order and world politics: crisis, change and continuity', *International Affairs*, 85(4): 669–87.

Goodhart, C. and Schoenmaker, D. (2009) 'Fiscal burden sharing in cross-border banking crises', *International Journal of Central Banking*, 5(1): 141–65.

Helleiner, E. and Pagliari, S. (2009) 'Crisis and the reform of international financial regulation', in Helleiner, E., Pagliari, S. and Zimmerman, H. (eds) *Global Finance in Crisis: The politics of international regulatory change*, London and New York: Routledge, 1–17.

— (2010) 'The end of self-regulation? Hedge funds and derivatives in global financial governance' in Helleiner, E., S. Pagliari and H. Zimmerman (eds), *Global Finance in Crisis,* London: Routledge: 74–90.

— (2011) 'The end of an era in international financial regulation? A postcrisis research agenda', *International Organization*, 65(1): 169–200.

Institute of International Finance (2010) *A Global Approach to Resolving Failing Financial Firms: An industry perspective*, May 2010, Washington, DC: Institute of International Finance.

— (2011) *Addressing Priority Issues in Cross-Border Resolution*, May 2011, Washington, DC: Institute of International Finance.

— (2012) *Making Resolution Robust – Completing the Legal and Institutional Frameworks for Effective Cross-Border Resolution of Financial Institutions*, June 2012, Washington, DC: Institute of International Finance.

King, M. (2009) 'Finance: a return for risk, working compass of international banks', speech to Worshipful Company of International Bankers, Tuesday 17th March 2009. http://www.bankofengland.co.uk/publications/Documents/speeches/2009/speech381.pdf. Accessed 12 February 2013.

Kudrna, Z. (2012) 'Cross-border resolution of failed banks in the European Union after the crisis: business as usual', *Journal of Common Market Studies*, 50(2): 283–99.

Mayes, D. G. (2009) *Banking Crisis Resolution Policy – Different country experiences. Staff memo no. 10*, Oslo: Norges Bank.

Pomerleano, M. (2009), 'A solution to financial instability: ring-fence cross-border financial institutions', *VoxEU.org*, 7 August. http://www.voxeu.org/debates/commentaries/solution-financial-instability-ring-fence-cross-border-financial-institutions. Accessed 6 October 2012.

Rodrik, D. (2009) 'A Plan B for global finance', *The Economist*, 12 March 2009.

Schoenmaker, D. (2009) 'The financial crisis: financial trilemma in Europe', VoxEU. org, 19 December 2009. http://voxeu.org/index.php?q=node/4420#fn. Accessed 11 June 2012.

— (2011) 'The financial trilemma', *Economic Letters*, 11(1): 57–9.

Tsingou, E. (2009) 'Regulatory reactions to the global credit crisis: analyzing a policy community under stress', in Helleiner, E., Pagliari, S. and Zimmermann, H. (ed.), *Global Finance in Crisis. The politics of international regulatory change*, London: Routledge: 21–36.

Véron, N. (2007) 'Is Europe ready for a major banking crisis?', *Bruegel Policy Brief*, 2007/03.

Wall, L. D. (2010) 'Too big to fail: no simple solutions', *Notes from the Vault 2010*. FRB of Atlanta.

Warwick Commission (2009) *The Warwick Commission on International Financial Reform: In praise of unlevel playing fields*, Warwick: Warwick University.

chapter five | offshore financial centres, shadow banking and jurisdictional competition: incrementalism and feeble re-regulation[1]

Thomas Rixen

Introduction

One reason why financial crises occur is that market participants make use of regulatory gaps in order to realise greater profits. In the process, they take on ever more risk, which they manage to hide from regulatory agencies, or to which regulators, if they are aware of the risks, turn a blind eye. Eventually, the bubble bursts and regulators try to close the particular regulatory gap that has led to the problem. In the current crisis, the main regulatory gap is the existence of a largely off-balance-sheet, non-bank financial system, the so-called shadow-banking system. Banks sponsored special-purpose vehicles (SPVs) in which credits were securitised and sold on the market. While securitisation in itself could lead to a more efficient allocation of risks, this business was to a large extent driven by regulatory arbitrage. By using off-balance-sheet vehicles, banks circumvented minimum capital requirements to hand out more credit, thus fuelling the credit bubble.

One element of this regulatory gap is offshore financial centres (OFCs). Most shadow-bank entities are incorporated offshore and enjoy the tax and regulatory privileges offered by these places. It was therefore warranted to target OFCs after the crisis – one of the most immediate and publicly discussed policy reactions of the G20. However, the regulatory response towards OFCs and shadow banking falls short of what would be needed. For one, we only see incremental rather than the radical reform that might have been expected given the severity of the crisis. The initiatives are at best minor improvements over the status quo. In addition, in many instances there is a remarkable misfit between the causes of the crisis and the content of policies. The policies adopted do not touch on those aspects of OFCs that are relevant to the shadow-banking strategy and financial instability. They merely intensify policies that were initiated earlier for different reasons. I argue

---

1. Jakob Ache, John Biggins, Reinhart Blomert, Sebastian Botzem, Peter Dietsch, Jan Fichtner, Philipp Genschel, Martin Höpner, Sonja Juko, Roy Karadag, Andreas Kruck, Peter Mayer, Manuela Moschella, Daniel Mügge, Lena Rethel, Peter Schwarz, Leonard Seabrooke, Matthias Thiemann, Eleni Tsingou, Cornelia Woll and Kevin Young offered helpful comments. Xaver Keller and Anne Siemons provided research assistance. Thanks to all of them.

that these policies serve a symbolic purpose, to appease popular sentiment without having actual effect. The case of OFCs and shadow banking is not only one of incremental but also of insufficient reform. While incrementalism clearly has its virtues, as Moschella and Tsingou point out in the Introduction to this volume, they do not apply in this case. How can we explain this feeble incremental regulatory response to OFCs and shadow banking?

This outcome is puzzling in some respects. Given the severity of the crisis, and the serious strain it put on the public finances of big, industrialised countries, many expected a different outcome, that is, swift and radical reform of the global and domestic financial systems. From a realist perspective, which focuses on the interstate dimension of financial regulation, one might expect that big and powerful countries, which see their regulatory intentions undermined by OFCs and shadow banking, could easily have pressured small offshore countries into compliance with stricter standards. From a rationalist perspective, which conceives of states as unitary actors and also focuses on the interstate dimension, one might expect the governments of big and wealthy countries to push for reform successfully. There should be room for mutually beneficial co-operation between big countries and OFCs; big-country governments should be able to offer efficient side-payments to OFCs in return for abstaining from their harmful policies. In a constructivist vein, which focuses not only on the interstate but also on the transnational dimension, one might perceive OFCs and shadow banking as manifestations of neoliberal ideology and ideas and thus expect more radical change, since the financial crisis, which could be perceived as a 'focusing event' (Kingdon 1984), put this ideology in question.

As Moschella and Tsingou discuss in the introductory chapter, one can also construct explanations in each of the three dimensions – interstate, domestic and transnational – that make incremental change the likely outcome. In this chapter, I want to propose an explanation for the incremental and feeble nature of regulatory reform that modifies the baseline expectation of the rationalist framework. I argue that the outcome of incremental and feeble reform can be explained within a rationalist framework, albeit one that gives up the unitary-actor assumption and instead models the situation as a two-level game. This means that my account focuses on both the interstate and the domestic dimension of financial governance and links both of these dimensions.

In a nutshell, my explanation is the following. Re-regulation is hampered by intensive jurisdictional competition over internationally mobile financial activity. Governments fear losing financial and economic activity to their competitor states. They are not able to solve the collective action problem to curb or ease competition with each other because they are influenced or even captured by domestic financial-interest groups, which lobby governments to refrain from effective regulation. Combined with the structural constraint of jurisdictional competition, these interest groups become effective veto-players. At the same time, governments are susceptible to popular and electoral demands for stronger regulation. The electorates in big onshore states can be seen as change-agents. This dual set of factors can explain why the outcome is not the absence of reform.

Subject to these different pressures, governments can only agree on incremental and ineffective reforms, which are symbolically potent enough to soothe popular demand for action.

The existing international institutions, which are responsible for developing standards and recommendations for financial governance, exhibit a surprising stability. The deadlock among governments makes significant institutional reform impossible. Despite some changes, like a stronger role for the G20 and an energised Financial Stability Board (FSB), the basic principles of the international governance structure of financial regulation remain unchanged. In particular, the institutional landscape remains fragmented (with different institutions working on different but strongly interlinked issues) and largely consists of club-like, expert-driven institutions, which at best achieve some minimum co-ordination of different domestic regulatory systems but do not possess any enforcement powers. Global financial regulation exhibits path dependence and continues on its previous trajectory. As the case of OFCs and shadow banking shows – and contrary to the expectations of some analysts – the basic mechanisms of jurisdictional competition and financial-interest-group pressure, which drove policy before the crisis, still hold the reins after the crisis.

The rest of this chapter is structured as follows. In the next section, I explain what OFCs and shadow banks are and how they have directly and indirectly contributed to the financial crisis. The third section presents a simple two-level game of jurisdictional competition and domestic interest-group politics, from which implications for both the expected outcome and the process of regulatory reform are derived. In the fourth section, I trace regulatory initiatives after the crisis and evaluate this record against the conjectures derived from the model. The conclusion summarises the main findings and draws out some implications for our understanding of incremental change.

What is the problem?

In this section, I explain how OFCs and shadow banking contributed to the financial crisis, taking each issue in turn. After that I briefly consider three counter-arguments and reject them by pointing out that they underestimate the effects of competition among governments.

Offshore financial centres

While there is no generally accepted definition of an offshore financial centre, the term generally refers to states or dependent territories which offer significantly lower taxes and/or laxer financial regulation than 'onshore' jurisdictions. OFCs intentionally create rules for the primary benefit and use of those not resident in their geographical domain. These rules are designed to circumvent the legislation of other jurisdictions. Often, OFCs create a deliberate, legally backed veil of secrecy that ensures that those making use of them cannot be identified to be doing so (Palan *et al.* 2010: 33–5). Analytically, two functions of OFCs can be distinguished – as financial-regulatory havens and tax havens. Tax havens offer very low or zero taxes and strict banking secrecy rules. They do not exchange tax-relevant information with other countries or do so only under very restrictive conditions. This way, they enable non-resident individuals or companies to avoid or evade taxation in their country of residence (OECD 1998: 15–16). A financial-regulatory haven offers light financial regulation and supervision, less stringent reporting requirements and trading restrictions. This often includes no or modest minimum capital requirements and opacity on the beneficial owners of the businesses incorporated there.

While the analytical distinction is valid, in reality most OFCs offer both tax and regulatory loopholes. For example, jurisdictions such as the Cayman Islands or the British Virgin Islands aim to attract business through both tax and regulation. On the other hand, Switzerland is a tax haven but not a financial regulatory haven. For the purposes of this paper, a jurisdiction will be considered an OFC if it offers at least one of the two functions. As will be shown, both the tax and financial regulatory aspects pose dangers to financial stability.[2]

Most financial institutions in regulatory and tax havens will be under the control of non-residents, who use them to channel funds to other non-residents. This means that the financial sector in regulatory havens by far exceeds the size necessary to finance the local economy (*cf.* IMF 2000). In order to benefit from regulatory and tax advantages, non-residents can register offshore corporations or international business corporations (IBCs), of which the infamous special-purpose vehicles (SPVs) and structured-investment vehicles (SIVs) are examples. Or they may purchase a banking licence and set up a subsidiary of a multinational bank.

Today, there are, depending on the classificatory scheme used, between 40 and 72 states or dependent territories that have positioned themselves as OFCs. Whereas International Governmental Organisations are more conservative in their classifications, the NGO Tax Justice Network (TJN), which campaigns against tax havens and for financial transparency, classified 72 jurisdictions as so-called 'secrecy jurisdictions'(Palan *et al.* 2010). Table 5.1 identifies OFCs according to TJN, the OECD and the International Monetary Fund (IMF).

Shadow banks and the crisis

OFCs are certainly not the sole cause of the crisis. But in the complex interaction of several factors that lie at the heart of the build-up of the credit bubble, the regulatory gaps offered by OFCs in combination with off-balance-sheet shadow banking have played a significant role. The financial crisis can be described as a bank-run on so-called shadow banks (Krugman 2009). Shadow banking consists of non-depositary banks, for example, investment banks, hedge funds and special-

---

2.   A third function for which OFCs have come under scrutiny, money laundering, will not be discussed. On this *see*, e.g., Tsingou (2010).

Table 5.1: Offshore Financial Centres according to TJN (and OECD and IMF)

America and Caribbean	Africa	Indian Ocean, Pacific	Europe	Asia, Near East
Anguilla[a1]	Liberia[a]	Cook Islands[a1]	Aland Islands	Bahrain[1]
Antigua and Barbuda[a1]	Mauritius[1]	Maldives	Alderney	Dubai
Aruba[a2]	Melilla	The Marianas	Andorra[a1]	Hong Kong[2]
Bahamas[a1]	Seychelles[1]	Marshall	Belgium	Malaysia
Barbados[1]	São Tomé and Príncipe	Islands[a2]	Campione	(Labuan)[a2]
Belize[a1]	Somalia	Nauru[a2]	(Italy)	Lebanon[2]
Bermuda[1]	South Africa	Niue[a1]	City of London	Macao[1]
British Virgin Islands[1]		Samoa[a1]	Cyprus[1]	Singapore[b1]
Cayman Islands[1]		Tonga	Gibraltar[a1]	Tel Aviv
Costa Rica[b1]		Vanuatu[a1]	Guernsey[1]	Taipei
Dominica[a1]			Hungary	
Grenada[a2]			Iceland	
Montserrat[a1]			Ireland	
Netherlands Antilles[a1]			(Dublin)[2]	
New York			Ingushetia	
Panama[a1]			Isle of Man[1]	
St Kitts & Nevis[a1]			Jersey[1]	
Saint Lucia[a1]			Liechtenstein[a1]	
Saint Vincent and the Grenadines[a1]			Luxembourg[2]	
Turks and Caicos Islands[a2]			Madeira	
Uruguay[a]			Malta[2]	
US Virgin Islands			Monaco[a1]	
			Netherlands	
			Sark	
			Switzerland[b2]	
			Trieste	
			Turkish Republic of Northern Cyprus	

On the OECD list, but not on the TJN list;
San Marino[a], Brunei[b], Chile[b], Guatemala[b], Philippines[a]

On the IMF list but not on the TJN list;
Palau[1]

a = On both OECD lists (2000; 2009). All jurisdictions considered co-operative.
b = On the OECD (2009) list, but not 2000 list. All jurisdictions considered co-operative.
1 = Co-operative jurisdictions on the IMF (2006) list (as of end January 2006).
2 = Unco-operative jurisdictions on the IMF (2006) list (as of end January 2006).

purpose vehicles (SPVs), such as structured-investment vehicles (SIVs) and asset-backed commercial paper (ABCP) conduits. It essentially provides the same functions as the traditional banking system, that is shadow banks engage in credit intermediation and maturity transformation – funding longer-term financial assets with short-term liabilities. But rather than relying on the money deposits of their customers as traditional banks do, shadow banks fund their investments with money-market instruments, such as mutual funds, short-term commercial paper, and repos. Traditional banks enjoy the privilege of a publicly provided safety net to prevent their collapse in bank runs. In return for this privilege, they are under tight regulatory control. Shadow banks, however, are not under the same regulatory obligations as traditional banks and, in theory, should not enjoy the privileges of a publicly provided safety net either (Ricks 2010).

The lack of regulatory oversight is an important incentive for creating shadow banks (Pozsar *et al.* 2010: 5–6). Significant parts of the shadow-banking system emerged through various techniques of capital arbitrage to realise greater rates of return than in the traditional banking sector. Driven by the desire for ever higher rates of return, the shadow-banking sector increased in size from $11.7 trillion to $26.8 trillion between 2002 and 2009 (IMF 2010). In the United States it outgrew the regular banking sector (Pozsar *et al.* 2010: 5). Traditional banks entered the market and sponsored SPVs, thus creating interdependencies between the traditional and the shadow-banking sectors (IMF 2010: 16–19). Importantly, shadow banks are not subject to the same capital-reserve requirements as traditional banks and therefore enjoy unrestricted possibilities for leveraged investments. In this way, the shadow-banking system has exacerbated the creation of the credit bubble (Adrian and Shin 2009). Additionally, and importantly, since SPVs are kept off the banks' balance-sheets, sponsoring banks do not have to increase their core capital buffers and can thus also (indirectly) benefit from unrestricted leverage.[3] This is because the calculation of core capital requirements is based on the banks' financial accounts.

When the market for mortgage-backed securities collapsed and the financial crisis took its course, the instability of shadow banking became apparent. Due to the connections between unstable shadow banks and traditional banks, the latter also got into trouble and some had to be saved by public intervention. At the height of the crisis, emergency policy response was almost entirely aimed at preventing shadow-bank defaults and their sponsoring banks from defaulting (Ricks 2010).

So far, the story is the familiar one but where do OFCs come in? One link is that most of the shadow banks are incorporated in OFCs. For example, around 60 per cent of all hedge funds are located offshore, with the Cayman Islands being the most prominent location (TheCityUK 2011).[4] Also, many of the SPVs that failed

---

3. In order to make sure that the SPVs could be kept off their balance-sheets, banks had to play a 'legal game, which relied strongly on an interpretation of the law according to the letter of the law rather than its spirit' (Thiemann 2011: 13).

4. Importantly, while hedge funds are incorporated offshore, the location of management is typically

in the crisis were also incorporated offshore. Well known and publicised examples are the German IKB Bank and Sachsen LB, which had managed their deals with mortgage-backed securities through SIVs in Ireland and Delaware. HSH Nordbank has about 150 off-balance-sheet subsidiaries in OFCs (Troost and Liebert 2009). Iceland's Kaupthing Bank, now state-owned, has engaged in CDS deals via SPVs in Bermuda (Weiner 2008). Cayman Islands were the largest foreign holder of US mortgage-backed securities (Lane and Milesi-Ferretti 2010).

Apart from these illustrative cases, the fact that offshore centres are major players in the global financial system and tightly interconnected with onshore jurisdictions also shows in aggregate data. In 2007, the Cayman Islands (6th), Switzerland (7th) and Luxembourg (9th) and Jersey (16th) rank among the biggest financial centres, as measured by their assets and liabilities (Palan *et al.* 2010: 25–7). On the basis of data from the Bank of International Settlements (BIS) Palan *et al.* (2010: 51) show that, in the same year, 51 per cent of the world's cross-border assets and liabilities were held in OFCs. In order to reveal some of the linkages between important economies and offshore centres, one can focus on bilateral data. For example, in 2007, foreign assets and liabilities of the United States against offshore centres amount to a sum that is about 45 per cent of US GDP (in comparison: 56 per cent against Euro-area countries and 19 per cent against Japan). The Euro area had assets and liabilities against offshore centres of about 52 per cent of its GDP, compared to 72 per cent against the USA (Milesi-Ferretti, *et al.* 2010). Importantly, however, funds also get channelled through OFCs. An analysis of financial flows shows that OFCs are used by large financial institutions in a few onshore financial centres as financial intermediaries (IMF 2010; Lane and Milesi-Ferretti 2010).[5]

Since hardly any real international investment occurs in OFCs, the strong involvement of OFCs in international financial flows can only be explained by the fact that they facilitate regulatory and tax arbitrage. OFCs increase financial risk in at least four ways. First, given their lax incorporation rules, they make it easier to register SPVs. Second, due to lax oversight and lack of co-operation with onshore jurisdictions, they allow onshore financial institutions to hide the risks involved in their offshore subsidiaries from regulators' view. Third, the low or zero taxes further increase profit margins and thus increase the incentive for risky behaviour. Fourth, and related, they foster the debt-bias of investments. One of the most common ways to minimise tax payments is thin capitalisation. As interest payments can be deducted as costs, whereas dividend payments cannot, most tax systems advantage debt over equity financing. Generally, the tax bias towards debt conflicts directly with financial regulation, which tries to lean against debt (*cf.* IMF 2009). This shows that a comprehensive approach to financial stability has to

---

onshore, with New York and London being the most important locations by far (TheCityUK 2011).

5. In fact, a closer analysis of the data suggests that the financial system is heavily concentrated in a few locations and, more importantly, a few big financial institutions (IMF 2010).

consider not only issues of financial regulation in a narrow sense but also, amongst other policies, taxation (IMF 2009).[6] This effect is exacerbated by the low or zero tax rates in OFCs; the interest payments reduce onshore tax burdens and the profit can be accumulated tax-free offshore. This increases the propensity to take on credit and to work with ever-higher leverage ratios in investments.[7] Taken together these features of offshore finance increase the investments' profit margins and make the shadow-bank strategy more attractive. To some extent, OFCs feed the shadow-banking system.

Three counter-arguments

Nevertheless, many observers argue that OFCs cannot have been a significant causal factor in the crisis because, first, SPVs in OFCs are only neutral conduits for investments made elsewhere (Rahn 2009). Second, it would have been possible to regulate offshore entities under a home state's mandate for consolidated supervision (de Larosière 2009: 75). Third, it is argued that OFCs cannot be made responsible because the establishment of off-balance-sheet shadow banks would also have been possible onshore (Loomer and Maffini 2009).

These counter-arguments have some merit and they show that it is not OFCs alone that can be accused of nurturing the shadow-banking system and excessive securitisation. Rather, OFCs are 'only' the most extreme manifestation of harmful competition among states, which has been joined by most countries' governments. It is the reality of this kind of competition, which these counter-arguments do not take seriously, that lies at the heart of the crisis.

But let us address the counter-arguments one by one. First, as has been shown, OFCs are not simply neutral pass-throughs; they allow investors to access significant regulatory and tax advantages, which, while not the only reasons for the creation of the credit bubble, certainly fuelled it. Also, the use of OFCs increases the complexity and opacity of financial transactions. This makes it more difficult for regulators to maintain adequate financial supervision but also hindered them in devising good rescue policies during the crisis (*cf.* Adrian and Shin 2009). Opacity also creates problems for market participants themselves. After the bubble burst, the main ensuing problem was the lack of trust among banks, who did not want to transact with each other because they could not trust their trading partners' balance sheets (Murphy and Christensen 2008). Admittedly, however, in the case of the

---

6. Given the focus on financial stability, I leave aside the adverse effects in terms of revenue foregone. On this *see* e.g. Rixen 2011b.

7. The sophisticated version of such thin capitalisation is the construction of hybrid instruments with many features of equity but enough features of debt to attract interest deductibility. It has been argued that the tax advantages offered by these instruments have been one of the major drivers of securitisation. In particular, Eddins (2009) has shown that, in theory, a trader can realise risk-free profits, which consist entirely in tax revenues foregone, by structuring his investments into CDSs in certain ways. In other words, tax differentials between equity and debt-financing and across jurisdictions are among the main reasons why securitisation has been undertaken.

current crisis, the opacity could probably have been managed had the SPVs been on the balance sheets of their sponsoring banks, which leads to the next argument.

Second, while consolidated supervision by the home state, coupled with co-operation and information-exchange by host states, has been one of the fundamental principles of financial regulation at least since 1983[8], it is also commonly known that cross-border co-operation of regulators does not work very well in practice, and is particularly difficult with OFCs (*cf.* Helleiner 1994: 187–8). Therefore it is often impossible for home-state regulators to get a clear picture of what is going on in offshore subsidiaries and branches. Significantly, not even home countries are very successful in implementing their part of consolidated supervision. In 2000, only 28 per cent of the countries assessed were fully compliant with it (IMF 2000). These practical problems do, however, not invalidate the more general point that onshore states could and should have effectively regulated their banks and could simply have asked them to lay open all their offshore activities, by passing regulation to require them to consolidate SPVs on their balance sheets. However, as I will show below, being in a situation of jurisdictional competition, onshore states did not want to do that.

Third, it is correct that the same or similar off-balance-sheet SPVs could also have been created in many onshore jurisdictions. However, as discussed above, in fact most of this activity occurs offshore, due to the additional benefits for investors stemming from tax and regulatory arbitrage. The reason why many onshore jurisdictions also allowed the shadow-banking sector to flourish is found in competition among jurisdictions. No one wanted to miss out on a profitable business. In that sense, OFCs can indeed not be blamed, they are merely extreme manifestations of the structural condition of competition among nation states, to which I turn now.

Jurisdictional competition

This description of the OFCs–shadow banking nexus shows that we are dealing with a phenomenon of supply and demand. On the demand side, firms, investors and other financial-market participants search for ways to minimise their regulatory and tax obligations, in order to increase their profit margins. On the supply side, sovereign jurisdictions are free to design their rules in ways that meet the demand. OFCs have pursued such policies in extreme ways and offer tailor-made solutions to investors. However, onshore states also try to attract financial activity and foreign tax bases. Examples are the US state of Delaware or the Netherlands, which enable the registration of shell companies to profit from very low tax rates. Other important financial centres with light regulation are the Japanese offshore market (JOM) and, most prominently, the City of London and New York. At the

---

8. The 'Basel Concordat' of 1975 foresaw co-operation between 'home' and 'host'' supervisors. It was revised in 1983 to take account of the growing need for consolidated supervision of international banking groups and thus prescribed prior responsibility to the home jurisdiction, aided by co-operation from the host country.

very least, big developed, that is, presumably, onshore, economies want to make sure that they do not lose the headquarters and well paid jobs of multinational companies. Thus, apart from creating certain regulatory gaps themselves, onshore jurisdictions have often allowed – or at least abstained from disallowing – their firms to access light regulations and taxes offshore. They have often followed Margaret Thatcher's advice: 'If you can't beat them, join them!' (quoted in Eden 1998: 659). Thus, it is sometimes difficult to draw clear dividing lines between onshore and offshore jurisdictions. Under globally liberalised capital flows, jurisdictional competition is a systemic condition.

Taken together this section has shown that OFCs and shadow banks are important players in global financial markets. They played a significant role in the build-up of the crisis and its development after the bubble burst. OFCs and shadow banks are an extreme manifestation of jurisdictional competition for financial activity and capital. We would thus expect that there would be a collective interest in regulating OFCs, shadow banking and jurisdictional competition. Under what conditions this collective interest can be expected to succeed, and what implications this has for the process of reform, is the question that the following model is designed to answer.

A two-level game of jurisdictional competition and capture

In regulatory competition, countries benefit individually from undercutting each other's regulatory standards to attract financial activity. The result is inefficiently low regulatory standards (a race to the bottom). Big and small countries are differently affected by this outcome and thus have diverging interests in such asymmetric competition (*see*, for example, Genschel and Schwarz 2011). Big, developed countries cannot sustain their economies on the basis of the activities of the financial sector alone but also have to guard the financial sector's interactions with the real economy. The domestic economic base, which would be subjected to inefficiently low taxes and may suffer from very low financial regulatory standards, is too big relative to the size of foreign financial activity that could be attracted.[9] For them, it should be *collectively* preferable to come to a co-operative agreement to curb regulatory competition.

For the political feasibility of reform however, the decisive question is, in how far governments have *individual* incentives to regulate. Relying on the logic of two-level games (Putnam 1988), governments have to mediate domestic and international pressures; they aim to stay within the win-set that satisfies both domestic and international demands. Thus, collective action and effective regulation will hinge on two important conditions at the international and domestic levels respectively. First, there is an international competitiveness constraint. While making it impossible for their banks and businesses to use shadow banking and

---

9. This, plus electoral pressure (*see below*) can explain why big countries do not turn into full-blown regulatory and tax havens themselves.

offshore devices would lead to better regulated markets and prevent tax revenue losses, the big-country governments would also run the danger of losing financial activity (and with it well paying jobs). To avoid these adverse effects they need to make sure that other big-country governments also implement such policies. They have to manage and overcome the *credible commitment* problem posed by their conflicting individual incentives to continue undercutting one another. In addition to the credible commitment problem, big countries also need to manage a *distributive* conflict amongst them. Some of the big countries, notably the UK and the USA, have larger financial sectors than other industrialised countries. The countries with big financial sectors have more to lose (or at least less to gain) from strict regulation and may thus be hesitant to support it.

Second, there is a domestic constraint in the form of social interests, which influence governmental preferences on financial regulation. We can distinguish between two conflicting pressures. On the one hand, domestic business and financial interests profit from regulatory and tax arbitrage possibilities offered by offshore banking. They lobby onshore governments to refrain from reform efforts. On the other hand, politicians in onshore states can be hypothesised to be under electoral pressure to push for reform. Given that the general public in onshore states suffers welfare losses, there should be majorities favouring effective reform. The logic of collective action (Olson 1965) suggests that the small group of business and financial interests, which enjoys significant and concentrated benefits, is able to exert more influence on governments than the general electorate.[10] This seems all the more likely in the field of finance. As it is a very complex matter, it will be difficult for the electorate to fully grasp the issues involved. Likewise, political decision-makers will depend to some extent on the expertise of financial-market actors. So there is an information asymmetry on top of the collective action problem of interest mobilisation. All in all, this makes it likely that financial interests can successfully capture governments. Nevertheless, we have to also account for the desire of elected politicians to accommodate popular sentiments in favour of stricter regulation. Note that, while governments cannot accommodate both demands in substance, they may try to square the circle symbolically, by passing regulations that seem to address the problems but which, in reality, leave loopholes for financial actors that are invisible to the public.

For small-country governments, the situation is different. Since their domestic economic base is small compared to the size of foreign financial activity that they can attract, they can over-compensate the potential welfare loss of lower regulatory standards. They oppose collective agreements to curb jurisdictional competition. There should also be no strong domestic opposition. As the entire economy is geared towards the offshore sector and profits from it, both economic

---

10. One might think that other domestic interests, most importantly organised labour, would counterbalance business influence on governmental policy. However, it is in theory not clear that organised labour will be in favour of regulating offshore finance (*cf.* Rixen 2011a). Empirically, while they have expressed preferences for regulation, trade unions have rarely campaigned or lobbied on the issue.

interest-groups and a majority of the electorate can be hypothesised to defend their country's status as an OFC.

Overall, this makes the strategic structure an *asymmetric prisoner's dilemma.* Big countries have classic prisoner's dilemma preferences and small countries have deadlock preferences. This means that, if the two conditions just discussed were met and big countries actually pursued regulatory efforts, they would either have to provide side-payments to OFCs or somehow use their power to force them into compliance with such an agreement. Overcoming an asymmetric dilemma is demanding, but possible. Big states would need to credibly commit themselves to collective action. What would be needed at the international level to achieve this is an institution able to define regulatory standards that were binding for all countries. Since the standards would not be self-enforcing under this particular strategic structure, the institution would also have to possess monitoring and punishment capacities. Moreover, the regime needs to encompass all big countries, to make it impossible to free-ride and exploit those adhering to the standards; i.e., a broad agreement is needed. It can be assumed that, as a group, big countries can pressure small states into compliance. If the big, developed countries collectively disallowed their resident financial actors to use offshore and shadow-banking devices, then it would no longer be profitable for OFCs to offer those services.[11] Based on this insight, we can concentrate on the international and domestic politics of big-country governments.

Conjectures on the reform process

Based on these theoretical considerations, we can make conjectures on the reform process after the financial crisis. Broadly speaking, the scenario is one of feeble and ineffective reform. While they feel pressured by their electorates to come up with stricter regulation, governments are unlikely to agree on and implement effective regulation and supervision if the international situation corresponds to a collective dilemma and if, at the domestic level, they are strongly influenced by interests opposed to reform (Putnam 1988; Zangl 1994). In such a situation, the international and domestic forces against reform combine and reinforce each other: competitive pressures at the international level make governments more susceptible to the domestic arguments of business interests; and these arguments are more credible because of the existence of jurisdictional competition. In other words, the interstate arena and the domestic arena are interlinked. As long as there is no effective and enforceable international mechanism that curbs competition among states, the competitiveness argument of domestic, financial interests can be expected to be successful. Under these conditions, the regulatory response should

---

11. Technically speaking, the k group, i.e., those countries which can sustain co-operation on regulation without hurting themselves, comprises the big, developed countries.

(at best) remain feeble – at both the domestic and international levels.[12] In addition to this general and broad expectation we can specify the following observable implications:

- Considerations of jurisdictional competition should play an important role in the reform process. We should find evidence at both the international and domestic levels that governments are aware of the competitive situation they are in.
- At the domestic level in particular, we should find that countries justify the absence or feebleness of domestic reform with concerns for their countries' competitiveness. We should see significant lobbying efforts by financial interests (veto-players) making extensive use of the argument that stricter regulation endangers a country's competitive position.
- At the international level, we should see big-country governments pushing for collective agreements on stricter regulatory standards. But we can also expect failure of these initiatives. In particular, we should see opposition from countries with big financial sectors. Given the need for an encompassing agreement, this will undermine effective regulation.
- Nevertheless, it is likely that governments wish to respond to the demands for reform by the electorate (acting as a change-agent). In order to square the circle between this need on the one hand and concerns for competitiveness and business pressures on the other, they will adopt tough rhetoric and some symbolic policies. But eventually they will, at best, implement incremental reform policies against OFCs and shadow banking.

Empirical illustration

To see if the conjectures are borne out, I describe and evaluate regulatory and supervisory activity related to offshore finance and shadow banking after the crisis. There are, in principle, three approaches to the regulation of shadow banking (FSB 2011a). The first considers shadow banking to be part of the banking sector and would simply subject it to the very same regulations in terms of capital requirements, supervision and so on as regular banks (*broad direct regulation*). This would, of course, only be effective if they were also implemented by OFCs; otherwise direct regulation could be circumvented. The second develops *specific*

---

12. Note that one could also argue for the following alternative hypothesis. Given that governments are in danger of capture by financial interests domestically, they should have an incentive to gang up at the international level. Acting collectively, they would not be susceptible to capture by small interest groups but could rather serve the interest of the broad electorate. However, given the additional distributive conflict at the international level and the fact that the electorate will be satisfied with symbolic politics (being largely ignorant of the important regulatory details) this conjecture is less likely to materialise.

direct regulations for each type of shadow-bank entity or activity. Examples would be special regulations for hedge funds or money-market funds, or certain restrictions on securitisation. Again, in order to be effective, OFCs would have to go along. The third approach eliminates the banks' vulnerability in relation to the shadow-banking sector by *indirect regulation* of the links between traditional banks and shadow banks. This would include measures such as risk-weights and additional capital buffers for banks dealing with the shadow banks they sponsor. Indirect regulation could be done by the home states of banks, that is, big developed countries, without OFCs' co-operation.

With the distinction between these three approaches in mind, I now turn to examine actual policy initiatives after the crisis. I first focus on the international level and then turn to the domestic level, in the United States and the European Union (EU), where I look at Germany, UK and France. These countries are major players in the international reform debate and were all affected, albeit to different degrees, by the breakdown of the shadow-banking system. Also, the size of their financial sectors varies. The financial sector makes up a more significant part of the economy in the USA (around 8 per cent of gross value added) and UK (around 9 per cent) than in Germany and France (around 4 per cent and 4.7 per cent respectively) (Broughton and Maer 2012). Accordingly, we expect the former to be more hesitant in re-regulation. Throughout, I will draw out the links between theory and empirical evidence.

The international level

After the crisis, arguably the most visible institutional change is the fact that the G20, rather than the G8, has taken the lead in crisis response. The enlarged club has held several summits since the peak of the crisis and has set the reform agenda. The G20 pledged 'to extend regulation and oversight to all systemically important financial institutions, instruments and markets' (G20 2009a). It also set (and continues so to do) more specific tasks for international financial institutions to pursue.[13] With respect to OFCs it set out 'to take action against non-cooperative jurisdictions, including tax havens. We stand ready to deploy sanctions to protect our public finances and financial systems. The era of banking secrecy is over' (G20 2009a). The fact that the initial steps have been taken by a group of big and developed countries shows that the model's expectation that those countries would have an interest in stricter regulation is borne out. Likewise, the enlargement of the group to twenty is evidence of the fact that actors understand the need to create a broad, multilateral initiative.

In the following, I provide an overview of the regulatory activity that has followed these strong and ambitious statements of the G20. I start with taxation and move on to financial regulatory aspects.

---

13. Among the more prominently discussed of the specific proposals are an early-warning system for financial risk, and supervisory colleges to ensure effective oversight of systemically relevant cross-border banks.

Taxation

One of the immediate political reactions to the crisis that received a lot of public attention was the attempt to exert pressure on OFCs to refrain from harmful tax practices. As instructed by the G20, the OECD reinvigorated its ongoing project on harmful tax practices. The project had been launched in 1998 and had so far made little progress. While it was initially envisaged as a broad effort to address (legal) tax avoidance and (illegal) tax evasion, it ultimately ended up targeting only tax evasion. The major reason for the curtailment of the project was successful domestic lobbying by business interests in the USA, who argued that if US firms could no longer use the offshore device they would have a competitive disadvantage against European firms whose foreign profits were exempt from home-country taxation (Rixen 2008). In response to US demands, the OECD settled for an ineffective standard of information exchange on request between national tax authorities.[14] This episode is an example of business lobbying and concerns for national competiveness reinforcing each other, as expected in my model. The required bilateral tax information exchange agreements (TIEAs) were, however, only forthcoming at a very slow speed, even though tax havens had quickly agreed to the rather soft standard of the OECD and were thus removed from a blacklist the organisation had drawn up (Rixen 2011a).

After the crisis, the OECD began to report regularly to the G20 on progress achieved. The OECD-sponsored Global Forum on Transparency and Exchange of Information for Tax Purposes – with 110 member countries the expected broad, multilateral forum – continues its peer reviews of the legal and regulatory frameworks for transparency and exchange of information in member jurisdictions. In April 2009, the OECD issued a new blacklist. The 46 listed countries were asked to reinforce their efforts at negotiating bilateral TIEAs. By the end of December 2011, the number of TIEAs had increased to 511.[15] One of the reasons why identified jurisdictions are so willing to enter into TIEAs is that the OECD has stated that, once a country has signed at least 12 TIEAs, it will be taken off the list. Tax havens therefore often conclude TIEAs between each other in order to get such a stamp of approval. Since all jurisdictions are considered co-operative, the G20 never had to prove that its threat of sanctions was credible.

While the willingness of OFCs to enter into TIEAs represents progress over the previous situation, this does nothing to ameliorate the major shortcoming, that is, the limitations of the OECD standard of information exchange on request. More important in the context of this paper, all the efforts to rein in evasion fail to address any of the tax distortions that cause financial instability. While the crisis provided the impetus for action, the policies pursued do not address the tax

---

14. Information exchange upon request is insufficient to curb tax evasion effectively because the requesting state needs initial evidence of evasion to post a request. Due to the secrecy offered by OFCs it is usually impossible to get such initial evidence (*see*, e.g., Sullivan 2007).

15. http://www.oecd.org/document/7/0,3343,en_2649_33745_38312839_1_1_1_1,00.html. Accessed 31 January 2012.

loopholes that contributed to the crisis. This shows that, as predicted, big-country governments engaged in symbolic policies to accommodate popular sentiments by continuing to pursue a project that they had agreed on earlier and that had already been curtailed to meet the needs of business interests and competitiveness concerns.

Financial regulation

From 1998 on, OFCs had been under the scrutiny of the BIS, the IMF, and the Financial Stability Forum (FSF). After the Asian financial crisis, developed countries launched an initiative to promote standards of financial regulation to be adopted by middle- and low-income countries and OFCs. The standards that were promoted were mostly already in place in high-income countries. Thus, as predicted, the initiative for stricter regulation came from the governments of big and wealthy countries. Often the standards had been developed by private actors from these countries, which also had a significant say in their development (Mosley 2010). In 2000, the FSF had drawn up a blacklist of 42 OFCs (FSF 2000) and delegated the task of assessing their regulatory systems to the IMF, which launched an OFC assessment programme and repeatedly reported on its progress. In the formulation of their policies, big-country governments were very much aware of the competitive situation they were in. All reports and statements by state representatives stressed the need to act collectively because individual initiatives would only lead to the diversion of financial activity to less regulated areas (*see*, for example, Drezner 2007).

In 2008, it was decided to integrate the OFC program into the regular Financial Sector Assessment Program (FSAP) carried out jointly by the IMF and the World Bank and thus to prepare the same Reports on the Observance of Standards and Codes (ROSC) that all countries are subject to. The main shortcoming in the FSAP framework is that the IMF (or any other international institution) does not have the authority to enforce the standards and codes. They can merely hope that publicising regulatory gaps and consequent implicit moral suasion will lead to improvements in the respective jurisdictions. Further, even in the case of positive ROSCs, there are often large but hidden gaps between the formal adoption of international standards and real compliance (Walter 2010). Also, the assessment by the IMF does not pay sufficient attention to the fact that regulators in OFCs often simply assume that they are only responsible for regulating their domestic banks – a task that they often fulfil very well and in line with the standards – and do not assume responsibility over foreign branches or subsidiaries (Troost and Liebert 2009).

The lack of enforcement capacity is due to a lack of political will on the part of big-country governments to act vigorously against countries that violate financial stability standards. Whereas in the Financial Action Task Force (FATF) initiative against money laundering, the USA, shaken up by 9/11, put its political clout and credible threats of sanctions behind the policies and consequently substantial progress was achieved (Drezner 2007; Tsingou 2010), there was far less resolve in the IMF/FSF case (*cf.* e.g. Palan *et al.* 2010). As expected by my model, concerns for the competitiveness of respective financial industries, which are irrelevant in the case of money laundering, can explain this difference. With respect to financial stability, big countries could not agree on effective measures but wanted to present regulatory activity to their electoral audiences.

After the crisis, the picture hardly changed. The FSAP remains the only international instrument for monitoring offshore and onshore jurisdictions. The renamed FSB was tasked to develop an effective peer-review programme to assess compliance with regulatory standards, which should explicitly include, but not be limited to, unco-operative OFCs (G20 2009b). Compared to the FSF, the FSB has a somewhat stronger mandate to promote financial stability (including the task of designing supervisory colleges and setting up an early-warning system), a wider membership (with all G20 countries joining), more resources and a more permanent internal organisational structure (with a full-time Secretary-General) than its predecessor. Nevertheless, just like its predecessor, the FSB merely aims at international policy co-ordination. While it is now allowed to assess countries' compliance records and publish its reports (Helleiner 2010), the FSB still does not command any 'hard' powers of enforcement. Instead, it will carry out its tasks by, essentially, relying on FSAP assessments. 'ROSCs have been an ineffective tool for promoting compliance in the past; nor did they prevent the build-up of financial fragility in the major centres before 2008' (Walter 2010). There is little change in the overall programme and these incremental reforms will not promote financial stability.

In addition to the FSAP programme, there are other policy initiatives concerned with better regulation and supervision of the shadow-banking sector. At the November 2010 Seoul Summit, the G20 asked the FSB to develop recommendations for improved regulation of the shadow-banking system. The FSB set up a task force, chaired by Adair Turner of the UK Financial Services Authority and Jaime Caruana, General Manager at the BIS. The task force shares the view that shadow banking is an important source of financial instability in the way described in this chapter. The FSB highlights the importance of a 'global approach to monitoring and policy responses' because of the danger of unhealthy competition for lower standards among jurisdictions (FSB 2011a) and thus echoes the issue of state competition at the heart of this chapter.

In a second report, prepared for the G20 meeting in Cannes, eleven recommendations, with a work-plan to further develop them in the course of 2012, are outlined. They consist of a mix of indirect regulatory measures, that is, measures that apply to banks sponsoring shadow banks – most importantly introducing risk-weights, stronger capital requirements and an improvement of accounting principles to force the consolidation of SPVs on their balance sheets – and specific direct measures, most importantly stricter supervision of money-market funds, securitisation and hedge funds (FSB 2011b). The task of devising indirect measures is delegated to the Basel Committee on Banking Supervision (BCBS), and that of devising direct measures to the International Organisation of Securities Commissions (IOSCO). While the G20 postponed discussion to its next meeting at the November 2011 Cannes summit (G20 2011), a progress report in April 2012 reports on the ongoing work in the relevant five work streams (capital requirements of banks interacting with shadow banks; money-market funds; other shadow-bank entities; securitisation and securities lending; and repo). The FSB also emphasises that it has begun to create and collect better data on the shadow-banking system, which is an important prerequisite of proper regulation and supervision. It will publish a first, detailed assessment of the shadow-banking sector at the end of 2012, together with its detailed recommendations for more effective regulation of shadow banking (FSB 2012).

So what kind of specific regulations have the international bodies that the FSB relies on proposed, so far? First, shortly after the crisis, the BCBS agreed on minor amendments to Basel II, specifically asking for heavier risk-weightings for securitisation exposure and off-balance-sheet vehicles, so that they cannot be used so easily to circumvent capital requirements (BCBS 2009).[16] These rules will also be part of the new Basel III agreement. While Basel III leads to a significant improvement of capital-reserve standards (with higher capital requirements and the introduction of leverage ratios) in the regular banking sector (Goldbach and Kerwer 2012),[17] most experts, including the FSB, agree that the rules are insufficient to seriously reduce risk in the shadow-banking sector (*see*, e.g. Turner 2011). Accordingly, there is a real fear that the stricter regulations for regular banks will increase the attractiveness of shadow banking. The FSB writes: 'Although Basel III closes a number of identified shortcomings, both the incentives for, and the risks associated with, regulatory arbitrage will likely increase as Basel III raises the rigor of bank regulation' (FSB 2011a).

Second, the International Accounting Standards Board (IASB) has revised IAS 27, a standard determining under what conditions a bank will have to consolidate its SPVs on the balance sheet. Negotiations at the IASB and FASB, which proved to be controversial, had been ongoing since 2003 and have renewed importance after the crisis. The revised standard can be expected to be a more detailed specification of the previous standard (IASB 2011). Importantly, however, the IAS had already been very strict even before the crisis, requiring the consolidation of off-balance-sheet Special Purpose Entities (SPEs) on banks' accounts. However, many national accounting rules, for example, those in the US, UK and Germany, which are binding for banks and the basis for prudential regulation, did not require this (Thiemann 2011).

---

16. Even in its pre-crisis formulation, Basel II had already required banks to adjust their capital reserves for SPV exposure. But during the phase-in stage of Basel II, this requirement was not obligatory. Interestingly, some countries, such as France, had implemented it in national legislation already, whereas others, among them Germany, had not, and were thus hit harder by the collapse of the shadow-banking system (Thiemann 2011).

17. Despite these improvements, many experts consider the Basel III capital requirements for traditional banks to be too low to guarantee stability (*see*, e.g., Admati *et al.* 2011).

As the work within the FSB is still ongoing, it is certainly too early for definite progress evaluations but one important observation can already be made. The regulatory approach taken by the FSB and the other international bodies has clearly been a combination of the second and third approaches outlined at the beginning of this section. This means that the clear-cut solution of subjecting shadow banks to regular banking regulation is off the table. Instead, the result will be a large number of specialised and detailed rules for individual cases. Also, delegating different aspects of the problem to different agencies implies a fragmentation of the regulatory effort. This is likely to make it easier for interested parties to water down the rules and create loopholes.

Admittedly, at this point, my sceptical evaluation involves some speculation. What is certain, however, is that any decisions of these organisations – be it the Basel III capital requirements or accounting rules – will have to be transposed into national laws to enter into force. As the case of the pre-crisis accounting rules reveals, domestic implementation is the decisive element. As we will see in the next section, and in line with the basic argument of this chapter, jurisdictional competition and business lobbying are major factors at the domestic level, which will very likely turn post-crisis domestic measures into merely incremental reforms that fail to address the shortcomings of the status quo.

Domestic and European politics

In this section I provide two brief case studies of the reform process in the USA and the European Union, where I focus on Germany, UK and France.

The reform process in the USA

In the US, the legislative process of financial reform in response to the crisis culminated in the Dodd-Frank Act (DFA). Most commentators welcomed the bill, saying that it represents progress towards safer financial markets. Nevertheless, it is also widely agreed that DFA contains significant loopholes that were inserted to accommodate business interest-group pressure. Also, the quite fragmented US regulatory landscape, which has received considerable criticism, has not changed. Most importantly, the construction of the DFA is such that it sets out regulatory goals that still need to be implemented by different specific regulators. Many fear that, in this process, some of the more strict rules will be watered down further (Woolley and Ziegler 2012).

And indeed, so far only 20 per cent of the proposed rules have been implemented. The regulatory agencies are confronted with intense lobbying efforts by the financial sector, which took out the bite of some of the regulations (*see*, e.g., Narayanswamy 2011). This is also true for the two measures that are considered to be the most significant for increasing the stability of financial markets. With respect to capital requirements, the DFA does not specify targets because it was argued by Republican legislators that the US should wait for the results of the Basel III negotiations – to protect the competitiveness of US financial markets, capital requirements should stay in tune with other countries' regulations (Johnson 2011). Second, while discussions about proper regulations for the shadow-banking sector played an important role in the legislative process, the final act did not contain specific rules on this aspect. Instead, the responsibility for crafting those rules lies with the Federal Reserve and the newly created Financial System Oversight Council (FSOC). The FSOC is subject to intense lobbying by financial firms, who argue against stricter capital requirements for both the traditional and shadow-banking sectors by pointing to the competitive disadvantage this may imply for US banks *vis-à-vis* their foreign competitors (Johnson 2011). In response, the FSOC pronounced that it may be dangerous to set capital requirements for banks too high because this may drive activity to the shadow-banking sector. Not only does this raise the possibility of capital requirements being too low for banks but it also means that the FSOC does not appear to be ready to regulate shadow banking further (Cooley 2011). All in all, these ongoing events nicely illustrate the logic of my model, with competitiveness concerns and interest-group influence reinforcing each other.

With respect to specific direct regulation of the shadow-banking sector, DFA requires hedge funds to register as investment advisers with the SEC. They will undergo periodic examinations and be required to disclose more information about their trades. Also, regulators are granted authority to freeze hedge funds' operations if they fear these are on the verge of collapse. However, there will be no *ex ante* restrictions on their activities or any increased capital requirements, meaning that these measures will not increase financial stability but merely improve crisis-reaction capacities. In the area of accounting, the relevant US generally accepted accounting principles (GAAP) standards on the consolidation of SPVs were tightened. As a result, $1 trillion were repatriated to balance sheets and an estimated equal size of SPE engagements were sold by banks (Thiemann 2011). This can certainly be viewed as a success. But it remains to be seen whether banks will find new loopholes in the regulations in the future.

The reform process in the European Union (Germany, France and UK)

In Europe, most of the regulatory rules for financial markets are made at the supranational level of the European Union and are then implemented in member states. Supervision, however, is mostly a national task. Therefore I will focus on the role that these three governments played in regulatory efforts at the EU level, but will also refer to domestic reforms.

Pre-crisis, Germany was a vocal supporter of stricter global regulations for hedge funds. At the same time, the SPD-Green government liberalised domestic financial markets with the so-called investment modernisation law in 2003, enabling, among other measures, securitisation and the introduction of private equity firms (Vitols 2005). The main reason for these moves was to improve the competitiveness of the financial sector *vis-à-vis* other countries (*see*, e.g. Asmussen 2006). Post-crisis, one can observe continuity in this general pattern. At the international level, the government is a strong supporter of stricter regulation, arguing for a financial-transaction tax and better regulation of the shadow-banking system. It is joined in these efforts by France. Former French president Sarkozy was probably the most vocal of all political leaders in calling for stricter regulation. Both Germany and France have stated a strong preference for acting on a European, if not a global level, rather than at the domestic level (Handke and Zimmermann 2012; Jabko 2012). However, it can be shown that the results at the European level have been meagre and that neither country has been successful in implementing stricter regulation and supervision domestically; but both have been concerned with the competitive position of their financial systems.

At the European level, the most visible change is the establishment of a new supervisory structure. It consists of the European Systemic Risk Board (ESRB) hosted by the ECB in Frankfurt and in charge of monitoring macroprudential risk; and three new bodies: the European Banking Authority (EBA) in London; the European Insurance and Occupational Pension Authority (EIOPA) in Frankfurt; and the European Securities Markets Authority (ESMA) in Paris. Their task is to co-ordinate the national supervisory agencies and promote co-operation among them. France supported this reform, while Germany was more hesitant, as the Bundesbank feared a loss of supervisory authority. The UK was even more sceptical. It considered the new agencies a 'French plot' to intervene in its financial markets (Jabko 2012). These fears seem to be wildly exaggerated, however. To the contrary, the new structure is too weak to be up to the task of cross-border banking supervision. For one, it would be preferable to have one agency that deals with banking, insurance and securities in a comprehensive fashion. Further, and more importantly, it is not enough to co-ordinate national supervisors. Stringent supervision would need supranational competence, ensuring that national supervisors will not turn a blind eye to 'their' banks' cross-border activities, including shadow-bank and OFC engagements.[18]

With the Capital Requirement Directive (CRD) the EU will implement Basel III in Europe. The legislative process is still ongoing but the current Commission draft (COM(2011) 453 final), like the Basel template, contains only few regulations aimed at the interface of regulated banks and shadow banks. In Germany, regulators have expressed similar sentiments to their US counterparts, stating that it was necessary to ensure that the stricter rules under Basel III would not drive activity into the shadow-banking sector. At the same time, however, the responsibility for strengthening regulations is pushed to the international level, with the argument that unilateral action would threaten the competitiveness of the European banking sector (Kuehnen 2011). France has generally showed little enthusiasm for strengthening capital requirements since it did not want to endanger the competitive position of its large, universal banks (*cf.* Jabko 2012).

In terms of accounting rules, the EU had urged the IASB to strengthen its standards on the valuation of securitisation and the consolidation of SPVs. When

---

18. The ongoing sovereign debt or Euro crisis seems to have led policy-makers to the same conclusion. At least for big, systemically important banks, there are now serious plans for a 'banking union', i.e., truly supranational supervision (*see* Carstensen in this volume).

the IASB delivered, however, the Commission did not approve the standards. Reportedly, the reason for this was resistance by French, German and Italian policy-makers and banks, which would have been seriously undercapitalised on the basis of the new rules (Quaglia in this volume). This fits the pattern of advocating reform internationally but not delivering domestically for fear of losing competitiveness. Likewise, while Germany modernised its law on GAAP (*Bilanzrechtsmodernisierungsgesetz*) in 2009, for the purposes of prudential supervision and determining capital-reserve requirements, banks are still not required to put SPVs on their balance sheets (Thiemann 2011).

The European Union has also pursued specific direct regulatory measures aimed at shadow-banking entities. The Alternative Investment Funds Manager (AIFM) directive targets hedge funds. The legislative process was accompanied by heavy lobbying of the fund industry. The UK, together with financial interests, opposed the directive. France (together with Germany) was the most important proponent. After a contested legislative process, the compromise solution saw the UK accept the legislation but France agreed that offshore funds could continue to be granted access to the EU market (Woll 2012). The new rules require the managers of AIFM to register with the competent authorities of the EU member country in which the management is located. Thus, the management will be subject to this requirement, irrespective of where the fund itself is incorporated. Upon registration, managers will receive a European-wide passport that allows them to market their services everywhere in the EU. Managers will be subject to the supervision of their home member state. They will be required to provide the competent authority with data on their business activities. However, apart from the requirement that the country in which the fund itself is incorporated has signed a TIEA (*see* above), there will not be any restrictions on AIFM's business models. Thus, it is not clear how the directive can help to improve financial stability in the shadow-banking sector. In addition, the Commission is currently reviewing existing legislation on Undertakings for Collective Investment in Transferable Securities (UCITS) and the Markets in Financial Instruments Directive (MiFID), with a view to broadening the transparency and oversight of non-equity instruments and enhancing consumer protection in the area of investment funds (European Commission 2012).

While these few paragraphs are too short to do justice to the complexities of financial regulation in the EU, it is apparent that the central predictions of my model are borne out: that even those countries which are in favour of reform at the international level do not come forward with domestic reform exemplifies the logic of the collective action problem inherent in jurisdictional competition. Only if big, developed countries move in lockstep can reform be effective. Also, we can see that countries with smaller financial sectors are more in favour of reform (Germany and France) than countries with bigger financial sectors (the UK and US). Likewise, the influence of business pressure is visible.

Conclusion

There are reasons to be sceptical that financial regulation could ever be good enough to prevent crises from occurring. It is very likely that market actors will always be able to find gaps in regulation that enable them to make greater profits.[19] And regulators will always only be able to engage in *ex post* corrections of the rules after a crisis has occurred. Apart from this principled scepticism that a capitalist financial system could be made fully crisis-resistant, this paper comes to the conclusion that, in the case of shadow banking, not even *ex post* re-regulation has occurred to the extent necessary. This means not only that, as may always be the case, we can expect new regulatory gaps to emerge but, worse, the 'old' gaps are still open. In addition, by raising capital requirements for traditional banks, the premium on using the OFC and shadow-bank device has been raised. It therefore seems plausible that the next crisis will be an even more damaging re-run of the last one.

Rather than end on this bleak outlook, I close by summarising my findings and linking them to the main theme of this volume, incremental change. I have shown that OFCs and shadow banks played a significant role in the financial crisis of 2007. Insofar, it is warranted to push for regulatory change in this area and political leaders have indeed made the connection and called for such reforms. However, overall, the regulatory activity after the crisis can broadly be summarised under the heading 'more of the same' – which had proven insufficient in the era preceding the crisis. While some institutions, most importantly the FSB, are strengthened, their basic workings and formal powers are not enhanced. They still merely aim at co-ordination. Also, the institutional landscape is still fragmented. Different institutions address OFCs with different regulatory agendas. In consequence, a coherent policy towards OFCs has not been formulated. The fact that the institutions of financial governance continue to develop along their established paths and within their established institutional routines may also explain why their crisis response sometimes did not even target the crucial links between shadow banks, OFCs and financial instability. In other words, the actual content of regulatory efforts after the crisis cannot necessarily be linked to the causes of the crisis.

I have argued that the reason for this reform trajectory can be found in governments' concerns about international competitiveness, coupled with capture by financial interests. There is ample evidence that big-country governments perceive themselves to be in a situation of jurisdictional competition. In particular, those

---

19. One reason for this is that big financial players have more and better manpower than financial regulators. They will be able to spot new regulatory gaps very quickly. But even if the oligopolistic market could be turned into a more competitive one with many small players, these would still be likely to find new regulatory gaps, quite simply because there is a premium on finding them. Once loopholes are found, others will have to follow because competition forces them to do so. Nevertheless, having a more competitive market would be an improvement, both because it could reduce the severity of crises and because the sector would likely lose political lobbying power, as it would face more severe problems of collective action.

countries with large financial sectors are hesitant to agree on strict and binding international standards. While we would expect governments to be able to overcome this collective action dilemma if we adopted a unitary state assumption, the failure to do so is due to capture by interest groups, which becomes visible if we adopt a two-level-game perspective. Competitiveness concerns and interest-group influence are even more apparent at the domestic level. Reforms are feeble in all four countries and are significantly slowed down by the interference of financial and business interests successfully marshalling the competitiveness argument. Even those countries that advocate a strong international reform agenda do not follow through domestically. On the basis of a two-level model that interlinks the two arenas of international and domestic politics, this becomes understandable. Nevertheless, the crisis has spurred regulatory activity. Policy-makers try to square the circle between jurisdictional competition and financial interest capture on the one hand and public demands for stricter regulation on the other by resorting to incremental, but often ineffective and symbolic, reform measures.

This speaks to the general point raised by Thelen (1999; 2003) and taken up by Moschella and Tsingou in the introductory chapter to this volume – the observation that stability (for example, in the broad principles of an institution) and incremental change (for example, in some rules) often occur at the same time. Streeck and Thelen (2005) argue that such small-scale changes may, over time, add up to significant and transformative change. While this is certainly true in many cases, it is not true in the case of OFCs and shadow banking. Here, we have a case of merely symbolic policies that lack real bite. As long as nation states conceive themselves to be in a position of jurisdictional competition, they do not have any interest in real change.

References

Admati, A. R., DeMarzo, P.M., Hellwig, M. F. and Pfleiderer, P. (2011) *Fallacies, Irrelevant Facts, and Myths in the Discussion of Capital Regulation: Why bank equity is not expensive*, Rock Center for Corporate Governance at Stanford University, Working Paper No. 86. 23 March 2011. https://gsbapps.stanford.edu/researchpapers/library/RP2065R1&86.pdf. Accessed 21 November 2011.

Adrian, T. and Shin, H. S. (2009) *The Shadow Banking System: Implications for financial regulation*, Federal Reserve Bank of New York, Staff Report No. 382. http://www.ny.frb.org/research/staff_reports/sr382.pdf. Accessed 11 January 2011.

Asmussen, J. (2006) 'Verbriefungen aus Sicht des Bundesfinanzministeriums', *Zeitschrift für das gesamte Kreditwesen*, 19: 1016–18.

Basel Committee on Banking Supervision (2009) 'Basel II capital framework enhancements announced by the Basel Committee', press release, 13 July 2009. http://www.bis.org/press/p090713.htm. Accessed 27 January 2011.

Broughton, N. and Maer, L. (2012) 'The financial sector's contribution to the UK economy', House of Commons, SN06193. http://www.parliament.uk/briefing-papers/SN06193. Accessed 16 August 2012.

Cooley, T. (2011) 'Regulatory architecture', in Acharya, V., Cooley, T., Richardson, M. and Walter, I. (eds), *Dodd-Frank: One year on*: VoxEU. http://www.voxeu.org/sites/default/files/file/Dodd-Frank_One_Year_On.pdf. Accessed 12 November 2011.

Drezner, D. W. (2007) *All Politics Is Global: Explaining international regulatory regimes*, Princeton: Princeton University Press.

Eddins, S. T. (2009) *Tax Arbitrage Feedback Theory*, manuscript. http://ssrn.com/abstract=1356159. Accessed 24 January 2011.

Eden, L. (1998) *Taxing Multinationals: Transfer pricing and corporate income taxation in North America*. Toronto: University of Toronto Press.

European Commission (2012) *Green Paper on Shadow Banking*. http://ec.europa.eu/internal_market/bank/docs/shadow/green-paper_en.pdf. Accessed 14 August 2012.

Financial Stability Board (2011a) *Shadow Banking: Scoping the Issues. A background note of the Financial Stability Board, 12 April 2011*. http://www.financialstabilityboard.org/publications/r_110412a.pdf. Accessed 20 July 2011.

— (2011b) *Shadow Banking: Strengthening Oversight and Regulation. Recommendations of the Financial Stability Board. 27 October.* http://www.financialstabilityboard.org/publications/r_111027a.pdf. Accessed 12 November 2011.

— (2012) *Strengthening the Oversight and Regulation of Shadow Banking: Progress report to G20 Ministers and Governors. 16 April.* http://www.financialstabilityboard.org/publications/r_120420c.pdf. Accessed 13 August 2012.

Financial Stability Forum (2000) *Report of the Working Group on Offshore Centres*, http://www.financialstabilityboard.org/publications/r_0004b. pdf?nof*rames=1*. Accessed 21 January 2011.

G20 (2009a) 'The global plan for recovery and reform', 2 April 2009. http://www.g20.org/Documents/final-communique.pdf. Accessed 26 January 2011.

— (2009b) 'Declaration on further steps to strengthen the financial system', meeting of finance ministers and central bank governors, London, 4–5 September 2009. http://www.g20.org/Documents/FM__CBG_ Declaration_-_Final.pdf. Accessed 26 January 2011.

— (2011) 'Building our common future: renewed collective action for the benefit of all', Cannes summit final declaration, 4 November 2011. *http://www.g20.utoronto.ca/2011/2011-cannes-declaration-111104-en.html*. Accessed 9 March 2012.

Genschel, P. and Schwarz, P. (2011) 'Tax competition: a literature review', *Socio-Economic Review*, 9(2): 339–70.

Goldbach, R. and Kerwer, D. (2012) 'New capital rules? Reforming Basel banking standards after the financial crisis', in Mayntz, R. (ed.), *Crisis and Control: Institutional change in financial market regulation*, Frankfurt: Campus, 247–62.

Handke, S. and Zimmermann, H. (2012) 'Institutional change in German financial regulation', in Mayntz, R. (ed.), *Crisis and Control: Institutional change in financial market regulation*, Frankfurt: Campus, 119–42.

Helleiner, E. (1994) *States and the Reemergence of Global Finance. From Bretton Woods to the 1990s*, Ithaca: Cornell University Press.

— (2010) *The Financial Stability Board and International Standards*, CIGI G20 Papers, No. 1, June 2010. http://www.cigionline.org/sites/default/files/G20%20No%201_2.pdf. Accessed 27 January 2011.

International Accounting Standards Board (2011) *Consolidation. Project update, January 2011*. http://www.ifrs.org/NR/rdonlyres/7ED0455B-1350-4BA1-A8D6-831200AB8F38/0/ProjectreportJan11.pdf. Accessed 27 January 2011.

International Monetary Fund (2000) *Offshore Financial Centers*, IMF background paper. http://imf.org/external/np/mae/oshore/2000/eng/back.htm. Accessed 31 January 2011.

— (2006) *Offshore Financial Centers. The assessment program—a progress report, 8 February 2006*. http://www.imf.org/external/np/pp/eng/2006/020806.pdf. Accessed 21 January 2011.

— (2009) *Debt Bias and Other Distortions: Crisis-related issues in tax policy, Prepared by the Fiscal Affairs Department, 12 June 2009*. http://www.imf.org/external/np/pp/eng/2009/061209.pdf. Accessed 12 January 2011.

— (2010) *Understanding Financial Interconnectedness, October 4, 2010*. http://www.imf.org/external/np/pp/eng/2010/100410.pdf. Accessed 12 January 2011.

Jabko, N. (2012) 'International radicalism, domestic conformism: France's ambiguous stance on financial reforms', in Mayntz, R. (ed.), *Crisis and Control: Institutional change in financial market regulation,* Frankfurt: Campus, 97–118.

Johnson, S. (2011) 'The big banks fight on', 15 June 2011. *http://economix.blogs. nytimes.com/author/simon-johnson.* Accessed 21 November 2011.

Kingdon, J. W. (1984) *Agendas, Alternatives, and Public Policies*, Boston MA: Little, Brown, and Company.

Krugman, P. (2009) *The Return of Depression Economics and the Crisis of 2008*, New York NY: W. W. Norton.

Kuehnen, E. (2011) 'Basel III no threat to growth, shadow banking a risk'. http://www.reuters.com/article/2011/11/15/us-bundesbank-regulation-idUSTRE7AE10N20111115. Accessed 21 November 2011.

Lane, P. R. and Milesi-Ferretti, G. M. (2010) *Cross-Border Investment in Small International Financial Centers,* IMF Working Paper WP/10/38.

de Larosière, J. (2009) *Report of the High Level Group on Financial Supervision in the EU.* http://ec.europa.eu/internal_market/finances/docs/de_larosiere_report_de.pdf. Accessed 31 January 2011.

Loomer, G. and Maffini, G. (2009) *Tax Havens and the Financial Crisis.* http://www.sbs.ox.ac.uk/tax. Accessed 26 June 2009.

Milesi-Ferretti, G. M., Strobbe, F. and Tamirisa, N. (2010) *Bilateral Financial Linkages and Global Imbalances: A view on the eve of the financial crisis*, IMF Working Paper WP/10/257.

Mosley, L. (2010) 'Regulating globally, implementing locally: the financial codes and standards effort', *Review of International Political Economy*, 17(4): 724–61.

Murphy, R. and Christensen, J. (2008) 'The threat lying offshore. Tax havens will sabotage attempts to re-regulate global finance. Democracy demands we tackle them.', *Guardian*.

Narayanswamy, A. (2011) 'Lobbyists swarm agencies as Dodd-Frank is implemented', *Sunlight Foundation Reporting Group* 19 July 2011. http://reporting.sunlightfoundation.com/2011/dodd-frank-lobbying. Accessed 13 November 2011.

OECD (1998) *Harmful Tax Competition. An emerging global issue*, Paris: OECD.

— (2000) *Towards Global Tax Co-Operation: Report to the 2000 Ministerial Council Meeting and Recommendations by the Committee on Fiscal Affairs: Progress in identifying and eliminating harmful tax practices.* http://www.oecd.org/dataoecd/9/61/2090192.pdf. Accessed 31 January 2011.

— (2009) *A Progress Report on the Jurisdictions Surveyed by the OECD Global Forum in Implementing the Internationally Agreed Tax Standard.* http://www.oecd.org/dataoecd/38/14/42497950.pdf. Accessed 20 May 2009.

Olson, M. (1965) *The Logic of Collective Action: Public goods and the theory of groups*, Cambridge: Harvard University Press.

Palan, R., Murphy, R. and Chavagneux, C. (2010) *Tax Havens: How globalization really works*, Ithaca: Cornell University Press.

Pozsar, Z., Adrian, T., Ashcraft, A. and Boesky, H. (2010) *Shadow Banking* Federal Reserve Bank of New York Staff Report No. 458. http://www.ny.frb.org/research/staff_reports/sr458.pdf. Accessed 23 December 2010.

Putnam, R. D. (1988) 'Diplomacy and domestic politics: the logic of two-level games', *International Organization*, 42(3): 427–60.

Rahn, R. W. (2009) 'In defense of tax havens', *Wall Street Journal*.

Ricks, M. (2010) *Shadow Banking and Financial Regulation*, Columbia Law and Economics Working Paper No. 370. http://papers.ssrn.com/sol3/papers.cfm?abstract_id=1571290. Accessed 4 February 2013.

Rixen, T. (2008) *The Political Economy of International Tax Governance*, Basingstoke: Palgrave/Macmillan.

— (2011a) 'From double tax avoidance to tax competition: explaining the institutional trajectory of international tax governance', *Review of International Political Economy*, 18(2): 197–227.

— (2011b) 'Tax competition and inequality: the case for global tax governance', *Global Governance: A Review of Multilateralism and International Organizations*, 17(4): 447–67.

Streeck, W. and Thelen, K. (2005) 'Institutional change in advanced political economies', in Streeck, W. and Thelen, K. (eds), *Beyond Continuity: Institutional change in advanced political economies*, Oxford: Oxford University Press, 11–39.

Sullivan, M. A. (2007) 'Lessons from the last war on tax havens', *Tax Notes* 116 (July 30): 327–37.

TheCityUK (2011) *Hedge Funds 2011*. http://www.thecityuk.com/assets/Uploads/Hedge-funds-2011.pdf. Accessed 20 July 2011.

Thelen, K. (1999) 'Historical institutionalism in comparative politics', *Annual Review of Political Science* 2: 369–404.

— (2003) 'How institutions evolve. Insights from comparative historical analysis', in Mahoney, J. and Rueschemeyer, D. (eds), *Comparative Historical Analysis in the Social Sciences*, Cambridge: Cambridge University Press, 208–40.

Thiemann, M. (2011) *Regulating the Off-Balance Sheet Exposure of Banks: A comparison pre- and post crisis,* Foundation for European Progressive Studies. http://www.feps-europe.eu/fileadmin/downloads/political_economy/1106_OffBalanceSheetExposure_Thiemann.pdf. Accessed 20 July 2011.

Troost, A. and Liebert, N. (2009) 'Das Billionengrab. Von Steueroasen und Schattenbanken', *Blätter für deutsche und internationale Politik*, 3: 75–84.

Tsingou, E. (2010) 'Global financial governance and the developing anti-money laundering regime: what lessons for international political economy?', *International Politics*, 47(6): 617–37.

Turner, A. (2011) *Leverage, Maturity Transformation and Financial Stability: Challenges beyond Basel III*, Cass Business School, 16 March 2011. http://www.fsa.gov.uk/pubs/speeches/031611_at.pdf. Accessed 21 November 2011.

Vitols, S. (2005) 'Changes in Germany's bank-based financial system: implications for corporate governance', *Corporate Governance: An International Review*, 13(3): 38–396.

Walter, A. (2010) 'Can the FSB achieve surveillance of systemically important countries?', in Helleiner, E., Woods, N. and Griffith-Jones, S. (eds), *The Financial Stability Board: An effective fourth pillar of global economic governance?*, The Centre for International Governance Innovation, 32–5. http://www.cigionline.org/sites/default/files/FSB%20special%20 report_2.pdf. Accessed 27 January 2011.

Weiner, J. (2008) 'Icelandic bank failure reveals tax haven links', *Tax Notes International* 10 (November 2008): 443–52.

Woll, C. (2012) 'The defense of economic interests in the European Union: the case of hedge fund regulation', in Mayntz, R. (ed.) *Crisis and Control: Institutional change in financial market regulation*, Frankfurt: Campus, 197–211.

Woolley, J. T. and Ziegler, J. N. (2012) 'The two-tiered politics of financial reform in the United States', in Mayntz, R. (ed.), *Crisis and Control: Institutional change in financial market regulation*, Frankfurt: Campus, 29–65.

Zangl, B. (1994) 'Politik auf zwei Ebenen. Hypothesen zur Bildung internationaler Regime', *Zeitschrift für Internationale Beziehungen*, 1(2): 279–312.

chapter | the Wall-Street—Main-Street
six | nexus in financial regulation:
business coalitions inside and
outside the financial sector in the
regulation of OTC derivatives[1]

Stefano Pagliari and Kevin Young

Introduction

What is the role of private-sector groups in determining the incremental character of the financial regulatory response to the recent crisis? As Moschella and Tsingou argue in the introductory chapter, the influence of those business actors that are advantaged by existing institutions and which have a vested interest in the continuation of the status quo is a primary cause of patterns of incrementalism in regulatory politics. Studies that have explored these dynamics in the financial regulatory arena have often unequivocally identified the financial-industry groups as the primary veto-players, frequently deploying a variety of strategies and resources in order to oppose significant attempts at regulatory reform that could generate a regulatory burden and place them at a competitive disadvantage. From this perspective, the paucity of regulatory reforms that significantly challenge the prevalent paradigm is a sign of the consistent power of the same financial-industry groups that drove much of de-regulatory policy before the crisis and of the continued political resilience of their capacity to veto more ambitious regulatory solutions.

In this chapter we contend that, while financial-industry groups have played an important role in shaping post-crisis regulatory reform, this influence has remained conditional on their capacity to adjust their advocacy strategies in response to the changes in the new regulatory environment triggered by the crisis. As the crisis has weakened the capacity of financial-industry groups to preserve the status quo by the usual means, the industry's capacity to shape the content of regulatory policies has been increasingly determined by its ability to tie its interests to those of a broader range of stakeholders outside the industry itself.

Consequently, in order to explain the incremental nature of the post-crisis regulatory response, we need to consider not just the financial-industry groups being directly subjected to regulation but also the mobilisation of non-financial business groups. Such a perspective, we argue, helps to explain how a broader

---

1.   We are grateful to Irene Spagna for helpful research assistance.

range of actors beyond the 'usual suspects' of financial-sector groups themselves have worked to veto more radical regulatory solutions that would challenge the existing paradigm; these measures would also have affected the patterns of financial intermediation more broadly within the real economy. Thus rather than 'Wall Street' acting as a veto-player to block more ambitious post-crisis reform, the incremental nature of the regulatory reforms introduced after the crisis must be understood as due to the demands of the wider business community, often working in tandem with financial groups: what could be called 'Wall-Street–Main-Street' nexus.

The chapter is structured as follows. The next section discusses the prevalent ways of thinking about private financial-industry groups and their power in the policy-making process. These are contrasted with the advocacy strategy employed by the financial industry during and shortly after the crisis. The following section discusses the role of non-financial actors within the business community and presents recent evidence of their importance in shaping the regulatory response to the global crisis. In the final section, we illustrate these dynamics at work in a high-profile, high-stakes case of financial regulatory policy-making: the reform of derivatives markets in the United States.

Our analysis thus engages with a specific dimension of Moschella and Tsingou's framework mapped out in their Table 1.1 – specifically the role of private-sector groups as veto-players who adapt to new challenges. While the focus of our empirical case study is on the national level, in the United States, our analysis has broader implications. Indeed, the changes in private-sector advocacy discussed in this chapter have informed regulatory changes at the global, regional and national levels of governance, as well as in the regulation of a broader range of sectors.

Financial industry groups: still dominant veto-players?

As Moschella and Tsingou argue in the introduction to this volume, the output of financial regulatory bodies at the national, regional and global levels has mostly fallen short of bringing a paradigm change and has been significantly less dramatic than the size and severity of the crisis might suggest. One of the most popular interpretations of this involves the role of the financial industry as a kind of veto-player, able to block or at least severely limit the extent of post-crisis regulatory reforms. While not possessing formal capacity to block change through formal rulemaking procedures, the financial industry is often seen to informally block policy process, for example through their close integration into the 'policy network' of finance. Such a sentiment is crystallised in the news media's discussion of the uneven reform process in the regulation of the derivatives sector, which explains that '[b]ig banks have been lobbying to block change' (*New York Times* 2010); that big banks have pursued a 'strangle it in the womb' strategy, leading to the result that 'most of them [the proposals for new regulation] wound up whittled down to such an extreme degree that they were barely recognizable in the end' (Taibbi 2012: 65). Other accounts portray a similar general narrative of the 'big-bank lobby' as voracious as ever (Kroll 2010), or depict 'Wall Street' making an 'assault...on new regulation' (Protess and Eavis 2012). Such sentiments also exist in commentary on the issue of post-crisis regulatory reform in academic circles. Acemoglu and Johnson (2012) have argued, for instance, that, after the crisis, the Fed 'has given way completely, at the higher level and with disastrous consequences, when the bankers bring their influence to bear' by 'resisting attempts to raise capital requirements by enough to make a difference'.

Such sentiments continue a long-standing tradition within academic scholarship of identifying financial-industry groups as the primary veto-players in the financial regulatory arena, capable of steering the direction of domestic and international financial regulatory reforms away from measures that could undermine their privileged position (Underhill 1995; Wood 2005; Wade 2008). Different resources have been identified by existing scholarship as bolstering this veto power. While some scholars have focused on the financial resources deployed by financial-industry groups in the policy-making process in the period before the crisis (e.g. Igan, Mishra, and Tressel 2009), other authors have argued that the capacity of the financial industry to veto regulatory policies was amplified by the same institutional context in which financial regulatory policies were developed over this period. In particular, the 'Olympian distance' of financial regulatory authorities from domestic political dynamics has been described as disguising the deep and institutionalised engagement these agencies had developed with financial-industry groups, reinforced by the shared 'professional ecologies', ideas and the so-called 'revolving doors' between individuals from the industry and regulatory personnel (Underhill and Zhang 2003, Seabrooke and Tsingou 2009, Underhill and Zhang 2008, Braun and Raddatz 2009). Finally, different authors have highlighted the capacity of financial-industry groups to shape regulatory policies through their 'cultural capital' and the attitude prevailing in countries such as the United States 'that what was good for Wall Street was good for the country' (Johnson 2009; *see also* Kwak 2013). Johnson argues that 'from this confluence of campaign finance, personal connections, and ideology there flowed, in just the past decade, a river of de-regulatory policies that is, in hindsight, astonishing' (Johnson 2009).

Such a perspective would suggest that the incremental change that characterises the regulatory response to crisis can be attributed to the continuation of the power of private financial-industry groups with a vested interest in preserving the status quo. Indeed, different scholars and commentators have warned of the fact that the crisis has not undermined the influence of the same 'Wall-Street–Treasury complex' that drove much of the de-regulatory policies before the crisis (Bhagwati 2008; Wade 2008; Johnson 2009; Tsingou 2009). For authors such as Johnson (2009), this particular situation 'gives the financial sector a veto over public policy, even as that sector loses popular support'.

As Moschella and Tsingou argue in the introduction to this volume, the identity of veto-players and change-agents can change with changing circumstances. While it is true that several of the protagonists of the regulatory process before the crisis have played important roles, works postulating the continuous dominance of financial-industry groups have, arguably, paid insufficient attention to changes in the policy-making context since the financial crisis. There are a number of significant factors that might be considered in this regard.

First, the identification of the roots of the crisis in core countries such as the US has altered the international political landscape within which the international regulatory response to the crisis has unfolded in a way less conducive to the continuation of the status quo. In the aftermath of previous major episodes of financial instability, emerging from peripheral countries (for example, the Mexican crisis of 1994; the East-Asian Crisis of 1997–8; the Argentinian crisis of 2001) US authorities had worked to narrow the scope of more ambitious regulatory initiatives that would undermine the competitive position of their domestic financial industry, often swaying the international approach towards market-based regulatory mechanisms (*see* Wood 2005; Drezner 2007). However, the origin of the crisis within the US has altered the incentives of US policy-makers. Rather than acting as an international veto-player on new regulatory initiatives, US authorities have been at the centre of efforts to re-regulate different markets and institutions domestically and internationally (Helleiner and Pagliari 2009; Fioretos 2010).

Besides the changed international political context of the regulatory response to the crisis, the intellectual landscape has also been altered in a way detrimental to financial-industry groups' traditional advocacy strategies. Unlike previous episodes of financial instability of the late 1990s, whose roots lied partly in fiscal imbalances, macroeconomic policies, and other government policies, the origin of the crisis in the activities of financial institutions has weakened the legitimacy of measures relying on the capacity of markets to discipline themselves, advocated in the aftermath of the emerging market crises of the late-1990s. These ideas have been challenged by some of the same important members of the international regulatory community that had championed them before the crisis (Foot and Walter 2010: 249). This shift in the ideational landscape has therefore reduced the capacity of financial firms to rely on claims regarding the superiority of market-based solutions in order to oppose more stringent forms of regulation.

Third, the financial crisis altered the institutional context in which financial regulatory policies have been designed. While the influence of financial-industry groups before the crisis was magnified by their privileged access to independent regulatory agencies and the insulation of this policy community from the 'rough and tumble of traditional policy making in democratic governments, such as in trade negotiations' (Underhill and Zhang 2008: 544; Underhill 1995), the deepening of the crisis moved the focal point away from the technocratic policy network and toward the agenda of elected politicians. Greater involvement in the design of financial regulatory reform initiatives of bodies such as the US Congress and the European Parliament has opened new access points in the policy-making process to a broader range of stakeholders. Moreover, while law-makers in bodies such as the US Congress had, before the crisis, in several instances taken the side of the financial industry and rejected calls for more stringent regulation (Tett 2009), the significant backlash against the financial industry generated by the crisis and the deployment of taxpayer money in support of the financial industry in most industrialised countries have weakened the willingness of elected officials in these countries, including the US, to stand up openly in defence of the interests of the financial industry. Furthermore, the greater salience of financial regulatory issues in the US and other industrialised countries has created a political environment in which a greater number of policy-makers have sought to extract electoral rewards by supporting tougher regulation of the financial industry (Helleiner and Pagliari 2011).

Thus there are a number of reasons why the institutional context in which regulation has been generated might have weakened the financial industry's previous veto power. This does not mean that financial-industry groups have not played a meaningful role in shaping the direction of post-crisis regulatory reform and its incremental nature. However, the influence of financial-industry groups over the design of regulatory policies has become more *conditional* on the capacity of financial-sector groups to adjust their advocacy strategies in to the face of the changes in the regulatory environment described above.

As Tsingou and Moschella write, when actors are faced with significant changes in the normal conditions within which they operate, they may realise that their advantage is better preserved by adapting existing rules and institutions, rather than by seeking to maintain the status quo as such (*see also* Scharpf 2000: 782). This pattern has also informed the behaviour of financial-industry groups in the aftermath of the crisis. With their sector's mishaps in the public spotlight, financial institutions have often found it strategically counterproductive to resist calls for (re)regulation of their activities actively and aggressively. Rather than simply trying to veto new regulatory policies, financial-industry groups have, since the very early phases of the crisis, sought to provide careful *support* for incremental changes in the existing regulatory regime.[2] This 'change-agent' behaviour reflected the acknowledgment that seeking to preserve the status quo at all costs would have damaged the public reputation of the sector at a moment at which public opinion was not on their side, potentially leading them to exclusion from the financial-policy network.[3] Moreover, support for incremental regulatory changes has allowed financial-industry groups to concentrate their opposition on those elements of the emerging regulatory framework most significantly threatening their positions.

---

2. For instance, unlike the aggressive lobbying by the banking industry in the early 2000s against some proposals by the Basel Committee (*see* Lall 2011; Wood 2005), bank-industry groups since the crisis have adopted a different tone, often endorsing new regulatory reforms rather than resisting them (IIF 2008a; IIF 2008b). Hedge fund-associations have endorsed the same requirements forcing managers to register with securities regulators that they had opposed and successfully fought in court in the years before the crisis (MFA 2004; MFA 2009; Helleiner and Pagliari 2009). Under regulatory scrutiny more than ever since the crisis, credit-rating agencies have jointly affirmed their commitment to amending their respective codes of conduct as recommended by IOSCO (A.M. Best *et al.* 2008). The main banks that act as dealers in the OTC derivatives markets have co-ordinated an extensive set of self-regulatory measures to reinforce the operational infrastructures of these markets (discussed below).

3. Interviews with financial-industry representatives routinely express the sentiment that the volume and character of recent financial regulation is driven by elected officials' responsiveness to perceived public demands, rather than the demands of regulators. This is also evinced by the fact that the climate of hostility toward the financial sector has been conceptually framed as the result of 'grandstanding' and populism (*see* Wearden 2009).

However, the influence of financial-industry groups has also been conditional on their capacity to adjust their advocacy strategies to a shift in the regulatory policy-making process towards highly politicised arenas, such as the US Congress and other national parliaments. This changed institutional context has weakened the capacity of financial-industry groups to counteract these proposals through their 'tools of quiet politics' (Culpepper 2011), such as their expertise and privileged access to decision-makers; and it has created channels of access for the mobilisation of a number of stakeholders outside the financial industry. As Culpepper argues in his analysis of high salience regulatory politics, the politicisation of regulatory policy-making forces business groups to alter their advocacy strategy in order to influence public opinion in their favour, as well as to form alliances with other interest groups (Culpepper 2011: 49). These dynamics have also informed the advocacy strategies adopted by financial-industry groups after the crisis, which have frequently sought to work alongside other groups in order to effectively oppose more radical changes.

In order to investigate this, the next section looks beyond the financial industry in isolation and considers finance's interaction with a broader range of stakeholders that has mobilised in an attempt to shape financial regulation in the aftermath of the crisis.

Beyond finance: non-financial end-users and new coalitions

Analyses of the veto-players and change-agents among the actors seeking to influence the content of financial regulatory policies have typically focused on the actors being subjected to regulation, that is, financial-industry groups themselves, largely neglecting the role of other, non-financial corporate actors, who may be indirectly affected by such policies. Existing scholarship has posited several reasons for this narrow focus. Interest-groups other than those in the financial industry have frequently been described as having neither the resources – either financial or technical expertise – nor the same incentives to mobilise and compete with financial groups in shaping financial regulatory policies (Mattli and Woods 2009; Baker 2010). Moreover, the close ties between the financial industry and regulatory agencies, strengthened by a common language, shared professional background and 'revolving doors' for personnel exchanges between regulators and industry, has been described as representing an almost insurmountable barrier to the capacity of other groups to break in to the relatively closed financial-policy network (Heinemann and Schüler 2002). As a result, the presence of non-financial-sector actors in shaping financial regulatory policies has been traditionally conceived as chronically weak and insignificant; authors who have analysed the politics of regulatory reform before the crisis have often lamented the lack of countervailing forces to the dominance of the financial industry (e.g. Helleiner and Porter 2010; Baker 2010).

This pervasive view does not reflect the fact that financial regulatory policy-making is actually associated with the mobilisation of a variety of business groups. A quantitative indicator of the importance of non-financial-sector mobilisation

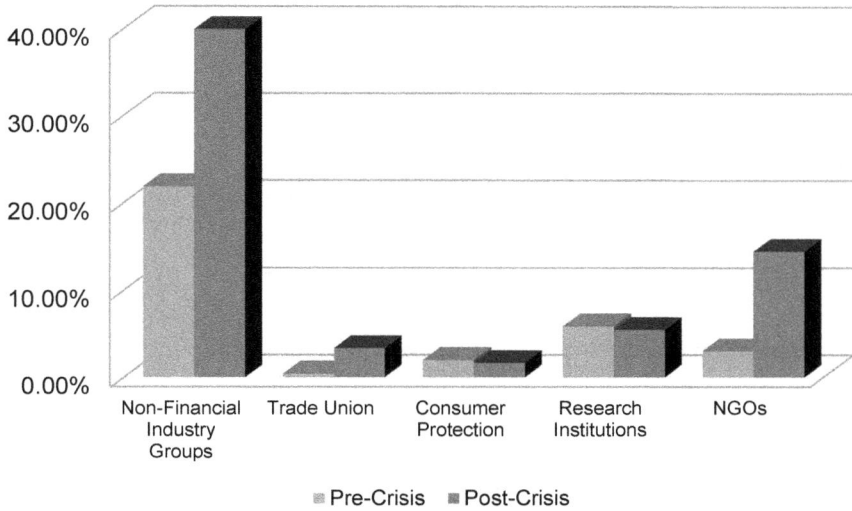

Figure 6.1: Financial consultation respondents, as a percentage of financial-industry group respondents

within financial regulatory policy-making can be found in an analysis of responses to financial-sector consultations. Figure 6.1 shows the results of such an analysis of the private respondents to a number of financial regulatory consultations before and after the crisis, differentiating private-sector respondents as a percentage of the private sector total.[4]

As these results illustrate, non-financial-industry groups have been an important component of the mix of private-sector respondents in the period before the crisis. Most importantly, non-financial corporate actors have significantly increased their mobilisation in the financial regulatory policy-making triggered by the global financial crisis. Indeed, as a percentage of total respondents, non-financial respondents have increased by 44.5 per cent.

These quantitative observations relate to qualitative changes in the policy-making environment. Not only has the financial crisis triggered a broader mobilisation of actors beyond the financial industry but the changes in the policy-making context described above have also increased the potential receptiveness of policy-makers to non-financial-industry groups' concerns. As argued above, the high salience of financial regulatory debates has weakened the incentives for

---

4.   From a selection of 146 financial-sector consultations, we collected a total of 6379 private-sector letters submitted to financial governance authorities at the national, regional and international levels. For each consultation, we categorised the different kinds of respondents in a given consultation. Specifically, we assessed whether or not the respondent was from within the financial sector itself, or from outside. We also coded for non-profit, private-sector groups, such as NGOs, research institutions, labour unions and consumer-protection groups.

elected policy-makers and regulators to heed the requests of the financial industry openly. However, it has remained highly unpopular for elected policy-makers to support regulatory policies that would have negatively affected corporate actors not at the origin of the crisis. Indeed, the importance of the impact of regulatory policies on employment and the overall economy has, arguably, been increased by change in the macroeconomic environment. As the crisis has pushed most Western countries into recession, elected politicians have become particularly sensitive to the implications of regulation on employment and unwilling to impose costs upon corporations that remain a crucial source of employment.

Furthermore, the influence of corporate actors has also been magnified by the change in the institutional environment in which financial regulatory policies are developed. As argued above, the deepening of the crisis has shifted the focal point of the policy-making process from the autonomous regulatory agencies towards government branches and parliamentary committees, which are more receptive to the claims of non-financial interest-groups, for example the US Congressional Agriculture Committee (Clapp and Helleiner 2012).

An important question in this context is what kind of regulatory preferences non-financial-industry groups have been expressing. Are they acting as a 'countervailing force' to the preferences of financial-industry groups and promoting more extensive regulatory changes? Or do the two groups share similar regulatory preferences in opposing more radical regulatory changes? The situation is difficult to generalise empirically. This reflects not only the wide diversity of non-financial-industry groups that have mobilised in response to post-crisis financial regulation but also the conflicting incentives of different non-financial business groups. On the one hand, non-financial business groups have repeatedly professed their support for stronger regulatory approaches, in order to mitigate the recurrence of financial crisis and its costs to the real economy. On the other hand, many of the same non-financial groups have also actively sought to mitigate the short-term negative impact that different regulatory measures targeting financial activities would have had on their financing and risk-management activities. Indeed, this latter set of incentives has frequently prevailed and non-financial end-users have often opposed parts of regulations introduced primarily to curb risk in the activities of financial firms.

For instance, business groups opposed the introduction of taxation on financial transactions that could have increased the cost of capital. According to the British Association of Corporate Treasurers, the proposal by the European Commission to tax bonds and derivatives failed 'to recognise that these sorts of transactions and the related markets assist in the provision of capital and risk reduction for companies and as such are essential for the operation of the economy' (ACT 2011; EACT 2012). The same corporate treasurers groups deplored how the implementation of Basel III in Europe would have 'push[ed] upwards the overall cost of capital and make productive investment more difficult to justify financially' (EACT 2011) while, at the international level, the mobilisation of non-financial-industry groups against the agreement was led by the International Chamber of Commerce (ICC 2010). The opposition to the directive presented to regulate hedge funds in Europe for the first time was not confined to the hedge-fund industry but also included charitable foundations and pension funds, which denounced the loss of return that the new rules would impose upon their investments (EFRP 2009; Jones 2009). The extension of scope of the directive to venture-capital funds triggered the mobilisation of 700 small and medium company-managers and -owners, who warned the European Parliament that it would be a 'mistake to think that its impact will be restricted to companies trading in financial instruments. This is about the real economy, and these proposals will directly affect tens of thousands of companies across every sector, from fashion to photovoltaics, and from sandwich making to waste recycling' (Brehler 2010). Almost 30 non-financial companies from different sectors such as retail, energy and medical research, co-ordinated by the US Chamber of Commerce, have mobilised to express their opposition to the 'Volcker Rule', that is, the provision in the US legislation limiting proprietary trading activities in the federally insured banking institutions, on the ground that it would negatively affect their 'ability to raise capital and manage risk' (Abbott Laboratories *et al.* 2012; *see also* Protess 2012).

Financial-interest groups have taken advantage of this mobilisation whenever possible. As argued above, the backlash against the financial industry in the US and other industrialised economies has deprived the financial industry of a number of the benefits it enjoyed in earlier times. In the place of arguments regarding the need to protect the financial sector *as such*, many financial-sector groups have engaged with new financial regulation by emphasising the 'economy-wide' negative effects that may result as consequence of a given regulatory policy. Examples of such advocacy behaviour permeate the post-crisis political economy. For instance, shortly after the Basel III proposal was released in June 2010, the IIF responded that implementation of the agreement would decrease economic growth eight times more than estimated by the Basel Committee (IIF 2010), costing 7.5 million jobs in five years in the industrialised economies (IIF 2011). Rather than stressing the effects on financial institutions, or on financial markets *per se*, the emphasis has been on the knock-on effects of re-regulating bank capital, as exemplified in the European Banking Federation's (EBF 2010: 2) statement that '[e]very Euro, Pound, or Kroner ore of core capital translates into a multiple reduction of the banks' lending capacities.' The Alternative Investment Managed Funds Association – the main hedge-fund association in Europe – has opposed the directive presented by the European Commission by claiming that it would have imposed a cost up to €25 billion a year on Europe's pension-fund industry. In the words of one of their advocacy documents:

> With Europe facing strong demographic pressures as a result of an ageing population, pension funds will need strong growth and reliable returns over the coming years in order to meet future demand. If they suffer lower returns as a result of the directive, it's not only Europe's pensions funds but Europe's pensioners of both today and tomorrow who will suffer (AIMA, 2009).

So prevalent has such a discursive turn been that important policy-makers such as the Bank of England's Robert Jenkins have accused the banking industry of supporting 'a lobbying strategy that exploits misunderstanding and fear' in this regard (cited in Masters and Goff 2011). Simon Johnson has defined the attempts 'to disguise this self-interest in a veneer of social interest' as a form of 'deceptive lobbying' or 'market power masquerading as lobbying on behalf of customers' (Johnson 2011). However such behaviour is characterised, this shift in the advocacy strategy and the greater emphasis on the diffuse costs that new regulations may impose upon the economy as a whole has allowed financial-industry groups to take advantage of the mobilisation of non-financial end-users and to signal to policy-makers the broader support behind some of their claims.

Financial-industry groups and non-financial end-users appear to have lobbied together in the formal sense only rarely. This has, for instance, occurred within existing cross-sectoral associations, such as the US Chamber of Commerce, which has argued in public reports that the new wave of US financial regulation would damage small businesses and entrepreneurship in the United States (Durkin 2009). In Europe, the main European business association has joined the European Banking Federation and the European Federation of Retirement Provisions in jointly proclaiming that 'financial reforms should not have a disproportionate impact on growth' (BusinessEurope et al. 2010). Yet the overlap between the preferences of these two parties does appear to represent an important source of veto power in the regulatory response to the crisis.[5] Their combined mobilisation had the effect of weakening support for those elements of post-crisis regulatory reformers seeking to challenge the dominant regulatory paradigm more extensively and to interfere in the activities of financial-market actors, as these proposals were frequently also those with the biggest impact on financial intermediation towards non-financial end-users.

In the remainder of this chapter, we illustrate the importance of the mobilisation of non-financial-industry groups and the attempts by financial groups to work alongside them, through one of the most important post-crisis regulatory transformations: the reform of derivatives regulation in the United States.

Banks, corporate end-users, and the new politics of derivatives regulation

Banks and the regulation of derivatives before and after the crisis

Derivatives have become associated in the collective imaginary with the aspect of global finance most detached from the needs of the real economy and most closely associated with 'casino' finance (LiPuma and Lee 2004). This is particularly the case for credit derivatives, the segment of the derivatives markets that has

---

5.   As Baumgartner et al. (2009) point out, for groups taking the same position to have an impact on policy outcomes, they need not be explicitly lobbying together in a formal coalition, since their signals and resources are often aggregated in 'sides' of an issue.

witnessed the most significant growth in recent years, in which only ten banks accounted for about 90 per cent of all the trading volume (Kiff *et al.* 2009)

Different authors who have analysed the political economy of derivatives regulation before the crisis have therefore highlighted how, in the decade before the crisis, the same banks that dominated these markets exercised a determining influence in keeping the parts of the markets that were traded bilaterally among financial institutions – or 'over-the-counter' (OTC) – outside the direct oversight of the regulatory agencies in the major jurisdictions. Working through the International Swaps and Derivatives Association (ISDA), banks that operate as derivatives dealers have, over the years, developed a set of self-regulatory arrangements that have made OTC derivatives markets the poster-child for private governance in finance (*see* Tsingou 2006). Moreover, when their regulatory status was threatened by various legislative proposals presented within the US Congress during the 1990s (Tett 2009), the threat that regulating derivatives markets could shift highly mobile derivatives trading away from New York towards London, and the importance of the financial industry as a source of political contributions (Coleman 2003), weighed heavily in dissuading Congress from regulating the sector. In fact, the US Congress consistently rejected measures to regulate these markets and, in 1999, approved the Commodity Futures Modernization Act, which formally exempted OTC derivatives markets from the oversight of federal authorities. This crucial bill was included with very little notice in an 11,000 page omnibus appropriations bill, approved by the Senate on a voice vote.

Events such as the collapse of the US investment bank Lehman Brothers in September 2008, and the emergency rescue by US authorities of Bear Stearns and of insurance giant AIG, had the effect of highlighting the opaqueness of and potential for systemic disruption originating from these markets. These events have also refocused the attention of policy-makers towards the limits of the existing industry-driven regulatory regime built over the decade before the crisis by derivative dealers. Since the early stages of the crisis, derivatives dealers have reacted to this renewed scrutiny by accelerating the implementation of a wide range of self-regulatory measures, co-ordinated during a series of closed-door meetings with the Federal Reserve Bank of New York, to bolster the operational infrastructures of derivatives markets. These measures included steps to enhance the processing of derivatives traded over the counter and to reduce the enormous volume of outstanding credit derivatives, as well as shifting parts of these markets into central clearing-houses (Federal Reserve Bank of New York 2008, 2009). This proactive engagement of derivative dealers in promoting incremental regulatory changes reflected, in part, their attempt to manage the regulatory risk by preserving a greater control over the emerging regulatory framework.

These initial measures were not sufficient to stem the strength of the political momentum in favour of regulation that was building up within the US Congress. Since the fall of 2008, various bills have been presented to Congress to tighten up the oversight of derivatives dealers by federal regulatory authorities. They included the proposal presented by the Obama administration in May 2009 to subject 'all OTC derivatives dealers and all other firms whose activities in those markets create large exposures to counterparties' to a 'robust regime of prudential supervision and regulation' (US Treasury 2009), thus reversing the decision taken a decade before to exempt OTC markets from federal oversight.

While previous Congressional debates over the regulation of derivatives before the crisis had occurred, they had come 'at a time of a high degree of coordination among US regulators and private market participants' (Levin et al., 1994: 15, cited in Tsingou 2003: 18). Yet Congressional debate during and after the recent financial crisis has been characterised by a much more adversarial tone. Derivatives dealers have complained that the US Treasury has intentionally blindsided them in an attempt to maintain control of the legislative output, giving it almost no opportunity to review the bill presented to Congress before its publication (Harper, Leising and Harrington 2009; *Derivatives Week* 2009). Indeed, the backlash against Wall Street and the high salience of the debate on the regulation of derivatives created strong incentives for members of Congress to take a hard line against derivative dealers and to oppose their claims. Even President Obama intervened in person, to declare that he would veto a bill if this did not regulate derivatives severely (Favole 2010) and his administration would have stood 'firm against any attempt by the financial sector to avoid their responsibilities: in any future crisis the big financial companies must pay, not taxpayers' (Obama 2010).

The changed political climate within Congress has significantly weakened the capacity of banks that had dominated the politics of derivatives regulation before the crisis to secure their preferences; and it has forced these dealers to alter their advocacy strategy. In 1994, when various legislative proposals for regulating derivatives appeared on the Congressional agenda, a coalition of financial-sector groups claimed that the bill was 'unnecessary' and that, if passed, it would increase the cost of risk-management, so market-liquidity would decline (Brickell 1994). This time around, however, the changed political climate within Congress has forced financial dealers to abandon their opposition to the introduction of mandatory regulation of the sector. For instance, ISDA immediately endorsed the legislation introduced by the US Treasury, describing this as 'an important step toward much-needed reform of financial industry regulation' (ISDA 2009). This does not mean that derivative dealers have not sought to scale-down the scope of legislation. On the contrary, this change in policy advocacy has better positioned dealers to focus their lobbying on opposing proposals that would have most significantly curtailed the size of these markets and their profits, such as attempts to force all contracts to be traded on regulated exchanges or proposals to ban so-called 'naked' trading of credit derivatives.

Beyond finance: the mobilisation of derivatives end-users

The shift in the regulatory process, from secretive closed-door meetings between derivative dealers and the Federal Reserve Bank of New York to Congress, exposed derivative dealers to competition from a broader range of financial groups. For instance, Congressional hearings gave significant space to clearing-houses and exchanges, which saw in the proposed legislation an opportunity to gain a greater share of the derivatives market (Helleiner and Pagliari 2009). Most importantly, although the legislation introduced in Congress represented a response to excessive risk-taking in the way credit derivatives were traded primarily among financial institutions, the broader scope of the legislation triggered an important mobilisation of groups from outside the financial sector.

The diversification of post-crisis private-sector mobilisation around the area of derivatives is striking. Following the same methodology described above, we analysed all US Congressional hearings since 1990 that concerned the regulatory treatment of derivatives. From 48 hearings in all, we divided the composition of private-sector participants represented in these hearings for both the pre-crisis period and the post-crisis period, into the groups represented in Figures 6.2 and 6.3, respectively.

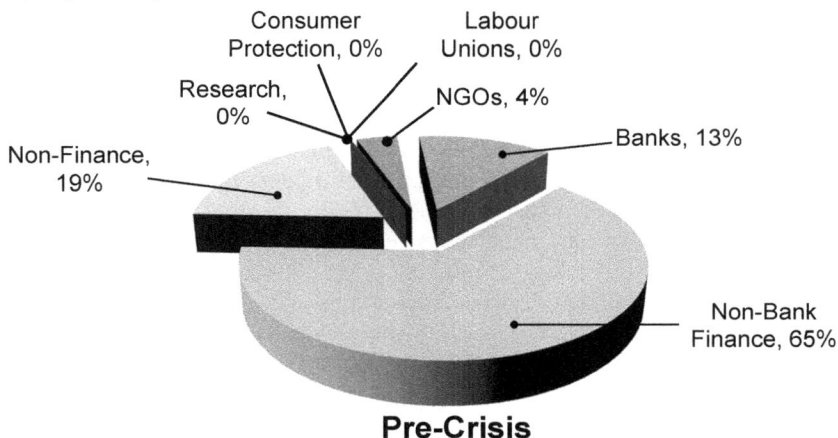

Figure 6.2: Composition of private-sector participants in US Congressional hearings on derivatives, 1990–August 2008

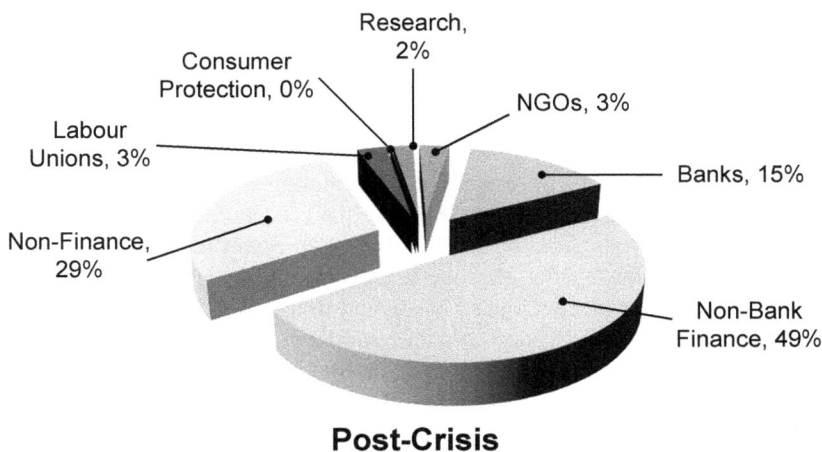

Figure 6.3: Composition of private-sector participants in US Congressional hearings on derivatives, August 2008–2011

According to this data, non-financial sector actors have increased their presence in US congressional hearings on derivatives by 56 per cent since the crisis. Who are these non-financial groups? One important group of non-financial actors that has mobilised to influence the regulation of derivatives is to be found among agricultural interests, who use derivatives to hedge fluctuations in the price of agricultural products. As Clapp and Helleiner argue, US agricultural interests had been active in demanding more stringent regulations to constrain speculative activities since the emergence of the agricultural futures markets in Chicago in the nineteenth century; but their activism and capacity to counter-act the financial industry had decreased since the 1980s. Yet the role of speculation in derivatives markets in creating commodity-price volatility has meant that these agricultural interests were now able to form a wide coalition of 'producers, processors, distributors, retailers and residential, commercial and industrial end-users in the agricultural, food, and energy sectors' named the Commodity Markets Oversight Coalition. These business groups were also able to join forces with various consumer advocacy groups, NGOs (the Institute for Agriculture and Trade Policy, Friends of the Earth, Public Citizen, New Rules for Global Finance), and different faith-based organisations in support of tighter regulation of commodity derivatives (Clapp and Helleiner 2012).

The mobilisation of non-financial business groups has not been limited to firms active in the commodity markets, however. Over 170 major American companies and the bulk of US national business associations joined forces in a single group named the Coalition for Derivatives End-Users. A letter sent to every member of Congress in October 2009 expressed concern that 'certain proposals for reform of the OTC derivatives market would place an extraordinary burden on end-users in diverse sectors of the economy – including manufacturers, energy companies, healthcare companies and commercial real estate owners and developers' (Coalition for Derivatives End-Users 2009a; *see also* 2009b). Table 6.1 lists some of the signatories in this group.

Coalition for Derivatives End-Users, US Chamber of Commerce, and National Association of Corporate Treasurers estimated that a '3% margin requirement on OTC derivatives could be expected to reduce capital spending by $5.1 to $6.7 billion per year, leading to a loss of 100,000 to 130,000 jobs' within the S&P 500 companies alone (Keybridge Research 2011).

Regulatory authorities have warned that granting broad exemptions to end-users could undermine the attempt to tame the risk in derivatives markets by creating loopholes that could be exploited by Wall Street (Gensler 2010; 2011). Despite this, when the legislative proposal presented by the US Treasury moved to the House of Representatives, the claims of end-users were quickly endorsed. The Dodd-Frank bill passed by Congress in the Summer of 2010 exempted 'commercial end-users' from the registration, capital, and reporting requirements, and other rules applied to derivatives dealers and other 'major swap participants', as well as from the requirement to have derivatives transactions that were sufficiently standardised centrally cleared and traded on a regulated exchange.

Table 6.1: Firm and association signatories to the Coalition for Derivatives End-Users

Individual firms	Business associations
3M	Electric Power Supply Association
Ford Motor Company	American Petroleum Institute
IBM	US Chamber of Commerce
Boeing	The Business Roundtable
Caterpillar	Financial Executives International
Apple	National Association of Real Estate Investment Trusts
Intel Corporation	Industrial Energy Consumers of America
Bayer	The Real Estate Roundtable
Cargill	National Association of Manufacturers
Coca-Cola	American Chemistry Council
Harley-Davidson	American Gas Association
Shell Oil	American Forest and Paper Association
Procter and Gamble	

The preferential treatment granted to corporate end-users, shows how end-users were more successful that bank lobbies in having their preferences incorporated in legislation, which did not grant the same exemption from central clearing and exchange trading to standardised derivatives trades between financial institutions. How do we explain the greater influence of corporate end-users despite the greater resources mobilised by financial industry? One explanation points to the impact of the crisis in shifting the institutional contexts in which the regulation of derivatives took place, away from contexts favourable to the financial industry, such as closed-door meetings between the Federal Reserve and the main dealers, towards institutional venues that maintained stronger links with corporate end-users (for example, the Agriculture Committee and the Energy and Commerce Committee within US Congress; *see also* Clapp and Helleiner 2012). A complementary explanation points towards the electoral incentives faced by policy-makers in these venues, and the greater resonance among elected policy-makers of the claims advanced by the end-users regarding the impact that regulation would have on employment, vis-a-vis traditional concerns regarding a potential migration of derivatives trades from New York to London.

In a moment in which the severity of the crisis had severely reduced their political capital in Washington, derivative dealers adjusted their lobbying strategy to take advantage of the mobilisation of their corporate customers. Financial-industry actors have followed in the footsteps of corporate end-users in highlighting the costs that legislation would have imposed, not only on Wall Street but also on Main Street. For instance, the ISDA has opposed Congressional proposals to tighten the regulation of derivatives markets, on the ground that they would 'increase the cost of doing business for industry participants' and 'put

American businesses at a significant disadvantage to their competitors around the world' (Pickel 2009). A study published in June 2010 argued that legislation on the table at that time would have cost US companies as much as $1 trillion in terms of capital requirements (ISDA 2010).

The Congressional leaders who had been shepherding the legislation through Congress saw this as 'playing on the fears of the end-users in order to obtain an exemption for themselves', as stated by Rep. Peterson (cited in Drawbaugh 2010). Barney Frank – chair of the House Financial Services Committee and main architect of the bill in Congress – publicly expressed his concern about 'financial institutions taking the end users in effect as hostages to get out from under some of these requirements' (cited by Paletta 2010).

End-users and Wall Street: source of incremental or radical change?

We have seen that end-users of derivatives, such as corporate actors, have played an important role alongside 'the usual suspects' of financial-industry groups. But what has been the impact that the mobilisation of end-users has actually had over the regulation of derivatives?

The large number of non-financial business groups that have mobilised within Congress, as well as in other policy arenas, has increased the challenge for the main target of re-regulation, that is, banks, in limiting the scope of regulation. For instance, as Clapp and Helleiner (2012) argue, the Commodity Markets Oversight Coalition and the different NGOs and consumer-advocacy groups that have mobilised over the regulation of commodity derivatives have successfully challenged the preferences of derivatives dealers and played a key role in achieving the introduction in the Dodd-Frank Act of mandatory position limits, which had been resisted by financial-sector groups. From the perspective of Clapp and Helleiner, non-financial end-users have been important change-agents in the regulatory debate. Yet in many circumstances the advocacy of corporate end-users of derivatives sought to restrain the scope of regulatory proposals rather than to expand it. A prominent example in this regard is the so-called Lincoln Amendment, that is, the measure introduced by Senator Blanche Lincoln requiring federally insured banks to spin off their swaps-trading desks into independently capitalised entities. This significant change in the structure of derivatives markets was supported by the various NGOs and trade unions comprising Americans for Financial Reform, which stated that this measure would 'sharply reduce the possibility of taxpayer bailouts for speculative activity that does not serve the real economy' (AFR 2010). However, corporate end-users from the Coalition for Derivatives End-Users opposed the same proposal on the grounds that it would have made it more difficult for them to find counter-parties and increased the cost of hedging their risk (Coalition for Derivatives End-Users 2010). This mobilisation contributed to watering down the measure, as subsequent legislation passed by Congress allowed banks to retain the bulk of their swap-trading operations on their books and to spin off only the trading of those derivatives perceived as more risky.

The mobilisation of corporate end-users also facilitated the attempt by derivatives dealers to veto other ambitious regulatory proposals. For instance, various legislative proposals introduced in Congress have sought to decrease the systemic risk posed by these markets: by forcing all derivatives contracts on to regulated exchanges (for example, the Derivatives Trading Integrity Act of 2009, introduced in January 2009 by Senator Tom Harkin), or by seeking to ban the development of the most customised products (for example, the Credit Default Swap Prohibition Act of 2009 introduced by Representative Maxine Waters). Banks naturally opposed these measures, which would have curtailed the volume of contracts traded on derivatives markets and barred the more profitable products; corporate end-users also opposed these measures, which would restrict their capacity to enter into customised transactions. From the perspective of the Coalition described above, the attempt to increase the safety of derivatives markets by increasing the level of standardisation would 'preclude companies from accessing customized derivatives to offset or reduce unique business risks' (Coalition for Derivatives End-Users 2009b). The legislation passed by Congress has safeguarded the capacity of financial institutions to develop and trade customised products outside regulated exchanges.

The opposition of a broad constellation of financial and non-financial actors was also important in influencing the position of Congress over so-called 'naked' trading, that is, the practice of trading in derivatives without owning the underlying asset upon which the derivatives contract was based. This practice received significant attention during the crisis and different commentators have called for making this practice illegal, on the ground that it represented a 'purely speculative gamble' without any social or economic benefit (Munchau 2008). The financier George Soros described these practices with the analogy of 'buying life insurance on someone else's life and owning a licence to kill him' (Soros 2009).

Congress considered different legislative proposals to ban such 'naked' derivatives trading and allowing only market actors owning the underlying bond to trade in the derivatives markets (*see* for instance Derivatives Markets Transparency and Accountability Act of 2009, introduced by Rep. Peterson, or the joint bill released by Peterson and the Chairman of the House Financial Services Committee, Barney Frank, in July 2009); Congress ultimately rejected this radical solution, given the widespread opposition to it from beyond the banking industry. As Congressman Barney Frank stated:

> When we first began to talk about this (prohibiting naked credit default swaps)… I did not expect people in the business of selling these, people in the financial industry, to be happy with that. They weren't … We didn't care whether they were or weren't. What we began to hear were objections to some of this from those people for whom derivatives are not an end for making money as they are for the financial institutions, but a means so that they can go about their business of producing goods and services with some stability, with some reasonable expectation about cost (US House of Representatives 2009: 2).

These examples demonstrate how the significant mobilisation of corporate end-users has not acted as a countervailing force to the power and preferences of the financial industry. Instead, corporate end-users have frequently expressed preferences that largely *converged* with those of financial-industry groups, thus reinforcing the attempt by the financial industry to veto the introduction of more radical solutions for regulating derivatives markets when these would also have impaired the capacity of end-users to use derivatives to hedge their commercial risks. The incremental policy change in the area of derivatives regulation can thus be attributed to a veto-block of corporations and financial-industry groups that prevented more radical regulatory proposals.

Conclusion

As the other chapters in this volume testify, there are a wide range of explanations for why post-crisis changes to financial governance have been incremental in character. In this paper we have centred our attention on the mobilisation of private-sector actors in response to financial regulatory reforms.

Through an analysis of the post-crisis attempts to reform the regulation of derivatives in the US, we have shown how incremental policy change appears to be driven in part by private-sector groups, not by the usual 'Wall Street' suspects, but rather coalitions comprising financial and non-financial business groups. The analysis of the broader mobilisation of non-financial business groups developed in Section 2 reveals how this represents a broader trend affecting the design of regulatory policies in different contexts and sectors after the crisis.

Our analysis here has not sought to challenge the notion that financial-industry groups remain important actors in shaping financial regulatory reforms but it calls for focused attention on two issues in any consideration of private-sector roles in shaping post-crisis reform. The first is the constraints that the policy-making environment places on the influence of financial-industry groups. From this perspective, the influence of financial-industry groups has remained conditional on their capacity to adjust their advocacy strategy to a changed environment, promoting incremental changes and tying their interests to those of other, non-financial interest-groups. Second, this analysis calls for greater attention to the mobilisation of non-financial-industry groups in shaping financial regulatory policies and the impact that this has on the capacity of financial-industry groups to shape regulatory policies. Thus we have argued that, in order to make sense of the role of the private sector in the incremental character of post-crisis financial regulatory change, we need to understand the broader network of private-sector groups outside the financial sector, and their important connections to recent regulatory changes. When the impact of corporate actors as a distinct set of actors is examined, corporate actors are frequently seen to act as veto-players, rather in the way that financial-industry groups might have been expected to perform.

References

Abbott Laboratories *et al.* (2012) 'Letter to Federal Regulators re: prohibitions and restrictions on proprietary trading and certain interests in and relationship with, hedge funds and private equity funds', 14 February 2012. http://www.centerforcapitalmarkets.com/wp-content/uploads/2010/04/2012-2.14-FINAL-Coalition-letter_Volcker-Rule-2.14.pdf. Accessed 30 April 2012.

Acemoglu, D. and Johnson, S. (2012) 'Who captured the Fed?' Economix Blog, *New York Times*, March 29. http://economix.blogs.nytimes.com/2012/03/29/who-captured-the-fed/. Accessed April 30 2012.

Association for Corporate Treasurers (2011) 'Comments in response to *'Call for Evidence: Towards a Financial Transaction Tax'*, issued by the House of Lords European Union Committee', 4 November 2011. http://www.treasurers.org/node/7521. Accessed 30 April 2012.

Americans for Financial Reform (2010) 'AFR supports the prohibition against federal government bailouts of swap entities', 3 May 2010. http://ourfinancialsecurity.org/2010/05/afr-supports-the-prohibition-against-federal-government-bailouts-of-swap-entities/. Accessed 30 April 2012.

Alternative Investment Management Association (2009) 'European directive could cost European pension industry 25 billion Euros annually', 4 August 2009.

A. M. Best, DBRS, Fitch, Moody's and S&P's (2008b) 'Joint response to the technical committee of the International Organization of Securities Commissions' consultation report on the role of credit rating agencies in structured finance markets', in IOSCO, *Comments Received in Relation to the Consultation Report 'The Role Of Credit Rating Agencies In Structured Finance Markets'*, May 2008. http://www.iosco.org/library/pubdocs/pdf/IOSCOPD272.pdf. Accessed 12 July 2012.

Baker, A. (2010) 'Restraining regulatory capture? Anglo-America, crisis politics and trajectories of change in global financial governance', *International Affairs*, 86(3): 647–63.

Baumgartner, F. R., Berry, J. M., Hojnacki, M., Kimball, D. and Lebon, B. (2009) *Lobbying and Policy Change: Who wins, who loses, and why*, Chicago: University of Chicago Press.

Bhagwati, J. (2008) 'We need to guard against destructive creation', *Financial Times*, October 17.

Braun, M. and Raddatz, C. (2009) *Banking on Politics*, Policy Research Working Paper 4902, World Bank Development Research Group.

Brehler, M. (2010) 'EU hedge fund rules will hurt small businesses. An open letter to the European Parliament from 700 business owners', *Wall Street Journal*, 10 May 2010.

Brickell, Mark C. (1994) 'Joint statement of the leading financial industry and professional associations in the United States of America on HR 4503', press release, New York, 11 July 1994.

Business Europe, European Banking Federation, European Federation for Retirement Provision, European Private Equity and Venture Capital Association, Federation of European Accountants (2010) 'Financial reforms and the recovery', 25 June. http://www.evca.eu/uploadedFiles/News1/News_Items/2010-06-25_Financial_reforms_and_the_recovery-June_2010.pdf. Accessed 30 April 2012.

Clapp, J. and Helleiner, E. (2012) 'Troubled futures? The global food crisis and the politics of agricultural derivatives regulation', *Review of International Political Economy* 19 (2): 181–207.

Coalition for Derivatives End-Users (2009a) 'Coalition for Derivatives End-Users views Senate discussion draft as significant step backward. Legislation would drive capital away from job creation and economic growth', 10 November. http://www.reit.com/PolicyIssues/OtherFederalLegislation/~/media/Portals/0/PDF/Dodd%20Discussion%20Draft%20Release.ashx. Accessed 12 July 2012.

— (2009b) 'Statement for the Senate Committee on Agriculture hearing, "Reforming U.S. Financial Market Regulation"', 18 November. http://www.nam.org/~/media/F68C770A9DDD49E89048C60ABD3934A5/FINAL_Coalition_Statement_for_Senate_Agriculture_Hearingpdf.pdf. Accessed 12 July 2012.

— (2010) 'Coalition for Derivatives End-Users comments to Title VII of the Lincoln/Dodd Substitute to S. 3217, The Wall Street Transparency and Accountability Act of 2010', 29 April.

Coleman, W. (2003) 'Governing global finance: financial derivatives, liberal states and transformative capacity', in Weiss, L. (ed.) *States in the Global Economy: Bringing domestic institutions back in*, Cambridge: Cambridge University Press, 271–92.

Culpepper, P. (2011) *Quiet Politics and Business Power: Corporate control in Europe and Japan*, Cambridge: Cambridge University Press.

Derivatives Week (2009) 'OTC proposals intentionally blindsided industry', 28 August.

Drawbaugh, K. (2010) 'Democrats deny margins for swap end-users in bill', Reuters, 30 June.

Drezner, D. (2007) *All Politics is Global: Explaining international regulatory regimes*, Princeton, Princeton University Press.

Durkin, T. (2009) 'The impact of the consumer financial protection agency on small business', Center for Capital Market Competitiveness, US Chamber of Commerce. http://www.uschamber.com/reports/impact-consumer-financial-protection-agency-small-business. Accessed 12 July 2012.

EACT (2011) 'Presentation to Committee on Economic and Monetary Affairs of the European Parliament by Richard Raeburn, Chairman of the EACT', 11 October 2011. http://www.europarl.europa.eu/document/activities/cont/201110/20111012ATT29103/20111012ATT29103EN.pdf. Accessed 30 April 2012.

— (2012) 'Presentation to Committee on Economic and Monetary Affairs of the European Parliament by Richard Raeburn, Chairman of the EACT', 6 February 2012. http://www.eactnew.org.uk/docs/ECON-Raeburn_06-02-12.pdf. Accessed 30 April 2012.

European Banking Federation (2010) 'Finding the right balance of the new Basel framework', policy paper, 16 April. http://www.ebf-fbe.eu. Accessed 12 July 2012.

European Federation for Retirement Provision (2009) 'EFRP response – European Commission consultation on hedge funds', Brussels, 31 January. http://www.efrp.org/. Accessed 30 April 2012.

Favole, J.A. (2010), 'Obama to veto bill that doesn't bring derivatives market under control', *Dow Jones Newswire*, 16 April 2010.

Federal Reserve Bank of New York (2008) 'New York Fed welcomes further industry commitments on over-the-counter derivatives', New York, 31 October. http://www.newyorkfed.org/newsevents/news/markets/2008/an081031.html. Accessed 12 July 2012.

— (2009) 'Market participants commit to expand central clearing for OTC derivatives', New York, 8 September. http://www.newyorkfed.org/newsevents/news/markets/2009/ma090908.html. Accessed 12 July 2012.

Fioretos, O. (2010) 'Capitalist diversity and the international regulation of hedge funds', *Review of International Political Economy*, 17(4): 696–723.

Foot, R. and Walter, A. (2010) *China, the United States, and Global Order*, Cambridge: Cambridge University Press.

Gensler, G. (2010) Keynote Address of Chairman Gary Gensler, OTC Derivatives Reform, U.S. Chamber of Commerce, Washington, D.C. 24 March 2010. http://www.cftc.gov/PressRoom/SpeechesTestimony/opagensler-36. Accessed 23 May 2013.

— (2011) 'Remarks, OTC derivatives reform, European Parliament, Economic and Monetary Affairs Committee, Brussels, Belgium, Commodity Futures Trading Commission', 22 March 2011. http://www.cftc.gov/PressRoom/SpeechesTestimony/opagensler-75. Accessed 12 July 2012.

Harper, C., Leising, M. and Harrington, S. (2009) 'Wall Street stealth lobby defends 35 billion derivatives haul', *Bloomberg*, 31 August.

Heinemann, F. and Schüler, M. (2002) 'A Stiglerian view on banking supervision', Discussion Paper No. 02-66, Mannheim: Centre for European Economic Research (ZEW). http://ftp.zew.de/pub/zew-docs/div/regconf/Heinemann_Schueler_2.pdf. Accessed 6 February 2013.

Helleiner, E. and Pagliari, S. (2009) 'The end of self-regulation? Hedge funds and derivatives in global financial governance', in Helleiner, E., Pagliari, S. and Zimmermann, H. (eds) *Global Finance in Crisis: The politics of international regulatory change,* London: Routledge.

— (2011) 'The end of an era in international financial regulation? A post-crisis research agenda', *International Organization*, 65(3): 169–200.

Helleiner, E. and Porter, T. (2010) 'Making transnational networks more accountable', *Economics, Management and Financial Markets*, 5(2): 158–73.

International Chamber of Commerce (2010) 'Letter to Basel Committee', 16 April. http://www.bis.org/publ/bcbs165/icoc.pdf. Accessed 12 July 2012.

Igan, D., Mishra, P. and Tressl, T. (2009) 'A fistful of dollars: lobbying and the financial crisis', IMF Working Paper WP/09/287, Washington, DC: International Monetary Fund.

Institute of International Finance (2008a) 'Final report of the IIF Committee on market best practices: principles of conduct and best practice recommendations', press release, July 2008. http://www.iif.com/press/press+75.php. Accessed 12 July 2012.

— (2008b) 'Systemic crisis requires extraordinary actions', press release, 2 October. http://www.iif.com/press/press+80.php. Accessed 12 July 2012.

— (2010) *Interim Report on the Cumulative Impact on the Global Economy of Proposed Changes in the Banking Regulatory Framework*, Institute of International Finance. June 2010. http://www.google.co.uk/url?sa=t&rct=j&q=&esrc=s&source=web&cd=1&ved=0CE8QFjAA&url=http%3A%2F%2Fwww.iif.com%2Fdownload.php%3Fid%3Di%2FQ%2B9bBo%2Fj8&ei=PKD-T7vVIIWi0QWS3LmpBw&usg=AFQjCNHprDAUa4KpcqcdKYoHexFbexBcvw&sig2=os8eTD298dVUhmvZh3sEog. Accessed 12 July 2012.

— (2011) *The Cumulative Impact on the Global Economy of Changes in the Financial Regulatory Framework*, September 2011. http://www.iif.com/press/press+203.php. Accessed 12 July 2012.

International Swaps and Derivatives Association (2009) 'ISDA comments on proposed regulatory reform or OTC derivatives', New York, 13 May 2009. http://www.isda.org/press/press051309otc.html. Accessed 12 July 2012.

— (2010) 'US companies may face US $1 trillion in additional capital and liquidity requirements as a result of financial regulatory reform' New York, 29 June. http://www.isda.org/media/press/2010/press062910.html. Accessed 12 July 2012.

Johnson, S. (2009) 'The quiet coup', *The Atlantic*, May.

— (2011) 'Deceptive lobbying on derivatives', *The New York Times Economix Blog*, 16 February. http://economix.blogs.nytimes.com/2011/02/16/deceptive-lobbying-on-derivatives/. Accessed 30 April 2012.

Jones, S. (2009) 'Hedge funds win Church of England blessing', *Financial Times*, 6 October.

Keybridge Research (2011) 'An analysis of the Coalition for Derivatives End Users' survey on over-the-counter derivatives', 11 February. http://www.chathamfinancial.com/wp-content/uploads/2011/02/OTC_Derivatives_Survey0211.pdf. Accessed 12 July 2012.

Kiff, J., Elliot, J., Kazarian, E., Scarlata, J. and Spackman, C. (2009) 'Credit derivatives: systemic risks and policy options', IMF Working Paper WP/09/254, November 2009, Washington, DC: International Monetary Fund.

Kroll, A. (2010) 'Exposing the big bank lobby', *Mother Jones*, 11 May.

Kwak, J. (2013), 'Cultural capture and the financial crisis', in Carpenter, D. and Moss, D. (eds) *Preventing Regulatory Capture: Special interest influence, and how to limit it*, Cambridge: Cambridge University Press.

Lall, R. (2011) 'Reforming global banking standards: back to the future?', in Ponte, S., Gibbon, P and Vestergaard, J. (eds), *Governing Through Standards: Origins, drivers and limitations*, London: Routledge, 75–101.

Levin, P., J. Luke and P. Sundaravej (1994), *New York in International Financial Law Review*, November: 10-16.

LiPuma, E. and Lee, B. (2004) *Financial Derivatives and the Globalization of Risk*, Durham: Duke University Press.

Masters, B. and Goff, S. (2011) 'Banks accused of "dishonesty" on reform', *Financial Times*, 23 November.

Mattli, W. and Woods, N. (2009) 'In whose benefit? Explaining regulatory change in global politics', in Mattli, W. and Woods, N. (eds) *The Politics of Global Regulation*, Princeton, NJ: Princeton University Press.

Managed Funds Association (2004) 'MFA issues warning on SEC hedge fund registration proposals', press release, Washington, DC, 17 September. http://www.hedgeweek.com/2004/09/17/mfa-issues-warning-sec-hedge-fund-registration-proposals. Accessed 12 July 2012.

—   (2009) 'Managed Funds Association announces support for registration of investment advisers including hedge funds', press release, Washington, DC, 7 May. http://www.managedfunds.org/. Accessed 12 July 2012.

Münchau, M. (2008) 'Time to outlaw naked credit default swaps', *Financial Times*, 28 February.

New York Times Editorial (2010) 'AIG, Greece, and who's next?', *New York Times*, 5 March.

Obama, B. (2010) 'Statement from the President on financial reform', Washington, DC, The White House, Office of the Press Secretary, 15 March.

Paletta, D. (2010) 'Late change sparks outcry over finance-overhaul bill', *Wall Street Journal*, 1 July.

Pickel, R. (2009) 'Testimony of Robert Pickel, Chief Executive Officer, International Swaps and Derivatives Association before the Subcommittee on Securities, Insurance and Investment Committee on Banking, Housing and Urban Affairs, United States Senate', 22 June. http://www.isda.org/press/press062209.html. Accessed 12 July 2012.

Protess, B. (2012) 'The Volcker rule's unusual critics', Dealbook, *New York Times*, 15 February 2012.

Protess, B. and Eavis, P. (2012) 'At Volcker rule deadline, a strong pushback from Wall Street', *New York Times*, 14 February.

Seabrooke, L. and Tsingou, E. (2009) 'Revolving doors and linked ecologies in the world economy: policy locations and the practice of international financial reform', CSGR Working Paper 260/09, Centre for the Study of Globalisation and Regionalisation, University of Warwick.

Sharpf, F. (2000) 'Institutions in comparative policy research', *Comparative Political Studies*, 33(6–7): 762–90.

Soros, G. (2009) 'One way to stop bear raids', *Wall Street Journal*, 23 March.

Taibbi, M. (2012) 'The slow, painful death of Dodd-Frank', *Rolling Stone*, Issue 1157, 24 May: 62–7; 86–7.

Tett, G. (2009) *Fool's Gold: How the bold dream of a small tribe at J. P. Morgan was corrupted by Wall Street greed and unleashed a catastrophe*, New York NY: Simon & Schuster.

Tsingou, E. (2003) Transnational policy communities and financial governance: the role of private actors in derivatives regulation. CSGR Working Paper No. 111/03.

— (2006) 'The governance of OTC derivatives markets', in Mooslechner, P., Schuberth, H. and Weber, B. (eds) *The Political Economy of Financial Market Regulation: The dynamics of inclusion and exclusion*, Cheltenham, Edward Elgar: 89–114.

— (2009) 'Regulatory reactions to the global credit crisis: analysing a policy community under stress' in Helleiner, E., Pagliari, S. and Zimmermann, H. *Global Finance in Crisis. The politics of international regulatory change*, London, Routledge, 21–36.

Underhill, G. (1995) 'Keeping governments out of politics: transnational securities markets, regulatory co-operation, and political legitimacy', *Review of International Studies*, 21(3): 251–78.

Underhill, G. and Zhang X. (2003 *International Financial Governance Under Stress: Global structures versus financial imperatives*, Cambridge: Cambridge University Press.

— (2008) 'Setting the rules: private power, political underpinnings, and legitimacy in global monetary and financial governance', *International Affairs*, 84(3): 535–54.

US Treasury (2009) 'Regulatory Reform Over-The-Counter (OTC) Derivatives'. Press Release, 13 May 2009. http://www.treasury.gov/press-center/press-releases/Pages/tg129.aspx. Accessed 23 May 2013

Wade, R. (2008) 'The first-world debt crisis of 2007–2010 in global perspective', *Challenge*, 51(4) (July/August): 23–54.

Wearden, G. (2009) 'Leave bankers alone, says BBA's Angela Knight', *Guardian*, 31 December.

Wood, D. (2005) *Governing Global Banking: The Basel Committee and the politics of financial globalization*, Aldershot: Ashgate.

chapter seven | continuity of expert rule: global accountancy regulation after the crisis

Sebastian Botzem

Introduction: continuity in times of crises

After the financial crisis of 2007–09, frequent comparisons were made to the market crashes in the late 1920s and to the Great Depression. When, after the Lehman collapse, housing prices declined, banks went bankrupt, production suffered and jobs were in danger, public discussions began about the causes of the crisis and the regulatory measures to be taken. In those discussions, accounting regulation figured prominently as one of the fundamental issues to be addressed in order to fix the current and prevent future crises. While accounting scandals in individual firms are nothing new, this time the standards themselves and the governance of rule-setting were both fundamentally questioned. Public discussions were not mainly about 'cooking the books' or negligent auditing. Instead, fair-value accounting, a core accounting principle, was put into question especially in relation to the procyclical dynamics it triggers. Criticism was thus directed to the very heart of accounting standardisation, questioning the content of standards, the mode of standard-setting and the governance structure of the standardisation body, the International Accounting Standards Board (IASB).

The G20 was among the first international bodies to question the appropriateness of private transnational standard setting in accounting and called for immediate action. Most notably, the G20 asked the IASB to review its membership, to enhance transparency, and to ensure appropriate relationships with public authorities (G20 2008: 6). However, several years after this pressure was first exerted, an assessment of the developments indicates that – above all – continuity can be detected in accounting standardisation. Changes are small and to some degree symbolic. Despite far-reaching initial demands, no major organisational reconfigurations can be detected. In line with the other contributions in this volume, this chapter examines the puzzle of marginal change in transnational accounting standardisation despite the fundamental criticism with which the IASB was initially faced.

For two reasons, continuity in transnational accounting regulation merits closer attention: first, the IASB's governance structure had been under criticism before the crisis and can therefore be interpreted as initially weak or vulnerable. Second and perhaps more important, accounting regulation is an icon of transnational self-regulation and, as such, a critical case of private, expertise-based rule-making. Both aspects underline the potential for fundamental change – and call for an explanation of why it has not materialised. Instead, the developments are characterised by incrementalism with only modest organisational modifications.

The chapter sets out to explain this, giving particular consideration to the relevance of professional expertise as a power resource at the disposal of established actors. More precisely, I focus on three interrelated aspects of transnational accounting (content of rules, procedures of rule-setting and governance structures) and the strategic responses of actors seeking to maintain the basic institutional configuration. To explain continuity in transnational accounting regulation, the chapter sets out to answer the following questions: How did the IASB meet and accommodate fundamental criticism? Who are the relevant actors and which strategies can be identified that ensured incremental development? Which lessons can be drawn from this case to contribute to the discussion of institutionalism and agency?

Transnational accounting regulation is characterised by professionalism and expertise-based standardisation. This chapter therefore highlights not only the crucial role of expert networks and large professional services firms in developing, maintaining and changing the institutional arrangement of private standard-setting. It shows the development through time of modernising organisational structures and also of the process of renewing social closure, which preserved the club-like nature of accounting regulation. In particular, I focus on the organised activities of the IASB to proactively manage institutional change at various levels. This contributes to the discussion of agency exercised by powerful insiders in the processes of incrementalism, as set out in the Introduction to this volume. The case of accounting regulation underscores how powerful veto-players interested in maintaining the status quo engage in a number of activities and at a number of levels, to preserve and also to renew their position within the wider governance structure of global financial regulation. Drawing on institutionalist ideas, I argue that transnational accounting regulation is characterised by a complementary set-up of the content of accounting standards, the procedures and governance structures in which they are developed and the actors involved. Accordingly, the IASB's reaction to the financial crisis can be interpreted as a strategic response combining avoidance of confrontation, reframing criticism and carefully renewing organisational leadership.

Transnational accounting regulation shares characteristics with other cases discussed in this book. Among them are the difficulties of unseating incumbents, the problems of enhancing ideational alternatives, and the challenges posed by institutional friction. However, some particularly pronounced aspects make accounting regulation a case that merits closer attention. Among these are the importance of professional expertise and its embeddedness within the IASB's governance structures. In addition, the IASB'S long trajectory, dating back to the early 1970s, and the large range of organisational activities in terms of rule-setting procedures and decision-making allow for interesting insights in historical institutionalist analysis.

This chapter recounts and explains the interrelatedness of three dimensions of transnational standardisation: the normative content of standards; the operational structure of standard-setting; and a close-knit network of decision-makers. The institutional complementarity of these three dimensions is central to understanding the high degree of continuity in accounting regulation. However, this is no attempt to privilege structure over agency. Instead, institutional change is explained by the balance between agency and the institutions within which agents operate. Establishing institutional density and renewing social closure are important activities in accounting regulation, from which actors derive additional resources to maintain their influence. The institutional continuity in transnational accounting-regulation is therefore not to be mistaken for stasis. Instead it is a case of insider-led, carefully mediated change.

The post-crisis situation of the IASB is not a case of business as usual. Instead, it shows how central players in accounting regulation reacted in a reflective and multifaceted way to the criticism with which they were confronted. Incremental change was sought to maintain the overall institutional make-up and to keep the IASB's position as a core actor in transnational regulation. Empirically it can be shown that the IASB sought to balance opening up to critics as much as needed while steering discussions over appropriate regulation in a favourable direction. Continuity was ensured by cautiously re-shaping the IASB and addressing criticism, without compromising its basic, expertise-based orientation.

Transnational accounting regulation as institution-building

Accounting standardisation epitomises a particularly far-reaching transnational private regulatory arrangement and the IASB is often seen as challenging national rule-making authority. In particular, the IASB's considerable autonomy and the strong influence of expert-based professionalism are somewhat incompatible with statist approaches, which usually emphasise the importance of national politics and the role of local regulators, such as the US Securities and Exchange Commission, or the European Commission (cf. Simmons 2001; de Lange and Howieson 2006; Posner 2009). Approaches focusing on private authority discuss additional sources of power. Porter (2005), for instance, argues that practical and professional expertise provides an independent source of 'technical' authority. Büthe and Mattli (2011) point to the role of professional associations and their capacities to organise their interests at both the national and transnational levels. More critical studies debate the influence of private business engaged in accounting-standard setting, above all the role of globally active auditing firms (Perry and Nölke 2005; Botzem 2008). Literature on accounting regulation also discusses the interrelation of national and international levels of standard-setting with regard to interest-group representation (Martinez-Diaz 2005; Perry and Nölke 2006) and the conditions of institutional fit between these levels (Büthe and Mattli 2011).

Economic dynamics are given particular attention in explaining accounting harmonisation. Martinez-Diaz (2005) traces the impact of national deregulation and privatisation during the 1980s and 1990s as a catalyst for global investment and cross-border listing of corporations, for which harmonised accounting standards are instrumental. Accounting standards are seen as one way of broadening and deepening the impact of globalised finance (Nölke 2009). In fact, they play a constitutive role in the 'financialisation' of the global economy, in particular, the spread of fair-value accounting (Perry and Nölke 2006; Boyer 2007). Fair value is a key tool for aligning corporate reporting with financial markets, mostly by accounting for assets and liabilities at market value. It should be noted, however, that while change is often driven by private actors, public and private regulation are no opposites, but rather interdependent elements of global private politics (Büthe 2010: 20).

Recent work on the IASB has a specific focus on actor constellations. For example, Leblond (2011) argues that the IASB's large degree of autonomy can be attributed to the fact that the organisation has more than one principal, namely the USA and the European Union (EU). Divergent interests among the principals and limited means of controlling the agent give the IASB much leeway to act independently (Leblond 2011: 458). Posner (2010) offers an historical explanation, tracing changes in transnational accounting regulation to a sequence of events that took place in the transatlantic political arena. However, most studies on the IASB underrate internal procedures and changes in the organisational set-up; and they devote scant attention to the content of standards and normative changes over time. The specificities of accounting, in particular the strong role of professional associations and experts' power in framing relevant expertise, are lacking in many political-economy approaches. Many contributions fail to conceptualise the club-like nature of transnational accounting standardisation, in which professionalism and expertise are core characteristics, adequately.

The sociology of professions has long focused on professional associations, individual experts and accounting firms and emphasises the self-organising capacity of professions. Capacity to develop and foster a distinct system of knowledge is a core explanation of professional influence. The framing of expertise not only becomes a key activity but is also used to organise social closure, making disputes and the settlement of controversies a key aspect of professional influence (Sugarman 1995; Covaleski et al. 2003). More recent work has shown that large, internationally active professional services firms – in addition to the IASB – have become important loci of expertise (Greenwood et al. 2002; Botzem 2012). One important feature of accounting professionalism is self-regulation. It is particularly pronounced in Anglo-American countries, where professions enjoy a large degree of independence and often invoke anti-statist rhetoric, arguing for a laissez-faire attitude toward regulation and oversight (cf. Macdonald 1995; Willmott 2000). Disposal of practical expertise is a central argument when professions demand independence from the state. The IASB has managed to claim a similar role at the international level of standard-setting. It is actively engaged in defining expertise in a way that reflects the knowledge base of prominent actors involved in the IASB (cf. Tamm Hallström 2004). Here again, the role of auditing firms is central, particularly due to the considerable resources and client-related expertise they control (Walton 2004: 121; Cooper and Robson 2006: 431ff.).

Institutionalists have interpreted the IASB as a case of institution-building beyond the nation state, in which transformative effects result from multilevel interactions (cf. Djelic and Quack 2003). Empirically, it can be shown that, over many years, the IASB effectively mediated conflicts inherent in cross-border standardisation: '[C]ontest and conflict, usually seen as an impediment to successful standardization, can become a driving force of international standardization if organized within a commonly accepted procedural framework' (Botzem and Quack 2006: 268). Effective governance structures are one explanation of why the IASB emerged as a private transnational standard-setter. Another equally important factor was the emergence of a coalition of 'accounting policy bureaucrats' (Power 2009: 329). The institutionalist account presented here focuses on organisational configurations as well as actor constellations in explaining transnational institution-building and its modifications after the financial crisis. The development and continuous reorganisation of the IASB, as well as its cumbersome process of recognition by public authority, are key features for understanding the decisions taken as a response to criticism after the financial crisis. For much of its existence, the IASB was faced with an environment to which it had to adapt.

Historical institutionalist accounts are well positioned to investigate the interplay of agency and structure in understanding how developments unfold. At the actor level, they argue for the importance of unintended consequences and bounded rationality; and with regard to institutional development, they discuss complementarity as an important concept. This makes it possible to consider how formal and informal arrangements at different levels evolve over time. In addition, it also rebuts claims that interpret the financial crisis as an external shock from which exogenous change can be expected. As is laid out in the Introduction to this volume, financial-market regulation is not an good field in which to search for punctured-equilibrium models of change. Accordingly, in the remainder of this chapter I draw on institutionalist work to analyse change in three interrelated dimensions of transnational standard-setting, namely, the content of accounting standards; the procedures and governance structures in which they are developed; and the actors involved.

As outlined in the Introduction to this volume, over time gradual developments may result in a substantial transformation. The development of the IASB is an example of such a process of incremental change that took more than four decades to unfold and was characterised by the emergence of complementary institutions, in which actors embedded their interests (Botzem 2012). In such a dynamic perspective on institutional development, the concept of complementarity plays an important role. Crouch (2005: 359ff.) has suggested three different meanings of complementarity: 1) various components of a whole compensating for each other's deficiencies; 2) in the economic sphere, the price-dependency of related goods; and 3) complementarity as similarity. For the study of incrementalism in global finance, the first meaning is the most promising as it also alludes to the 'functional performance' (*cf.* Höpner 2005) of an institutional setting. As will be shown in the empirical section, it is this notion of complementarity as compensation in which the three dimensions outlined above are connected. Complementarity explains both stability and adaptation and therefore a good deal of IASB persistence after the crisis.

Seeking to explain the actions and reactions of core actors requires an understanding of institutions that leaves enough room for agency. On the other hand, there have to be institutional arrangements at the transnational level in which agency can unfold. Such 'institutional density' (Pierson 2000) draws on institutionalist elements such as path-dependence and underlines the complexity of institutional structures and how they favour continuity:

In contexts of complex social interdependence, new institutions and policies are costly to create and often generate learning effects, coordination effects, and adaptive expectations. Institutions and policies may encourage individuals and organizations to invest in specialized skills, deepen relationships with other individuals and organizations, and develop particular political and social identities (Pierson 2000: 529).

In accounting regulation, such complex interdependencies have emerged over more than four decades. Timing and sequence are as important in understanding the emergence of the IASB as they are in making sense of reactions to the financial crisis. However, simply referring to the central position the IASB has enjoyed is not sufficient to explain the organisation's persistence and how it reacted to criticism. Instead, the emphasis of this paper will be on showing how actors have engaged in these processes. It will focus on how change was organised, mediated and actively managed by powerful insiders. In line with agency-centred approaches in institutionalism (Djelic and Quack 2007), reflexive behaviour of actors is assumed and acknowledged. Consequently, this chapter aims to uncover the role of dominant actor-groups and to show how they carefully orchestrated reactions to criticism made after the financial crisis. This allows considering conflicts and compromise as characteristic of transnational standardisation at a more abstract level. And it makes it possible to analyse concrete reactions concerning the norms, procedures and actor networks of transnational accounting regulation. In the following empirical section, three modes of managing change that core actors of transnational accounting regulation championed will be outlined: conflict-avoidance through temporarily suspending the application of fair-value accounting; framing organisational reform to address accountability gaps; and carefully replacing the leadership of the organisation.

Effective crisis reaction: defending standards, procedures and actor networks

For the longest time, transnational accounting standardisation has been the business of practitioners and experts. Founded as a loose federation of national professional associations, today's International Accounting Standards Board (IASB) has grown into a potent private standard-setter.[1] At present the IASB employs more than 100 individuals, half of them exclusively tasked with standard-setting, and disposes of an annual budget of more than £12 million sterling. Since 1973 it has worked on developing a set of coherent standards (International Accounting Standards, IAS, and International Financial Reporting Standards, IFRS).

---

1.   The complete 40 year history of the IASB is covered elsewhere. *See* for instance Camfferman and Zeff (2007), Botzem and Quack (2009), Botzem (2012) and Zeff (2012).

Throughout its history, IASB's development has been contested. First, the nascent organisation competed with intergovernmental harmonisation attempts within the European Union and at the United Nations level. Both started to bring about more uniform rules for disclosure in corporate reporting during the 1960s. In close co-operation with private and public actors, mainly from Anglo-American countries, the IASB managed to outcompete the rival initiatives of inter- and supranational organisations (Rahman 1998; van Hulle 2004). After 2001, the IASB solidified its position as the sole transnational standard-setter. After close collaboration with international regulators, such as IOSCO and the Securities and Exchange Commission in the US, the early 2000s saw the breakthrough of IFRS. The most important move was the EU's decision to make the IASB's standards mandatory for consolidated accounts in all of Europe from 2005 onwards.

The IASB has a long tradition of interacting with public and private organisations in deliberating and bargaining over standards, competence and resources. These abilities were applied in the three dimensions outlined above, although to varying degrees. A holistic approach, as is suggested here, assumes the interrelatedness of standards, procedures and actor-networks. For analytical purposes, however, I will treat the three dimensions successively, showing the IASB's reaction to the financial crisis from 2008 onwards.

The content of international accounting standards: avoiding open conflict

During the last four decades, IASB's regulatory output grew at a steady rate. Standards were set, revised and interpreted by the IASB with an ever-expanding scope. In addition to quantitative expansion, the content of transnational standardisation has also undergone substantial change. Originally, IAS were combinations of various national standards and therefore of a pluralist nature. They were mainly composed of national rules that were merely redrafted and reformatted. This led to a vague catalogue of international normative prescriptions that neither fulfilled national legal requirements nor satisfied the information needs of private actors such as banks, stock exchanges, analysts and institutional investors (cf. Thorell and Whittington 1994). At the end of the 1980s, the IASB began to review and revise all its standards, excluding most alternatives that were not in line with capital-market orientations. The revision of standards is still not entirely completed but once-rival principles such as historical-cost accounting or replacement cost are today marginalised. Now, a clear-cut capital-market orientation prevails, in which market values play an increasing role for financial reporting, most notably as fair-value accounting (FVA).

Fair value has received more and more backing over the years, even though some resistance was always maintained (Power 2010). FVA thus became the dominant philosophy in international standardisation but, after the crisis, it encountered increased criticism, in particular due to the procyclical nature of IAS/IFRS (Lagneau-Ymonet and Quack 2012). It has to be noted, however, that discussions about FVA are debates about detailed accounting rules and can rarely be decided at an abstract level. Advocates try to introduce as many market values as possible – or econometric models of market values as substitutes when no market values are available – while opponents stress the problems of FVA, most notably its cyclical nature. Adversaries of fair value usually defend a more conservative approach to accounting, such as historical-cost accounting. They criticise FVA's 'inflation' of financial reports in times of boom and its contribution to harsh losses in times of bust. The application of FVA in Germany's biggest listed companies, for example, led to an increase of net profit in 2005 of between 10 and 15 per cent, simply due to converting from German standards to IASB provisions (Botzem 2012: 10). During the crisis, such a dynamic also unfolded, this time as a downward spiral 'destroying' values when banks in particular had to continuously account for a loss in market values, thereby reporting lower values and triggering further downward dynamics in the market prices of assets they held.

The dominance of fair value is intricately linked to the information needs of capital-market actors. Today's IAS/IFRS are clearly tailored toward the information requirements of investors who rely on market values (or calculative practices) for their investment decisions (for a critical perspective *see* Perry and Nölke 2006). As a consequence, FVA privileges the information needs of capital-market actors over other economic, social or political stakeholders, such as creditors, employees or tax authorities. Ultimately, this has distributional effects, benefiting shareholders and management at the cost of personnel, public entities or other stakeholders (Biondi and Suzuki 2007; Boyer 2007; Gallhofer and Haslam 2007).

Reaction to the financial crisis

As the financial crisis hit, accounting standards were quickly identified as highly problematic because of their procyclical nature (G20 2008). Accounting for derivatives in particular became an object of criticism, exemplified by Warren Buffet's famous labelling of them as 'weapons of mass destruction'. Subsequently, much of the debate initially concentrated on accounting provisions for financial instruments (ECB 2004: 74), a matter which has been highly controversial in Europe, where criticism of wide-ranging destabilising effects was particularly pronounced (Lagneau-Ymonet and Quack 2012). Prompt actions were taken which essentially allowed the reclassification of financial instruments retrospectively into a different category, defining July 2008 as the date when market values were to be recognised (*cf.* Zeff 2012). Both the US standard-setter the Financial Accounting Standards Board (FASB) and the IASB resorted to reinterpreting existing standards for financial instruments (Botzem 2012: 81–3). Reclassification, albeit initially not approved by the IASB's Board, emerged as a concession to critics, especially from Europe, who saw banks and financial actors disadvantaged compared to the US. The discussion about reclassification is tightly connected to an interpretation of the underlying causes of the crisis. Lagneau-Ymonet and Quack (2012) provide an in-depth characterisation of the different actors involved and the various approaches to problem-definition, as well as their changes over time.

In October 2008, FASB was the first standard-setter to react to pressures – mainly from banks – to issue guidance on how to reclassify assets held by financial institutions such as banks. In practice, this led to redefining assets, which were originally considered to be held for trading at their respective fair values, into another category in which fair value did not have to be applied ('held for maturity'). The IASB quickly followed suit in order to allow for the application of similar accounting rules in both the US and the EU. The temporary reclassification of assets – which essentially suspended accounting them at fair value – was intended to end the downward, procyclical dynamic inherent to FVA. To deliver an official justification for this move, the financial crisis was framed as a 'rare circumstance' in which no reliable measures of fair value were available. Behind this seemingly 'technical' reclassification unfolded a complex process of political bargaining, in which standard-setters, banks, supervisory bodies and regulators participated (Lagneau-Ymonet and Quack 2012; Zeff 2012). The EU's Council of Economic and Finance Ministers (ECOFIN) and the G8 also discussed accounting of financial instruments. In addition, the European Commission actively supported changes in IAS 39 and IFRS 7 (including additional disclosure requirements), to cushion the effects of the crisis.

Even after this initial post-crisis period, accounting for financial instruments remains controversial. IAS 39 was amended a number of times and will eventually be superseded by IFRS 9, which is divided into three sections. Criticism continues to be particularly pronounced in Europe: 'The European Commission pressured the IASB to make the fair value rules even more flexible (i.e., allow more opportunities for financial institutions to use purchase prices, as opposed to market prices, in valuing financial instruments in order to limit volatility in the financial statements)' (Leblond 2011: 456).

Some years after the Lehman collapse and the 'rare circumstances' it triggered, FVA continues to be the dominant accounting principle. A rupture with procyclicality is nowhere in sight. Instead, the crisis was used only to suspend FVA periodically. The IASB's decision to allow reclassification was controversial even within the organisation. Apparently, IASB Chairman Tweedie even considered resigning over the issue (Zeff 2012). With hindsight, the decision to give in to pressures mounting immediately after the Lehman collapse appears to have been a rather smart move. The IASB avoided open confrontation with politicians, regulators and much of the banking industry. What appeared to be a lost battle might, in fact, have been the winning of the war, because the threat to the IASB's legitimacy, had it stuck to its principles, could have fundamentally threatened the organisation. Declaring the financial crisis a 'rare circumstance' might thus have strengthened the logic of fair value in the long run. Opting for a short-term suspension of FVA and avoiding a showdown with European publics and regulators, in practice, led to acceptance of FVA in 'normal times'. The IASB has proceeded with the development of IFRS 9 (Financial Instruments), which builds on IAS 39 in a more systematic way; but it is not departing from FVA. The procyclical nature of IAS/IFRS remains untouched.

Framing organisational reform as crisis reaction

Immediately after the Lehman's collapse in September 2008, the criticism of the governance structure of the IASB, pointing to the accountability deficiencies of expert-based self-regulation in accountancy, which had been heard for some time before, intensified. The European Parliament and interest-group representatives of small- and medium-sized enterprises were among the critics of the private nature of the IASB (*cf.* Radwan 2008). Particular attention was devoted to the Trustees of the IASC Foundation, which formally oversees the activities of standard-setting and selects the members of the Board, the organisation's decision-making body. The Trustees' lack of accountability had also been regarded as problematic by market-friendly think tanks (*cf.* Verón 2007).

In January 2009, the Trustees of the IASB Foundation approved a modification of the IASB constitution. As of February that same year, an additional organisational body was established, the Monitoring Board. The Monitoring Board assembles regulatory agencies of the US and Japan, the EC and two working groups of IOSCO (Emerging Markets Committee and Technical Committee) (Nölke 2009). In addition, the Basel Committee on Banking Supervision participates as an observer (Zeff 2012).

The IASB explicitly refers to the changes in the constitution as having 'established a formal public accountability link to a Monitoring Board of public capital market authorities'.[2] It cultivates the appearance of having installed a new supervisory body with closer ties to national and international regulators, implying more influence for public authority. This perception is also reflected in some of the academic literature (Posner 2010). The IASB's organigram represents this message by depicting the Monitoring Board as the supreme organisational body.

In practice, however, the Monitoring Board's role is not yet clear and, given its relatively short existence, its impact is difficult to assess. This also has to do with its rather unspecific mandate: its powers are largely limited to the recruitment of Trustees. More remarkably, the IASB's constitution includes the requirement to reach all decisions by consensus (IASCF 2010: para. 23). For now, it can be concluded that the newly installed Monitoring Board is only a marginal player when it comes to overseeing the IASB's Trustees (Botzem 2012: 99).

Reaction to the financial crisis

The lack of accountability was a recurring criticism of the IASB's standard-setting practices and the organisation's governance structure. During a routine revision of the organisation's constitution in 2007, this issue was taken up and a consensus about integrating regulators into the IASB emerged. The introduction of the Monitoring Board was therefore not a reaction to criticism that arose after the crisis. Instead, the IASB took advantage of its long-planned decision to

---

2. Webpage, accessed May, 28 2012: http://www.ifrs.org/The+organisation/Governance+and+accountability/governance+and+accountability.htm. Accessed 6 February 2013.

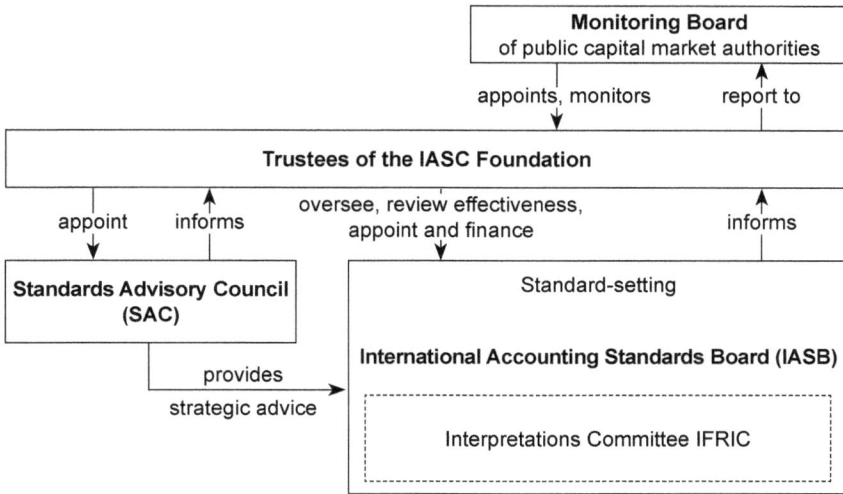

Figure 7.1: IASB structure as of 2012

Source: Botzem 2012: 99, based in IASB web presentation http://www.ifrs.org/The+organisation/How+we+are+structured.htm. Accessed 17 May 2012.

amend its organisational structure and merely framed the decision to set up the Monitoring Board as a reaction to the crisis: 'The formation of the Monitoring Board and changes to the composition, geographic diversity and size of the IASB are consistent with the G20 recommendations, and the Trustees expressed their support for the steps being taken by the IASB in responding to the crisis' (IASB press release 29 January 2009).

The Monitoring Board is an example of 'institutional layering', with largely symbolic content and little substantial consequence, at least for the time being. It is not clear whether an increase in public oversight will materialise (*see* Posner 2010). Adverse effects have also to be considered: national and international regulators are committed to be engaged in the IASB's activities and to endow the organisation with their legitimacy – without being able to exercise substantial influence. The Monitoring Board might simply protect the organisation's independence while its influence remains limited, because decision-making on standards as well as the deliberations preceding it are exclusively left to the Board of the organisation.

In the long run, a socialisation effect might take place. At least for SEC representatives, being more closely connected to the IASB might create a more in-depth understanding of the organisation's activities and decisions (*cf.* Zeff 2012). For the time being, however, a more critical interpretation seems appropriate: since modifications are largely superficial it can be concluded that the IASB uses the Monitoring Board to continue to shield its decision-making body from unwanted external influence. The IASB continues to uphold expert-based self-regulation instead of questioning it. Framing the organisational reform as an immediate reaction during the crisis enabled the organisation to regain ground and to re-establish credibility, of which the IASB was in desperate need in the winter of 2008–9.

Changing of the guard: carefully replacing decision-makers

The most important decisions in transnational standard-setting are taken by the IASB's Board. The Board now comprises 15 members appointed by the Trustees and is to have 16 members in the near future. All standard-setting decisions, including final decisions on standard interpretations, rest with the Board. In the terminology of the organisation, these 'technical decisions' are taken by high-profile individuals well acquainted with accounting matters. Recruitment criteria are sufficiently vague, so for a long time a close-knit expert community has dominated international standard-setting. Over many years, the Board's composition has been remarkably stable. Between 2001 and 2008 it consisted of 12 full-time and two part-time members. During the first seven years, only three newly selected individuals joined the Board. If we include membership in the Board's predecessor, the IASC Board established in 1973, some individuals show astonishing tenure (*see* Table 7.1): until recently, two persons had been members of the decision-making body since the 1980s. One member first attended IASC Board meetings in 1986; another in 1989; four others joined in 1995. When the Board was newly re-formed in 2001 and switched to the full-time employment of most of its members, it could already draw on an average of five years of experience. The average length of Board membership has steadily increased up to 2009, when it reached close to ten years. Recently, however, there has been considerable change and the close-knit insider group is dissolving, due to the term-limits in the IASB's constitution.

A longitudinal view brings to the fore the remarkable stability of the Board, to which five individuals belonged for more than a decade, two exceeding twenty years of membership. This group had made up an inner circle of standard-setters who had been responsible for key strategic decisions over many years. The core consisted of IASB Chair Sir David Tweedie (from the UK), his Vice-Chair Tom Jones (from the US), and the Australian Warren McGregor. The ties among the group go back to the early 1990s, when they were active in national accounting standard-setting (Botzem 2012: 133ff.). Moreover, they are all trained accountants and most have been partners in accounting firms at some time in their careers. Thus, this inner circle shares a professional background in accounting that is rooted in an appreciation for private-sector self-regulation. It also favours an approach to standardisation geared toward pragmatism and problem-solving, usually in tune with capital-market requirements. The experience of working for accounting firms operating on a global scale constitutes an important common denominator. Working for the Big Four auditing firms also involves experiences (soft skills) that can only be acquired in that specific environment (*see* Ramirez 2007). Table 7.1 shows IASB membership from 2001 to 2011. It testifies to the personnel continuity of the body over many years but also shows remarkable change more recently. These two trends are underlined by the average membership per person and the maximum time in office.

A closer look at today's Board members' biographies points to a subtle shift in the overall composition of membership (Botzem 2012: 136ff.). While trained accountants remain important, three characteristics of change are noteworthy:

over time, the IASB intensified efforts to integrate individuals with more specific knowledge about the information needs of the users of financial statements, such as analysts and investors. In addition, efforts were made to include members who had previously worked in oversight and regulation. Another recent trend is to bring in persons who have specific knowledge about emerging markets, namely China, India and Brazil (Zeff 2012).

Reaction to the financial crisis

More substantial alterations in Board membership during the last two years show that the long-lasting inner circle of a few Anglo-American individuals has been dissolved. These changes, however, are no immediate reaction to the crisis but resulted from constitutional provisions. The IASB's charter initially contained a term-limit of ten years (two five-year terms) and current prescriptions are even more stringent. As of 2010, Board members are selected for a five-year term, which might be extended by the Trustees for an additional three years.

As Table 7.1 shows, the average time in office dropped from ten years in 2008 to less than four years in 2011. Ten of today's fifteen members, including both the Chair and the Vice-Chair, started their term in office in July 2009 or later. In 2011, Dutchman Hans Hoogervorst became the new Chair, succeeding Sir David Tweedie who had held office from 2001 onwards and who was also the last Chair of the IASC board during the 1990s. Hoogervorst has been active with regulators at the national and international levels and had chaired the Monitoring Board before joining the Board. The newly elected Vice-Chair, Ian Mackintosh, is a well connected and experienced standards-setter who previously chaired the UK Accounting Standards Board.

Given the dual challenges the IASB faced after the financial crisis, regarding the general accountability deficit and constitutional constraints concerning Board membership, it can be noted that the renewal of the decision-making body was enacted without notable friction. Continuity was also ensured by promoting Paul Pacter to the Board, who had previously concurrently been IASB Director of Standards for Small and Medium-sized Entities (SMEs) and Director in the Global IFRS Office of Deloitte Touche Tohmatsu in Hong Kong (*cf*. Zeff 2012). Despite the rupture in some of its leadership positions, the IASB appears to continue the course set out in earlier years. Nevertheless, the old boys' network, which was instrumental in getting the IASB going and in establishing a clear-cut dominance of capital-market logics, has been dismantled. Now, more individuals have previous experience with analysts and other users of financial statements.

In addition, the most recent constitutional revision introduced a geographical quota for Board members – for the first time since 2001. Paragraph 26 suggests having four members from Asia/Oceania, Europe and North America, one each from Africa and South America and two members without specific background (IASCF 2010: para. 26). At first sight, these decisions indicate that representation of developing countries is to be strengthened and accountability is to be improved. It has to be noted, however, that despite reference to geographical origin, Board

Table 7.1: Board Composition of IASB as of 31 Dec 2011 and length of tenure in years (including previous experience at the IASC)

	Before 2000	2001	2002	2003	2004	2005	2006	2007	2008	2009	2010	2011
	Years of IASC membership	Name	Total years of membership / Name of newly appointed member									
Chair	6	Tweedie	8	9	10	11	12	13	14	15	16	Hoogervorst
Vice-Chair	6	Jones	8	9	10	11	12	13	14	--	--	Mackintosh
Member		Barth	2	3	4	5	6	7	8	McConnell	2	3
Member		Bruns	2	3	4	5	6	Cooper	2	3	4	5
Member	5	Cope	7	8	9	10	11	12	--	Kalavacherla	2	3
Member		Garnett	2	3	4	5	6	7	8	9	Scott	2
Member	12	Gelard	14	15	16	17	18	19	20	21	Koenig	2
Member		Herz	Smith	2	3	4	5	6	7	8	9	10
Member		Leisenring	2	3	4	5	6	7	8	9	Pacter	2
Member	14	McGregor	16	17	18	19	20	21	22	23	24	--
Member		O'Malley	2	3	4	5	6	Zhang	2	3	4	5
Member	6	Schmid	8	9	Engström	2	3	4	5	6	7	8
Member		Whittington	2	3	4	5	Danjou	2	3	4	5	6
Member	6	Yamada	8	9	10	11	12	13	14	15	16	Ochi
Member										DeOliveira	2	3
Member										Finnegan	2	3
Mean time in office (years)		4.9	5.9	6.9	7.2	8.2	8.9	9.7	9.8	9.7	6.6	3.7
Max. time in office (years)		15	16	17	18	19	20	21	22	23	24	10

Source: Author's composition based on annual reports.

members are explicitly not representing any particular jurisdiction. Geographical origin is therefore little more than an indicator of the intent to increase cultural diversity, a move that should be helpful in opening up to the global south and emerging markets to improve the worldwide spread of IFRS in the future. The IASB has renewed the personnel of the Board without substantially changing the organisation's course and seems to have taken the hurdle of having to replace the leadership of the IASB Board in challenging times without difficulty.

The IASB after the crisis: lessons for institutional theory

The financial crisis serves as a magnifying glass to understand the dynamics of transnational accounting regulation. In particular, it can be interpreted as a catalyst that intensified debate over the nature of IFRS and the organisation's accountability deficit. In its Washington meeting in November of 2008, the G20 prominently criticised the IASB, namely its membership and governance structure.

> [We] request our Finance Ministers to formulate additional recommendations, including in the following specific areas: mitigating against procyclicality in regulatory policy; reviewing and aligning global accounting standards, particularly for complex securities in times of stress' (G20 2008: 4).

Such clear assignments are a sign of urgency caused by the financial crisis and the high degree of political pressure with which the IASB was confronted. Throughout IASB's 35-year history, such explicit interference by public bodies in the realm of profession-based, private self-regulation has hardly been seen. After the Lehman's collapse, however, the IASB was fundamentally challenged regarding its norms and governance structure. In fact, similar criticism had been heard before but it was now introduced into the debate by a wider range of actors. Given the fundamental character of the criticism, the degree of continuity is striking and needs explanation. Therefore, I return to the puzzle outlined at the beginning of the chapter and provide explanations of the absence of more profound change in the aftermath of the financial crisis. In particular, I discuss how criticism was met and accommodated by the IASB, characterise the relevant actors dominating reform and outline their strategies for ensuring only incremental changes in accounting regulation.

In line with the institutionalist approach of this volume, conclusive answers need to consider formal and informal rules as well as the activities of core actors, specifically their engagement in processes of decision-making and in framing their actions. To explain incrementalism in transnational accounting regulation after the crisis I first revisit the three dimensions analysed above and discuss actors' strategic responses. I will then provide an overview of changes in the three dimensions and finally provide conclusions with regard to institutional theory.

Three strategies of crisis management

In hindsight, it can be concluded that the IASB's decision-makers quite effectively steered the organisation through dire straits. They did so drawing on different strategies depending on rules, structure and actor involvement, which can be characterised as follows:

Avoidance: Despite opposition to repealing fair-value accounting, in late 2008 the IASB gave in to pressures from political actors and the banking industry to effectively suspend FVA. They opted for allowing the reclassification of financial instruments from 'held for trading' to 'held for maturity'. This made it possible for financial institutions to counter the procyclical, downward dynamic of market values assigned to their financial instruments. While in conceptual terms this meant departing from long-standing accounting principles, the practical consequences for standard-setting were less drastic. In fact, taking this controversial decision can be interpreted as a successful move, relieving political pressure in stressful times. Interpreting the crisis as a rare circumstance allowed for the merely temporary reclassification of financial instruments at crucial times. By avoiding a showdown with political actors and parts of the financial industry, the IASB made it possible to preserve FVA in the long run.

Reframing: Constitutional reform addressing the accountability deficit of the IASB had been ongoing since the mid 2000s. After the crisis it was used to accommodate criticism that intensified after the Lehman collapse. In its public announcements, the IASB framed the establishment of the Monitoring Board as a solution to accountability gaps, despite the fact that the decision to establish the new body emerged in much earlier deliberation. In addition, a closer look reveals that national and international regulators are not given a strong mandate to supervise IASB's Trustees but rather an advisory position and only limited influence to oversee the recruitment of Trustees. The premature interpretation by some practitioners and scholars that this move brings public authority into accounting standard-setting indicates the success IASB has had with its framing of the constitutional modifications.

Leadership renewal: The need to follow constitutional provisions for recruiting members to the organisation's Board provided a significant constraint for the IASB. An additional term for long-serving Board members was not an option, so replacements had to be found for the inner circle of the Board. At the same time, the body's size was increased and additional Board members had to be integrated. The newly constituted Board mirrors these trends and assembles members from developing countries. Most importantly, however, the leadership of the Board was carefully renewed. Central positions were staffed with individuals well networked with the old elite, namely Vice-Chair Ian Mackintosh and Paul Pacter. The IASB was able to strike a balance between formal constitutional requirements and demands to open the Board to developing countries and users of financial statements, while including well versed Anglo-American standard-setters with close ties to the IASB. Despite having new members, the Board is set to continue the course initiated by its predecessors.

Professionalism and expertise as continuing characteristics of self-regulation

An analysis of the three institutional dimensions of accounting regulation (norms, procedures and actor-networks) reveals different strategies that help to explain the incrementalism observed. Differences in reacting to the challenges mainly stem from institutional conditions, such as formal rules or ongoing reform activities. Leadership renewal and reframing are examples of how IASB's dominant actors reacted to criticism and re-positioned the organisation in critical times. The most complex strategy identified here is avoidance. By giving in to mounting political and economic pressure – while declaring the circumstances exceptional – the IASB allowed its adversaries to gain ground early on. In the long run, however, the reformulation of a standard of financial instruments (IFRS 9) remains, despite some disagreement over its application, under IASB control. Avoiding open conflict in the short term and making concessions to critics allowed the IASB to regain lost ground later on. Such a strategy is only possible if actors have sufficient ideational and material resources at their disposal to enable them to take the lead in standard-setting later – an aspect shared by all three dimensions of transnational accounting regulation.

One core explanation for insider-led institutional change is the central role private actors, mainly accounting practitioners and standard-setters, enjoy in the established dense institutional network of accounting regulation. The normative consensus continues to rest on self-regulatory practices embedded in a tradition of anti-statist professionalism. While much criticism was focused on the IASB's governance structures, the role of expertise as a common denominator remains largely unchallenged. The power to define what the relevant expertise is and who is allowed to enter the inner circles to acquire expertise is perhaps IASB's single most important resource in support of incremental change. It enables the organisation and the leading actors to define relevant expertise and thereby exercise social closure, essentially upholding the exclusive and club-like nature of transnational accounting standardisation. This makes the IASB largely independent from public authority but also from reporting corporations (Botzem 2012). One additional explanation of IASB effectiveness has been its capacity to organise the procedures of standard-setting dominated by accounting professionals and their firms. Other organisations, such as professional associations, have been replaced as loci of expertise. This proved to be essential for moderating change in times of crises.

More importantly, the three strategies identified above complement each other. Not only was their orchestration 'functional' with regard to fending off criticism; the three strategies compensate for each other's deficiencies and thereby enable the IASB to provide a holistic answer, mirroring the interrelatedness of norms, procedures and insiders' interests.

Managed change: strategies of incrementalism

Transnational accounting regulation provides an instructive case of incremental institutional change because it shows how a private transnational standard-setting organisation addressed challenges and stabilised its position. Due to the organisational and intellectual capacities assembled within the organisation, the IASB provided comprehensive answers, playing its advantages. More importantly, by staying engaged in a number of discussions it remained the single most important locus of deliberation and decision-making, maintaining the capacity to frame problems as well as solutions.

IASB's unique position is underlined by the absence of alternative standard-setting organisations and procedures of standard-setting. Despite substantial criticism, there was never a serious discussion about other arenas or fundamentally different principles. Debate focused on improving instead of replacing the IASB. This is also true for the normative foundations of its standards. Even though FVA was criticised widely, alternative measures such as historical cost or amortised cost were also seen critically for they, too, have drawbacks when accounting for financial instruments (*see* Lagneau-Ymonet and Quack 2012). Discussing the range of fair-value accounting and market-to-market practices most often takes place within a neoliberal, market-friendly ideational framework. The main goal was not to substitute market values but to better understand the price signals they provide. The normative base of IFRS of addressing capital providers first and foremost was at no point seriously challenged.

In institutional terms, incremental change in accounting regulation highlights features common to many fields of global financial governance. Institutional friction remains a characteristic of the transnational level, even in accounting where one organisation dominates standard-setting. Transnational accounting regulation therefore contributes more general insights to the debate about incremental change.

First, it is important to remember that the transnational institutional arrangement of accounting standardisation was well established before the crisis and showed a high level of institutional density. This allowed the IASB and its core actors to draw on pre-existing channels of influence, directly and also through its established formal procedures of rule-making. Agents and institutions were intertwined. The transnational organisational structure and the institutional density in which it was embedded, continued to expand after the crisis, in part due to the purposeful influence of core actors. The introduction of national and international supervisors and regulators into the Monitoring Board can be seen as an indication of this. While institutional density is not a sufficient condition for incrementalism, it is a necessary requirement for upholding the dominant paradigm, both ideationally and organisationally.

Second, formal and informal institutions are not simply 'empty' governance structures. Instead, the rules of the game are tilted in favour of accounting professionalism and expertise-based discourse. The observed continuity is not to be mistaken as a case of non-change. Instead, it can be explained by insider-led, carefully mediated modifications that renewed the influence of dominant actors. Looking at the temporal dimension of developments shows that standards continue to be geared towards the information needs of capital-market actors; the organisational structure has been modified to include national and international regulators, albeit in a rather ceremonial fashion; and key individuals seem to be committed to continuing the self-regulatory practices of their predecessors. The continuity to be observed should, however, not be misinterpreted as stasis. On the contrary, the IASB made many efforts to react to challenges strategically. Its most valuable resource were close relations with networks of experts that existed before the crisis, with both public and private actors, and its organisational capacity to continue controlling access to its decision-making body. The renewal of leadership and the establishment of the Monitoring Board are two indicators of the prevalence of expertise-based, private rule-setting as a core institutional feature.

Third, while not necessarily intentionally co-ordinated from the beginning, the three strategies used to counter criticism complement each other well (*cf.* Mahoney 2000). They address all relevant aspects of accounting regulation and they compensate for each other's deficiencies: while *avoidance* is a rather defensive reply, *reframing* openly addresses the challenges upfront. The careful *renewal of leadership* shows a balanced approach with regard to organisational evolution. New individuals are included but IASB never compromised on its basic, expertise-based orientation. Its composition might change but the community of 'accounting policy bureaucrats' (Power 2009) remains dominant.

In sum, self-regulation was preserved by strategically managing the challenges the standard-setter was facing during the financial crisis. The IASB has maintained its position as the core actor in transnational regulation of accountancy and continues to co-operate closely with national standard-setters and big auditing firms in its daily activities. As an organisation it has proven to be highly adaptive to turmoil in its environment. With no ideational and organisational alternative in sight, the IASB seems to be in a comfortable position to influence standard-setting in the future and is well prepared for future institutional challenges. Whether the continuation of the professional self-regulatory model should be considered a success is, however, another matter. While incrementalism might be an indicator of effectively managing political change, it is not a criterion for assessing the appropriateness of regulatory policies for global financial governance with regard to social participation and the distribution effects resulting from its standard-setting activities.

References

Biondi, Y. and Suzuki, T. (2007) 'Socio-economic impacts of international accounting standards: an introduction', *Socio-Economic Review*, 5(4): 585–602.

Botzem, S. (2008) 'Transnational expert-driven standardisation: accountancy governance from a professional point of view', in Graz, J.-C. and Nölke, A. (eds) *Transnational Private Governance and its Limits*, London: Routledge, 44–57.

— (2012) *The Politics of Accounting Regulation: Organizing transnational standard setting in financial reporting*, Cheltenham: Edward Elgar.

Botzem, S. and Quack, S. (2006) 'Contested rules and shifting boundaries: international standard setting in accounting', in Djelic, M.-L. and Sahlin-Andersson, K. (eds) *Transnational Regulation in the Making*, Cambridge: Cambridge University Press, 266–86.

— (2009) '(No) limits to Anglo-American accounting? Reconstructing the history of the International Accounting Standards Committee: a review article', *Accounting, Organizations and Society*, 34(8): 988–98.

Boyer, R. (2007) 'Assessing the impact of fair value upon financial crises', *Socio-Economic Review*, 5(4): 779–807.

Büthe, T. (2010) 'Global private politics: a research agenda', *Business and Politics*, 12(3): Art. 12.

Büthe, T. and Mattli, W. (2011) *The New Global Rulers: The privatization of regulation in the world economy*, Princeton, NJ: Princeton University Press.

Camfferman, K. and Zeff, S. A. (2007) *Financial Reporting and Global Capital Markets: A history of the International Accounting Standards Committee 1973–2000*, Oxford: Oxford University Press.

Cooper, D. J. and Robson, K. (2006) 'Accounting, professions and regulation: Locating the sites of professionalization', *Accounting, Organization and Society*, 31(4): 415–44.

Covaleski, M. A., Dirsmith, M. . and Rittenberg, L. (2003) 'Jurisdictional disputes over professional work: the institutionalization of the global knowledge expert', *Accounting, Organizations and Society*, 28(4): 323–55.

Crouch, C. (2005), 'Three meanings of complementarity', *Socio-Economic Review*, 3(2): 359–63.

de Lange, P. and Howieson, B. (2006) 'International accounting standards setting and US exceptionalism', *Critical Perspectives on Accounting*, 17(8): 1007–32.

Djelic, M. L. and Quack, S. (2003) *Globalization and Institutions: Redefining the rules of the economic game*, Cheltenham: Edward Elgar.

— (2007) 'Overcoming path dependencies: path generation in open systems', *Theory and Society*, 36: 161–86.

European Central Bank (2004) *Monthly Report February*, Frankfurt: European Central Bank.

G20 (2008) 'Declaration summit of financial markets and the world economy' November 15, 2008. http://www.g20.org/Documents/ g20_summit_ declaration.pdf. Accessed 1 November 2011.

Gallhofer, S. and Haslam, J. (2007) 'Exploring social, political and economic dimensions of accounting in the global context: the International Accounting Standards Board and accounting disaggregation', *Socio-Economic Review*, 5(4): 633–64.

Greenwood, R., Suddaby, R. and Hinings, C. R. (2002) 'Theorizing change: the role of professional associations in the transformation of institutionalized fields', *Academy of Management Journal*, 45(1): 58–80.

Höpner, M. (2005) 'Epilogue to "Explaining institutional complementarity": What have we learnt? Complementarity, coherence and institutional change', *Socio-Economic Review*, 3(2): 383–87.

IASCF (2010) *Constitution*, London: International Accounting Standards Committee Foundation.

Lagneau-Ymonet, P. and Quack, S. (2012) 'What's the problem? Competing diagnoses and shifting coalitions in the reform of international accounting standards', in Mayntz, R. (ed.) *Crisis and Control: Institutional change in financial market regulation*, Frankfurt am Main: Campus, 213–46.

Leblond, P. (2011) 'EU, US and international accounting standards: a delicate balancing act in governing global finance', *Journal of European Public Policy*, 18(3): 443–61.

Macdonald, K. M. (1995) *The Sociology of the Professions*, London: Sage Publications.

Mahoney, J. (2000) 'Path dependence in historical sociology', *Theory and Society*, 29(4): 507–48.

—   (2001) 'Beyond correlational analysis: recent innovations in theory and method', *Sociological Forum*, 16(3): 575–93.

Martinez-Diaz, L. (2005) 'Strategic experts and improvising regulators: explaining the IASC's rise to global influence, 1973–2001', *Business and Politics* 7 (3): Art. 3.

Nölke, A. (2009) 'The politics of accounting regulation. Responses to the subprime crisis', in Helleiner, E., Pagliari, S. and Zimmermann, H. (eds.) *Global Finance in Crisis: The politics of international regulatory change*, London and New York: Routledge, 37–55.

Perry, J. and Nölke, A. (2005) 'International accounting standard setting: a network approach', *Business* and *Politics*, 7(3): Art. 5.

—   (2006) 'The political economy of international accounting standards', *Review of International Political Economy*, 13(4): 559–86.

Pierson, P. (2000) 'Increasing returns, path dependence, and the study of politics', *American Political Science Review*, 94(2): 251–68.

Porter, T. (2005) 'Private authority, technical authority, and the globalization of accounting standards' *Business and Politics*, 7(3): Art. 2.

Posner, E. (2009) 'Making rules for global finance: transatlantic regulatory cooperation at the turn of the millennium', *International Organization*, 63(4): 665–99.

— (2010) 'Sequence as explanation: the international politics of accounting standards', *Review of International Political Economy*, 17(4): 639–64.

Power, M. (2009) 'Financial accounting without a state', in Chapman, C. S., Cooper, D. and Miller, P. (eds.) *Accounting, Organizations, and Institutions: Essays in honour of Anthony Hopwood*, Oxford: Oxford University Press, 325–40.

— (2010) 'Fair value, financial economics and the transformation of accounting reliability', *Accounting and Business Research*, 40(3): 197–210.

Quack, S. (2007) 'Legal professionals and transnational law-making: a case of distributed agency', *Organization*, 14(5): 643–66.

Radwan, A. (2008) *European Parliament Resolution of 24 April 2008 on International Financial Reporting Standards (IFRS) and the Governance of the International Accounting Standards Board (IASB)* (2006/2248(INI)) A6-0032/2008. Brussels: European Parliament.

Rahman, S. F. (1998) 'International accounting regulation by the United Nations: a power perspective', *Accounting, Auditing & Accountability Journal*, 11(5): 593–623.

Ramirez, C. (2007) 'Exporting professional models: the expansion of the multinational audit firm and the transformation of the French accountancy profession since 1970', *Les Cahiers de Recherche* 864, Département Comptabilité-Contrôle, HEC School of Management, Paris.

Simmons, B. A. (2001) 'The international politics of harmonization: the case of capital market regulation', *International Organization*, 55(3): 589–620.

Suddaby, R., Cooper, D.J. and Greenwood, R. (2007) 'Transnational regulation of professional services: governance dynamics of field level organizational change', *Accounting, Organizations and Society*, 32(4): 333–62.

Sugarman, D. (1995) 'Who colonized whom? Historical reflections on the intersection between law, lawyers and accountants in England', in Dezalay, Y. and Sugarman, D. (eds) *Professional Competition and Professional Power: Lawyers, accountants and the social construction of markets*, London: Routledge, 226–37

Tamm Hallström, K. (2004) *Organizing International Standardization: ISO and the IASC in quest of authority*, Cheltenham: Edward Elgar Publishing.

Thorell, P. and Whittington, G. (1994) 'The harmonization of accounting within the EU. Problems, perspectives and strategies', *The European Accounting Review*, 3(2): 215–39.

van Hulle, K. (2004) 'From accounting directives to international accounting standards', in Leuz, C., Pfaff, D. and Hopwood, A. G. (eds) *The Economics and Politics of Accounting: International perspectives on research trends, policy, and practice*, Oxford: Oxford University Press, 349–75.

Véron, N. (2007) *The Global Accounting Experiment,* Brussels: Bruegel.

Walton, P. (2004) 'IAS 39: Where different accounting models collide', *Accounting in Europe*, 1: 5–16.

Willmott, H. (2000) 'Organising the profession: a theoretical and historical examination of the development of the major accountancy bodies in the UK', in Edwards, J. R. (ed.), *The History of Accounting: Critical perspectives on business and management, Vol. IV – Professionalisation of Accounting*, London: Routledge, 233–69.

Zeff, S. (2012) 'The evolution of the IASC into the IASB and the challenges it faces', *The Accounting Review*, 87(3): 807–37.

chapter eight | still in the market for change: the mass public as a veto-player in US and Danish mortgage-systems reform

Iver Kjar

Introduction

The United States and Denmark have similar liberal residential mortgage systems, in spite of many other profound differences in their socio-economic models. In this chapter, I show that these systems were important catalysts for their economic growth before the global financial crisis and explain that both systems have proved surprisingly resistant to substantial institutional change in its aftermath. This is especially worthy of attention in light of the emphasis on housing and housing finance as a root of the crisis (*see* for example, Sachs 2009; Ferguson 2009; Roubini 2008; Bernanke 2008; Stiglitz 2008; Krugman 2008).

In line with the general focus of this volume I aim to give an account of how 'vested interests in dominant institutional positions' at the domestic level were able to block meaningful institutional change beyond slight regulative adaptations (Moschella and Tsingou in the Introduction to this volume). I argue that the main veto-actor in both countries was home-owners, who, in spite of not actively organising as a political group, had significant political leverage thanks to their electoral power.

This chapter explains that the lack of institutional reform can be accounted for with reference to the domestic sources of institutional change and its necessary legitimisation in the broad public. This legitimisation is conceptualised as 'economic patriotism' (Seabrooke 2012). I argue that support from the broad public is crucial for any growth model as well as for institutional reform. Further, though the global financial crisis removed the structural and economic prerequisites for the success of the US and Danish mortgage-fuelled growth models, the economic patriotism that legitimised it persists in both countries. The mass public has therefore acted as a veto-player with regard to reforms of policies concerning taxes, property and credit, referred to as the 'financial reform nexus' in the analysis that follows (Seabrooke 2006: 3). This is in spite of negative consequences for continued economic growth and a pervasive ideational shift towards macroprudential regulation, especially among transnational governance networks in Basel (BCBS 2010a; BCBS 2010b; Baker 2013; Baker in this volume). As such, this chapter also speaks directly to the book's themes, including the observation that an incremental policy-change model concerning (inter)national financial regulation is a more appropriate way to think about reform; this is especially the case when dealing with issues of access to credit and the financialisation of everyday life (Moschella and Tsingou in this volume).

At the onset of the global financial crisis in 2008, a complete lack of credible information about some of the largest American financial institutions' collateralised debt obligations (CDOs) led to mistrust, panic and a destruction of assets worth $24 trillion, which in turn brought about a global liquidity crisis (Blackburn 2008: 5; Sinclair 2009; Gowan 2009: 18). During the 'long 1990s' (from 1990 to 2007), the OECD countries were blessed with high growth rates. The crisis therefore also marked the end of one of the longest periods of sustained economic growth in modern history, and was followed by slow economic recovery and a spike in unemployment (Roxburgh *et al.* 2009: 8; Bjørsted 2011; US Bureau of Labor Statistics 2011).

Colin Crouch's (2009) 'privatised Keynesianism', arguably, characterised the situation before the global financial crisis in the US and Denmark. Under privatised Keynesianism it is no longer the state that injects money into the economy by taking on debt; instead, increasing private indebtedness fulfils this function. Such a model assumes that property is individually held for people to put down as security. Therefore, home-ownership is the prerequisite for this mode of accumulation, along with the continued inflation of property value and increasingly effective financial intermediation by banks.

Denmark and the US both exhibit unrepressed financial systems (Schwartz and Seabrooke 2009: 9). Denmark has the largest housing bond market in Europe, combined with a generous welfare state, whereas the US is the most interesting example of a liberal system, primarily because of its size and significance for the world economy (*ibid*: Table 1.1). They also both provide mortgage bond securitisation systems that offer 20- to 30-year fixed-interest mortgage bonds as financial options for investors.

This chapter is organised in four sections. The first section outlines the theoretical approach to legitimacy and institutional change guiding the analysis. In line with the call in the introduction for analytical accounts inspired by historical institutionalism, in the second section I turn to an empirical analysis of the American and Danish financial reform nexuses and their consequences for economic growth before the global financial crisis. I further argue that Denmark was able to 'piggyback' on to this financialised economic world order, thanks to a liberalisation of its residential housing system during that period. In the third section, I argue that a certain asset-based domestic legitimacy has evolved that was instrumental for the financialisation of mortgages in both countries, while also allowing for the devolution of social responsibility. The crisis and its consequences have therefore created a need for institutional reform of the financial reform nexuses that moves away from privatised Keynesianism, if renewed growth is to occur. In the final section, I argue that, although these reforms might have been seen as necessary by economic experts for a return to economic growth, they have been politically untenable after the crisis, due to home-owners' unbroken economic patriotism concerning the appropriate interaction between credit, property and taxes at the domestic level.

The financial reform nexus and domestic legitimacy

Finance is based on promises, social conventions, and widespread confidence in its legitimacy. We lend each other money on the premise that we can expect to be repaid according to existing norms of economic conduct (Seabrooke 2006: 1). If this convention did not exist, and was not backed by the state through legal rights and contractual agreements, credit markets could not exist and economic enterprise would come to a complete standstill (Keynes 1949[1936]: 147). As outlined in the first section, the term financial reform nexus refers to the interaction between credit, property and tax politics. I will briefly touch on all three in turn.

In *The Philosophy of Money* (1990[1907]), Georg Simmel differentiated between a common man and a gentleman by their access to credit. Access to credit is desirable because it allows rearranging the spending of your lifetime income so that it corresponds to your present needs and preferences. It also allows you to raise capital for investment or entrepreneurship. Banks have historically been hesitant to extend credit to just anyone, for fear of default. The cut-off point for mortgage-credit access in any economy corresponds to a point below median individual income, depending on the makeup of the financial reform nexus. It then follows that how relatively poor you can be and still have access to credit can be affected by positive state intervention on behalf of hopeful home-owners in the financial reform nexus (Seabrooke 2006: 193).

In Denmark and the US, buying a house represents the largest loan any ordinary citizen will ever take out. If you were an average house-owner in the US in 2003 you had a mortgage debt equal to 77.8 per cent of your annual household disposable income, while it was a whopping 188.4 per cent in Denmark (OECD 2005: 131).

Tax politics concern how state revenue is achieved. Any tax affects the disposable incomes of individuals. Unsurprisingly, if a tax is socially regressive or fundamentally changes the economic outlook of an economic group, this will affect the material wellbeing of group members. But taxes also change economic incentives and can quickly alter the broad populace's behaviour in a desired direction.

Legitimacy and axiological rationality

Three social groups are crucial in shaping the financial reform nexus: the broader population of home-owners, the rentiers, and the state. According to Max Weber, it is the everyday consent or dissent of the mass public that ultimately decides the institutional makeup of the national economy. Without public legitimacy, no political construct can function efficiently. Thus, everyday politics supports the status quo, depending on its perceived legitimacy, or favours institutional change (Seabrooke 2006: 12). Just like home-owners, rentiers will attempt to win concessions that benefit their group interest and allow them to secure financial gains. Ultimately, the state is viewed as an arena for contestation, where collective actors engage with each other, the state, and its existing financial institutions. Different ideas and claims to legitimacy are put forward and solutions or compromises concerning the financial reform nexus are arrived at through belief-driven action. Which solutions prevail in this political struggle is quite open, albeit strongly affected by the existing political and institutional set-up and already dominant ideas (Seabrooke 2006: 44).

Following Seabrooke, I combine economic constructivism's focus on ideas and norms with a Weberian perspective on legitimacy to understand this struggle and how it results in change in the financial reform nexus. Individuals aggregated into collective actors might confer legitimacy on elites that lay claim to it by propagating ideas that are able to resonate widely. Legitimacy is bottom-up *and* top-down. Ideas can then be understood as weapons that are used for belief-driven action in a political struggle over legitimacy.

What people find legitimate is based on their *axiological beliefs*. Axiological rationality (axiorationality) can be understood as reasoned behaviour based on strong cognitive reasons that the individual holds to be important (Boudon 2003; Boudon 2001). This avoids universalistic and essentialist claims about the nature of human rationality and acknowledges that axiorationality is historically defined and socially constructed. Through their axiorationality, people positively embrace ideas and institutional solutions in favour of others according to what they 'consider to be procedurally fair and morally and ethically 'valid behaviour' (Seabrooke 2006: 46). Further, 'support for the institutions that underpin citizens' welfare can be understood as a form of "economic patriotism" – where there is a consistent preference for economic activity to be channelled through particular institutions that serve a defined population' (Seabrooke 2012: 1).

As such, my study refers to the struggle for legitimisation through an ideal-type that describes the mechanisms surrounding change in the financial reform nexus (Weber 1949[1904]: 90). This ideal-type comprises three mechanisms. Initial *contestation* by home-owners and rentiers with the state about the existing institutional and social environment essentially attempts to change the way the state intervenes in the economy. This is followed by *redistribution* of political and material assets, as well as credit access by the state, that supports either home-owners or rentiers. Then follows *propagation*, whereby the state attempts to promote the new order to society, hoping to gain renewed legitimacy. This propagation then provides important feedback for the next round of contestation, after home-owners and rentiers have reflected on the new order and its consequences. This mechanism is continual in the everyday politics of economic life and does not depend on crises or external shocks in order to keep changing the financial reform nexus; similarly, legitimacy fluctuates along a continuum from high to low rather than swinging between the binaries of legitimacy or illegitimacy *per se* (Seabrooke 2006: 51).

The financial reform nexus and economic growth

The US exhibits a weak welfare state combined with a rather commodified[1] housing system. It is a liberal market economy with high rates of owner-occupied housing and low amounts of social-rental housing, combined with a large amount of mortgage debt relative to GDP. Denmark is instead an economically quite equal society, with high taxes and high welfare, and provides a large amount of social housing (Schwartz and Seabrooke 2009: 10, 19). Half of all housing in Denmark is rentals and half of that is social housing (Realkreditraadet 2010). This creates less need for the Danes to build assets through their lifetime, and public pensions are both universally inclusive and quite generous (Esping-Andersen 1990: 21). American individuals cannot expect the government or public pension system to ensure their comfortable retirement, unlike the Danes. Home-ownership is therefore one of the most important ways to accrue lifetime assets to ensure financial independence in old age.

Through the years, widespread home-ownership has therefore become a natural policy priority for US politicians, because society needs to provide its elderly with income. Denmark, on the other hand, is a small and homogenous society. Based on a strong romantic nationalism (Hansen, K. 2008: 82; Hansen, L. 2002: 57) the Danish welfare state's development was led by a strong system of local communities, communal ownership of production facilities, social housing, and credit collaborations – also known under an umbrella term as the Danish co-operative movement (Ravnholt 1943). Denmark and the US thus represent the two opposite ends of the spectrum in the 'welfare trade-off' (Kemeny 2005: 65).

As it turns out, not everyone in the US is able to obtain a mortgage and buy a house on strict market terms. Many poorer Americans are ineligible for mortgage loans and are forced to rent, rather than buy, housing; they are thus excluded from building up assets through their lifetime. Although Americans typically view the high income inequality in their society as legitimate, and as an important driving force in their economy (Glyn 2006: 177), the same does not hold for inequality in access to home-ownership. Owning your own house is an integral part of economic patriotism in the US, something perhaps best described as an integral part of the American dream (Seabrooke 2012: 9). Many interest groups and lobby organisations[2] have therefore taken the issue to heart and contested for better access to owner-occupied housing, even for the poorest potential home-owners. For these reasons, the US state has a long history of positive intervention in the housing market, to facilitate home-ownership through credit subsidies. They also continually propagate the American housing dream as the legitimate solution to the welfare trade-off (Seabrooke 2006: 108).

---

1. The extent to which housing is said to be 'commodified' (versus 'decommodified') depends on the degree to which access to housing depends on market income as opposed to some form of social right.

2. Such organisations include the Fair Housing Advocates Association and the National Association of Affordable Housing Lenders.

Thus, in the pursuit of increased access to home-ownership, the US state created its first privately held government-sponsored enterprise (GSE) the Federal National Mortgage Association ('Fannie Mae') in 1938 (Jeske and Krueger 2005: 1). In the 1960s, concerns were raised about credit-access discrimination against particular, often racially determined, residential areas; consequently, the Government National Mortgage Association ('Ginnie Mae') was created as a public enterprise specifically to extend credit to poor Americans. Finally the Federal Home Loan Mortgage Corporation ('Freddie Mac') was chartered in 1970 to fulfil the same role as Fannie Mae and to widen the supply of mortgages. At the same time the GSEs were allowed to begin securitising mortgages, to create a pool of debt securities for investors to buy. This move essentially endorsed their competing in the private market for housing capital and lowered the cost of capital for home-owners substantially (Seabrooke 2008: 10).

The Danes tackled the same issue with a communal approach that included strong regulation of the Danish mortgage credit institutions (MCIs),[3] to combine public value with private capital. MCIs became mutual borrowers' associations in which 'borrowers were jointly responsible for payments within a pool of mortgages' (Seabrooke 2008: 16). The Danish housing market was therefore decommodified, all thanks to strong positive intervention on behalf of home-owners by the state, through strict regulation of rented housing and tax incentives to indebtedness (Andersen *et al.* 2008; Mortensen and Seabrooke 2009: 128). This positive intervention reflects the economic patriotism that dominated up until the 1990s, whereby housing was viewed as a social right rather than a market asset for investment.

This development in the housing market in the US coincided more or less with the collapse of the Bretton Woods system, which was accompanied by stagflation and a general decline in American competitiveness in manufacturing that created protracted recession and unemployment (Montgomerie 2009; Frieden 2007). Thus, there was a dire need for a new growth model for the US economy. The Glass-Steagall Act, which, since 1933, had prevented American banks from underwriting securities, was gradually relaxed; and the first structured investment vehicles were introduced in the 1980s, enabling banks to transform liabilities into assets off the books. The Glass-Steagall Act was eventually repealed in 1999 and opened up opportunities for greater creativity by US banks concerning financial products and services (Best 2010: 34; Solomon 2010: 132). Thus, the securitisation of mortgages was crucial for increased access to credit for home-owners *and* the deepening of financial markets: 'The US government was actively involved in making the trade in MBS [mortgage backed securities] possible, in delinking investment from place, and in facilitating liquidity/tradability, thereby creating opportunities for both risk-averse and high-risk investors.' (Aalbers 2008: 154).

This securitisation led to an effective financialisation of mortgage securities, as securities became something you could invest in to accrue financial profits (Smith

---

3.   *Realkredit Institutter.*

2009: 210; Langley 2008: 179). Due to the aforementioned need for individuals to build assets over their lifetime, massive private pension funds created a large demand for low-risk assets with decently high yields (Seabrooke and Tsingou 2009: 458). Thanks to another financial innovation, collateralised debt obligations (CDOs), MBS was restructured and bundled with other assets to further the delinking of space and, it was thought, effectively diversify default risk through advanced mathematical algorithms. For pension funds, this created perfect investment assets that provided unprecedented high yields combined with perfect AAA credit rating scores (Best 2010: 35; Valdez and Molyneux 2010: 265).

In spite of impressive stability in the financial reform nexus concerning the provisioning of decommodified housing, Denmark also saw widespread reform in this area. This was in the context of weak economic growth and austerity in Denmark during the late 1980s and early 1990s (Østrup 2010: 9). After a government-induced housing crash in 1987, changing governments tried to revive the housing market from 1990 onwards (Mortensen and Seabrooke 2009), coincidentally, at the same time as pressure from the US to liberalise and harmonise capital markets globally began to mount. The European Union (EU) implemented capital-market liberalisations following the move towards the Single European Market in 1987 (Compston 1998; Abdelal 2006) and the Second Banking Directive in 1989 (Abdelal 2007). In a typical case of Europeanisation (Hix and Goetz 2000), Denmark adopted EU standards and deregulated and re-regulated its mortgage system accordingly, to allow more competition from private enterprises in the mortgage market.

This created an impetus for reform and the formerly strictly regulated MCIs were allowed by the government to change the way they operated: rather than dealing only with banks on a wholesale basis as a provider of bonds for mortgages, they could deal directly with estate agents and individuals on a retail basis and compete with the newly introduced private-market actors. Also, more flexible mortgage-repayment possibilities, such as interest-only repayment and more flexible interest rates, were allowed (Mortensen and Seabrooke 2009). Covered mortgage bonds were also introduced, which permitted the delay of amortisation by more than ten years. Much like in the US, both helped to increase the amount of issued mortgages as borrowers could postpone the financial headache till their house had increased in value and the mortgage could be refinanced on better terms. While global interest rates were kept low by the high American supply of securities, Danish regulation allowed house-buyers to provide a down-payment of just 5 per cent and borrow the rest, allowing all manner of potential home-owners to gain access to mortgage credit.

Turning to US tax politics, we can observe that owner-occupied housing has been directly incentivised in the last 25 years. This was achieved by allowing the deduction of mortgage interest payments and owner-occupied property tax credits, while at the same time failing to tax capital gains from rising house prices effectively. Similar provisions are not in place for rental housing: 'The net effect is to raise the after-tax cost of rental relative to owner-occupied housing capital' (Green and Malpezzi 2003: 106, 109). In Denmark, the tax value of deductible interest rates on houses bought after 1998 was lowered from 46 per cent to 33 per cent, favouring existing home-owners and disadvantaging first-time buyers. But with rising house prices this led to a widespread use of 'parent buy',[4] in which parents would refinance their own mortgages to free capital that was then reinvested in housing for their children, increasing demand even more as long as prices were rising (Mortensen and Seabrooke 2009: 128). Home-owners who did not have reason to invest in a second property instead converted their higher property value into private consumption (Gjede 1997: 33).

Danish mortgage debt can very easily be refinanced through the buying of bonds at equal value at the present rate, with no penalty. The Danish bond market achieved very good credit ratings. It proved very popular for foreign investors because of high transparency and a history of no losses for bondholders from mortgage defaults. The Danish bond market therefore quickly grew to become the largest in Europe after the German, in turn helping to keep Danish interest rates at a record low (Seabrooke 2008: 17).

Housing prices naturally rose following the increasing amount of available cheap credit. This created a situation where the market value of US houses rose by $14 trillion while the amount of mortgage debt rose by $7 trillion from 1991 to 2006 (Schwartz 2009: 4; Martin 2010: 8). Danish housing prices also boomed. Owner-occupied housing prices rose from DKK 5.777 per m^2 in 1995 to above DKK 20.000 per m^2 in 2005, when the prices reached a plateau before dropping in the fourth quarter of 2008. Since then, prices have stabilised around DKK 18.000 m^2 (Realkreditraadet 2010). Residential mortgages soon followed and rose from already high 70.1 per cent of GDP in 1992 to 88.4 per cent in 2004 (Schwartz and Seabrooke 2009: Table 1.1) in spite of Danish GDP growing in nominal terms from $150,195 billion to $244,728 billion in the same period (World Bank 2011). This effectively translated into a massive injection of purchasing power (Martin 2010: 8). These factors in combination thereby fuelled impressive economic growth in Denmark in much the same way as they did in the US, in spite of Denmark's being a co-ordinated market economy.

The only problem with perpetual Keynesian creation of aggregate demand is that it is, after all, based on credit. Put crudely, the only negative effect of the positive intervention by the American and Danish state on behalf of home-owners was the massive rise in private and sovereign debt. Besides that, both home-owners and rentiers benefitted greatly from the financialisation of mortgages. But although credit might have been practically unlimited, the bill always has to be paid eventually.

---

4.   *Forældrekøb*.

Asset-based domestic legitimacy

As explained above, housing is viewed as an asset in the US and is quite commodified, partly due to the chosen American solution to the welfare trade-off. Before the 1990s, the opposite was true in Denmark, where housing was a social right above anything else and particularly decommodified. Due to changes in the financial reform nexus created by Europeanisation and a conscious attempt by the state to reinvigorate the housing market, a new liberal, asset-based common sense (Rupert 1995: 659) entered the scene in Denmark. Home-owners soon adopted it as house prices rose quickly and seemed to make everyone better off.

This was possible because, in the triangular relationship between the state, rentiers, and home-owners, the latter are often in a position of structural inferiority. Home-owners' axiorationality depends on the representations that the state and the financial sector enact. At the same time, households' consent is crucial for the legitimisation upon which the system depends (Jacoby 2009: 18). But individuals also respond to economic incentives within the bounds of social legitimacy. Given the economic context and emergent common sense, it simply did not make sense not to buy a house in Denmark in the long 1990s, rather than to rent one. This was because renting did not provide you with access to housing-asset inflation which, through re-mortgaging, gave access to more goods and services than would otherwise have been possible.

In accordance with the previous point that home-ownership works as a substitute for welfare provisions, Paul Langley has argued that there has been a generalised shift from 'socialised' to 'privatised' actuarialism, as part of a tactic to decrease the pressure on social-welfare budgets. These social-welfare provisions create a need for financial intermediation that is conducive to asset price bubbles (Langley 2008:91). In order to teach people to 'live by finance' and insure themselves instead of relying on the government to do it, it is necessary that the average yield accrued from deposits is higher than inflation, so as to create an incentive to save today in order to increase consumption greatly in the future. That is generally not the case unless asset price inflation is higher than general price inflation. This characteristic generally increases lifetime consumption for savers, provided that the financial market does not crash and is not hit by asset price deflation. As we have seen, this was the case in the long 1990s, until the crisis hit.

The important point is that continuous asset-price inflation is a prerequisite for the success of privatised actuarialism as a model for social-welfare provisioning. Langley describes the notion that one should 'live by finance' as the Foucauldian 'conduct of conduct' that morally obliges people to take care of their own welfare through prudential credit consumption and saving (Langley 2008: 91). This consumption of credit, and thereby risk, has been made mundane, through the discourse of diversified risk and the notion that credit was available to everyone along with an increased imperative as social-welfare provisions were retrenched. Privatised actuarialism thereby plays into the broader context of economic patriotism and growth through privatised Keynesianism in Denmark and the US.

Remembering the history of Danish economic patriotism, the housing boom could only attain broad social legitimacy because it was relatively inclusive. In Denmark, housing soon changed from purely being a social right into also being a means to wealth. As a result communal housing associations[5] slowly lost legitimacy as demands for a fair share in asset inflation led to their gradually being disbanded in the 1990s. The holders of communal shares (that is, apartments) were greatly enriched as apartments were transferred to the open market as a result (Mortensen and Seabrooke 2009: 131). This commodification of a long-standing communal housing solution would have been viewed as incredibly short-sighted and illegitimate just 15 years earlier but, in the late 1990s, that had changed thanks to the growth success of privatised Keynesianism and consequent change in Danish economic patriotism.

The GSEs' special status in the US economy was also justified through economic patriotism, with reference to a social right for all Americans to have access to owner-occupied housing on market terms. Thus, while housing is seen as a commodity that is instrumental for accrueing assets, the ability to buy such an asset is, at the same time, conceived as a social right that the state should support through its GSEs. Thus, tax politics should intervene positively to ensure, essentially, a form of decommodification on market terms. The GSEs legitimacy was increasingly contested in the 2000s by poorer home-owners and their interest groups, because the GSEs were gradually allowed by the state to relax their charter standards surrounding mortgage securitisation. They moved away from their public-purpose mandate of helping first-time buyers gain access to the housing market and towards the refinancing of mortgages for profit (Seabrooke 2008: 13). The most telling example of this transformation of the GSEs' perceived role from public to private enterprise is perhaps the accounting scandal of 2004, in which executives in Fannie Mae were found to have cooked the books to hide earnings worth $10.8 billion dollars from 1998 to 2004 and thus ensure their bonuses (Day 2006). At the same time, the securitisation model became increasingly successful at delivering cheap mortgages to an unprecedented number of home-owners and impressive profits to rentiers (Martin 2010: 9). This made it difficult to contest the legitimacy of the successful American mortgage system from within, thus increasing its global appeal, leading to institutional isomorphism of the financial reform nexuses in countries such as Denmark.

Gradually, these changes constituted a rentier-shift in the US, which increased the possibilities for profit in the new financialised economy through deregulation and by the relaxation of the concept of housing as a social right in favour of one of housing as an investor's asset. The profit rates in the financial sector have been rising disproportionately since the 1980s, due to financialisation (Khatiwada 2010: 2), and the sector is now the largest contributor to political campaigns for democrats and republicans alike. Exactly because of the economic patriotism around mortgage securitisation and the liberal appeal of Wall Street to the American dream, the last

---

5.   *Andelsboligforeninger.*

two decades have resulted in a dominating notion, embedded in the legitimacy of the American economy, that 'What is good for Wall Street is good for the country.' (Johnson 2009: 5) The general impetus towards securitisation of mortgages and continued high demand resulted in increasingly predatory marketing of mortgages to even the poorest families, who clearly would be unable to service a mortgage by any measure, unless their newly acquired property's value inflated quickly. As such, the crisis can be understood as a case of over-inclusion, where even the famous NINJAs[6] were included in the financialisation of the American economy (Aalbers 2009: 288).

Calls for change but lack of reform in the US and Danish mortgage systems

The self-reinforcing cycle that created the prerequisites for successful US and Danish growth has been disturbed. Andrew Baker (2010) argues that the prevailing 'crisis of debt' discourse only serves to justify even further public-sector retrenchments and austerity. An alternative crisis of growth discourse would not only be more descriptive; it would also lead to radically different policy recommendations, since it would include the recognition that privatised Keynesianism, and the devolution of social responsibility (Guthman 2007: 472), no longer constitute a feasible growth model. When the housing bubble finally burst, housing prices in the US dropped markedly as credit markets froze (Angelides 2011: 239; Sinclair 2010: 101). The ensuing bank bail-outs and high inflation did not solve poor home-owners' problems in keeping up their mortgage payments, especially as falling house prices made people technically insolvent. The stark reality of declining real wages and rising unemployment made default rates skyrocket, exacerbating the crisis (Schwartz 2009; Montgomerie 2009).

Most importantly, as Keynes reminds us, asset prices are affected by average investor sentiment and a general trust that the existing state of affairs will continue indefinitely, despite a complete lack of guarantees (Keynes 1949[1936]: 152). The conventional belief that the housing market would keep booming has been decisively undermined. American and Danish individuals are no longer willing to take the risks in their everyday economic lives that they were prepared to take before the crisis. This effectively disables the ability of privatised Keynesianism to create economic growth from the bottom up. Global aggregate demand has therefore imploded, as people attempt to get their personal debt under control (Rogoff and Reinhart 2009: 237). Without the required everyday legitimacy and social trust, the given economic order has become unable to provide economic growth.

Nonetheless, both in the US and Denmark, politicians have insisted that the crisis is a debt crisis and that severe austerity measures and retrenchment of the (welfare) state was, and still is, of paramount importance, rather than mortgage-

---

6.   No income, no jobs, no assets.

system reform. Borrowing from Layna Mosley (2005) one might wonder if financial globalisation has finally diminished the room to move? The crisis was certainly triggered by extremely large amounts of private and public debt. But the resulting problem is not debt *per se* but rather the lack of growth (Hay 2011). For political purposes it is therefore important to stress that it was the financialisation of mortgages and privatised Keynesianism, in combination with imbalances in the global economy between China and the US, that led to historically high growth rates. This imbalance is now gradually correcting itself and housing prices have stopped rising. It is therefore necessary that the broad public is made to realise that the structural prerequisites for privatised Keynesianism have been made obsolete by the crisis (Crouch 2009: 394). Because of the way the financial reform nexus has been legitimised through the propagation of privatised actuarialism, this necessary change of direction has proven to be extremely difficult to achieve politically in the period after the global financial crisis, as the domestic level becomes an arena for veto-players to hold up institutional reform.

The financial crash was quickly dubbed 'the subprime crisis' by experts at large and much effort was made to blame the over-inclusion of so-called NINJAs (Aalbers 2009). The Basel Committee on Banking Supervision (BCBS) were also quick to begin work on an overhaul of the Basel II capital requirements, only months after the accord's full implementation, finally resulting in the Basel III paper in 2010 (BCBS 2010a; BCBS 2010b). Moreover, talk at G20 of a new Bretton Woods for finance surfaced and was backed by then French President Nicolas Sarkozy (Sarkozy 2010; Rodrik 2009). In all these arenas, the focus on housing and the effects of 'subprime' was especially strong.

Yet, despite pervasive criticism of housing regulators and policies in general (Angelides 2011; Wallison 2009) there has been surprisingly little reform. To understand this lack of reform, attention must return to domestic veto-players as expert consensus apparently was not sufficient to secure institutional change after 2008. In accordance with prevailing liberal common sense and the dominant conception of economic patriotism concerning finance, Anna Leander argues that the 'taken-for-granted understandings of reform' (Leander 2009: 465), what she calls the reform *doxa* (*see also* Bourdieu 2005), assumes the neoliberal understanding of markets as self-regulating and the devolution of responsibility as natural. Danish and American politicians are, arguably, unable to imagine feasible solutions outside the liberal common sense of privatised Keynesianism, due to this strong prevailing conception of economic patriotism. 'They are therefore singularly unlikely to develop radical reform proposals or to consider these desirable.' (Leander 2009: 467). The same applies to home-owners, who are unable to imagine an acceptable alternative society where easy access to credit and housing is a thing of the past. Home-ownership has become too important a part of everyday life and individual subjectivity to allow institutional change. Further, the big mortgage-market players in both Denmark and the US have, as discussed previously, benefitted greatly from this pervasive legitimisation of the financialisation of mortgages. Following the crisis, and backed by continuing economic patriotism, they have deftly lobbied policymakers to ensure that little real reform has been adopted. Therefore the positions of the GSEs in the US and the MCIs in Denmark have not drastically changed following the crisis, despite frequent negative publicity about their role. In contrast to the big transnational banks, mortgage-players have not come under much more critical regulatory scrutiny, let alone been subjected to regulatory action.

Given this chapter's account of US economic patriotism, this is not surprising. Access to mortgage credit through securitisation is still an integral part of the concept of welfare provision in the US and a component of the American dream, in spite of the end of the financialised-growth miracle. Social cohesion and everyday legitimacy depends on this because the welfare system in the US is so limited. Minor symbolic changes did occur but either they were not very intrusive or were quickly reversed. Thus, Fannie Mae and Freddie Mac were put under conservatorship by the US government and a cap was introduced on the size of the securities they could underwrite. But this cap only lasted until Christmas Eve 2009, when the Obama administration removed it again, and by the end of 2010 the two GSEs were again securitising 98 per cent of all mortgages in the US (Seabrooke 2012: 19).

In Denmark, the mortgage-credit institutions were under less pressure. No real subprime sector existed in Denmark and individuals were able to take on much larger financial risk due to more generous welfare provision. The bank crashes were seen to be caused by the general market downturn rather than a Danish subprime crisis *per se* (Schrøder 2007). Also, the Danish state softened the blow for home-owners through its automatic welfare provisions when the crisis hit. But, as previously discussed, the 1990s fundamentally transformed the Danish residential housing system in a more neoliberal direction. Communal housing associations continued to be disbanded and replaced by the owner-occupation model.

As more and more Danes become home-owners, they constitute an increasingly large and congruent interest-group in Danish society. Because mortgages bind such a large part of a household's disposable income, the constituencies supporting redistributive taxes on personal income and capital gains have shrunk, while continued tax incentives for home-ownership and low interest rates are increasingly favoured. This is reflected in the complete absence of parties in the Danish political mainstream that are willing to advocate complete abolition of tax deductions on interest-rate payments, in spite of calls for this step from numerous economic experts (Mortensen and Seabrooke 2009: 131). Instead, the large banks were subjected to more stringent regulatory requirements and the prospect of 'bail-in' measures, something from which the MCIs have been completely exempted (Alloway 2011).

To put it bluntly, the home-owner has become the single largest and most pampered voter-group in Denmark, precisely because, prior to the crisis, they delivered desirable consumption-led growth. No party coalition can hope to win an election without promising this group that their situation will remain unchanged. This was unproblematic when home-owners provided the consumption boost necessary to uphold economic growth but this is no longer the case. Thus, in Denmark, economic patriotism legitimises home-ownership as a right *and* as an investor asset. This has created an effective political veto surrounding technical insolvency and housing-asset speculation that is only strengthened by the very attentive and politically active association for Danish mortgage issuers.[7] The argument in the political debate in Denmark goes that if the tax-deductibility of interest payments is removed, many home-owners will have to sell their houses to get out of their expensive mortgages, something that will leave the most unfortunate insolvent (Valentin 2008). The fact that many Danes speculated too heavily in housing-price inflation before the financial crisis is not viewed as justification for making these people shoulder a larger part of the national financial burden after the crisis. That notion simply lies outside the perspective of the current economic patriotism.

This effective domestic veto associated with economic patriotism has consequences at the global level as well. I would argue that the exorbitant privilege that the US has enjoyed has been severely diminished. The debt that was previously privately held has been nationalised and the bill needs to be paid. Because no significant policy change can be successfully propagated in the US, trust in US creditworthiness and willingness to pay its debts is quickly declining. Not only is US creditworthiness in doubt but also US politicians' willingness to avoid a default (Boak 2011). This resulted in Standard & Poor's downgrading of the US to an AA+ country in August 2011 (Swann 2011) and the immediate downgrading of the GSEs, since they are government backed.

At the same time, the Danish mortgage system came under pressure at the beginning of the Basel III process in 2010. Basel III aims, through the CRD IV at the EU level, to change how long prior to maturity covered bonds can be considered liquid. Further, only 40 per cent of the liquidity requirements can be fulfilled by covered bonds, unlike previous legislation under which the entire requirement could be fulfilled. This in effect would punish financial systems such as the Danish with heavy amounts of debt related to housing (Seabrooke 2012: 269). If implemented, this would necessitate pervasive reform of the financial products sold to house-buyers in Denmark. It would force MCIs to securitise differently, leading to higher interest rates, while disregarding that the Danish system is still an origin-and-hold system, in which MCIs issue bonds and hold them when issuing mortgages. Albeit, through a strong concerted effort by Danish ministers, members of the European Parliament, and Danish financial institutions some of these provisions have been softened while others are to be implemented gradually and evaluated until 2015 or 2018 (Realkreditraadet 2011; 2012). It is striking that while the Danish financial sector more broadly has gotten much criticism after the financial crisis in the Danish public debate, no one blames the inflated housing market and the MCIs, and there is a general public consensus about safeguarding the mortgage credit system as much as possible from European intervention.

Thus, it would be beneficial for both growth and the international environment if there was less positive intervention on behalf of home-owners in Denmark and the US, for reasons that are different but which all originate from the end of the congruence between the global economy and the financialisation of mortgages. But Denmark and the US are unable to reform their financial-reform nexuses because both home-owners and rentiers have a short-term interest in the status

---

7.   *Realkreditrådet.*

quo. Both Denmark and the US can probably continue for another decade or two without implementing any serious reform of their financialised economies. But recent history shows the consequences that are likely for economic growth when domestic legitimacy concerns go against institutional reform. Japan, for example, has yet to manage a proper showdown with the country's powerful banks and to implement deep structural reform. The financial-reform nexus has therefore allocated investments inefficiently and experienced low legitimacy since the 1980s, producing disappointing growth year after year (*The Economist* 2011).

Conclusion

In this chapter, I have argued that it is especially pertinent to focus on everyday legitimacy as a prerequisite for institutional change in the financial sector. Throughout the chapter I have focused on the axiorationality of everyday political actors, conceptualised on the macro-level as economic patriotism. I showed how the US mortgage market became financialised and exhibits a form of liberal common sense that was also adopted in Denmark during the 1990s. A historical analysis of the two countries has explained how a number of different financial factors related to housing came together to ensure the growth success of privatised Keynesianism in the long 1990s.

I have shown how regulative reforms of the mortgage systems in Denmark and the US have not been achieved after the financial crisis in 2008. The mass public in both countries has acted as an effective veto-player, due to pervasive economic patriotism in both countries. A strong legitimacy concerning home-ownership has come to surround mortgages in both the US and Denmark. Thus, the mass public can be viewed as important institutional actors in their own right when trying to understand incremental change or non-change concerning issues of financial policy. Further, by viewing legitimacy as a two-way street, I was able to show how financial mortgage institutions in both Denmark and the US avoided real regulative reform, by attaching themselves to existing economic legitimacy and lobbying politicians effectively, with the might of the masses at their backs. Meanwhile, other financial institutions, such as the transnational banks, have been less fortunate in their conferred legitimacy after the crisis.

I have thus, in my contribution to this volume, showed that institutional change is not only affected at the domestic level by elite institutional entrepreneurs and policy-makers but also by the non-elite – the mass public. In this particular case, this was partly because the mode of accumulation in the US and Denmark was based on individual home-ownership and housing-asset inflation, thus placing the individual home-owner in a structurally advantageous position. But the analysis also has wider implications for the study of the politics of financial regulation, in which the mass public is typically completely overlooked in favour of a focus on the transnational policy space. The real stakeholders in the financialised economy are, after all, home-owners, who have to cope with a continuously changing economic context; their say is likely to have more institutional significance than generally perceived and can limit the political solutions available to decision-makers, despite clear negative consequences for economic growth.

References

Aalbers, M. B. (2008) 'The financialization of homes and the mortgage market crisis', *Competition and Change*, 12: 148–66.

— (2009) 'The sociology and geography of mortgage markets: reflections on the financial crisis', *International Journal of Urban and Regional Research*, 33: 281–90.

Abdelal, R. (2006) 'Writing the rules of global finance: France, Europe, and capital liberalization', *Review of International Political Economy*, 13: 1–27.

— (2007) *Capital Rules: The construction of global finance*, Cambridge: Harvard University Press.

Alloway, T. (2011) 'Concerns grow over Denmark's bail-in rules', *Financial Times*. http://www.ft.com/intl/cms/s/0/281c7f70-855f-11e0-ae32-00144 feabdc0.html#axzz289Vg7fBG. Accessed 2 October 2012.

Andersen, P. K., Clausen, N. J., Edlund, H. H., Iversen, B., Michelsen, A. and Pedersen, H. V. (2008) *Dansk Privat Ret*, Copenhagen: Jurist- og Økonomiforbundets forlag.

Angelides, P. (2011) *The Financial Crisis: Inquiry report*, Washington, DC: US Government.

Baker, A. (2010) 'Austerity in the UK: why it is not common sense but politically driven nonsense'. http://www.qub.ie/schools/SchoolofPolitics InternationalStudiesandPhilosophy/FileStore/Stafffiles/AndrewBaker/ Filetoupload,224825,en.pdf. Accessed 7 February 2013.

— (2013) 'The new political economy of the macroprudential ideational shift' *New Political Economy*, 18(1): 112-139.

Basel Committee on Banking Supervision (2010a) *'Basel III: A global regulatory framework for more resilient banks and banking systems'*, Basel: Bank for International Settlements.

— (2010b) *'Basel III: International framework for liquidity risk measurement, standards and monitoring'* Basel: Bank for International Settlements.

Bernanke, B. S. (2008) *Federal Reserve Policies in the Financial Crisis,* Federal Reserve. http://www.federalreserve.gov/newsevents/speech/ bernanke20081201a.htm. Accessed 25 September 2012.

Best, J. (2010) 'The limits of financial risk management: or what we didn't learn from the Asian crisis', *New Political Economy*, 15: 29–49.

Bjørsted, E. (2011) *Historisk langsomt opsving i dansk økonomi*, København: AE–Arbejderbevægelsens Erhvervsråd.

Blackburn, R. (2008) 'The subprime crisis', *New Left Review*, 50: 63–6.

Boak, J. (2011) 'S&P: Debt default skeptics fueled ratings downgrade', Politico. http://www.politico.com/news/stories/0811/61147.html. Accessed 14 August 2012.

Boudon, R. (2001) *The Origin of Values: Essays in the sociology and philosophy of beliefs,* London: Transaction Publishers.

—   (2003) 'Beyond rational choice theory', *Annual Review of Sociology*, 29: 1–21.

Bourdieu, P. (2005) *The Social Structures of the Economy,* Cambridge: Polity Press.

Compston, H. (1998) 'The end of national policy concertation? Western Europe since the Single European Act', *Journal of European Public Policy*, 5: 507–26.

Crouch, C. (2009) 'Privatised Keynesianism: an unacknowledged policy regime', *The British Journal of Politics & International Relations*, 11: 382–99.

Day, K. (2006) 'Study finds "extensive" fraud at Fannie Mae', Washington: *The Washington Post.* http://www.washingtonpost.com/wp-dyn/content/article/2006/05/23/AR2006052300184.html. Accessed 11 August 2012.

The Economist (2011) 'Turning Japanese', *The Economist*: London.

Esping-Andersen, G. (1990) *The Three Worlds of Welfare Capitalism*, Cambridge, Polity Press.

Ferguson, N. (2009) 'Beyond the age of leverage: new banks must arise'. http://www.ft.com/intl/cms/s/0/85106daa-f140-11dd-8790-0000779fd2ac.html. Accessed 25 September 2012.

Frieden, J. A. (2007) *Global Capitalism: Its fall and rise in the twentieth century,* New York: Norton.

Gjede, T. (1997) 'Mortgage finance in Denmark', *Housing Finance International*.

Glyn, A. (2006) *Capitalism Unleashed: Finance, globalization, and welfare,* Oxford: Oxford University Press.

Gowan, P. (2009) 'Crisis in the heartland', *New Left Review*, 55: 5–29.

Green, R. K. and Malpezzi, S. (2003) *A Primer on U.S. Housing Markets and Housing Policy,* Washington DC: Urban Institute Press.

Guthman, J. (2007) 'The Polanyian way? Voluntary food labels as neoliberal governance', *Antipode*, 39: 456–78.

Hansen, K. (2008) *Det tabte land,* København, Gads Forlag.

Hansen, L. (2002) 'Sustaining sovereignty: the Danish approach to Europe', in Hansen, L. and Wæver, O. (eds) *European Integration and National Identity*, London: Routledge.

Hay, C. (2011) 'Pathology without crisis? The strange demise of the Anglo-liberal growth model', *Government and Opposition*, 46: 1–31.

Hix, S. and Goetz, K. (2000) 'Introduction: European integration and national political systems', *West European Politics*, 23: 1–26.

Jacoby, B. (2009) 'Everyday agents and economic regimes: What can EIPE tell us about the Credit Crisis?', BISA IPEG. http://www.bisa.ac.uk/index.php?option=com_bisa&task=download_paper&no_html=1&passed_paper_id=38. Accessed 11 August 2012.

Jamieson, A. (2011) 'China blasts US "debt addiction" and calls for new global stable reserve currency', *Daily Telegraph.* http://www.telegraph.co.uk/news/worldnews/asia/china/8685655/China-blasts-US-debt-addiction-and-calls-for-new-global-stable-reserve-currency.html. Accessed 11 August 2012.

Jeske, K. and Krueger, D. (2005) *Housing and the Macroeconomy: The role of implicit guarantees for government-sponsored enterprises*, Working Paper Series. Atlanta: Federal Reserve Bank of Atlanta. http://ideas. repec.org/e/pkr7.html. Accessed 12 February 2013.

Johnson, S. (2009) 'The quiet coup', *The Atlantic:* Atlantic Media Company.

Kemeny, J. (2005) '"The really big trade-off" between home ownership and welfare: Castles' evaluation of the 1980 thesis, and a reformulation 25 years on', *Housing, Theory, and Society*, 22: 59–75.

Keynes, J. M. (1949[1936]) *The General Theory of Employment, Interest and Money*, London: Macmillan and Co., Limited.

Khatiwada, S. (2010) 'Did the financial sector profit at the expense of the rest of the economy? Evidence from the United States', discussion paper, Geneva: International Labour Organization.

Krugman, P. (2008) *The Return of Depression Economics and the Crisis of 2008*, New York: W. W. Norton & Company.

Langley, P. (2008) *The Everyday Life of Global Finance: Saving and borrowing in Anglo-America*, Oxford, Oxford University Press.

Leander, A. (2009) 'Close range: targeting regulatory reform', *International Political Sociology*, 3: 465–68.

Martin, R. (2010) 'The local geographies of the financial crisis: from the housing bubble to economic recession and beyond', *Journal of Economic Geography*, 1–32.

Montgomerie, J. (2009) 'The pursuit of (past) happiness? Middle-class indebtedness and American financialisation', *New Political Economy*, 14: 1–24.

Mortensen, J. L. and Seabrooke, L. (2009) 'Egalitarian politics in property booms and busts: housing as social right or means to wealth in Australia and Denmark', in Seabrooke, L. and Schwartz, H. M. (eds) *The Politics of Housing Booms and Busts*, Basingstoke: Palgrave Macmillan.

Mosley, L. (2005) 'Globalisation and the state: still room to move?', *New Political Economy*, 10: 355–62.

Neogy, A. and Anishchuk, A. (2011) 'BRICS demand global monetary shake-up, greater influence', Reuters. http://uk.reuters.com/assets/ print?aid=UKTRE73D0XL20110414. Accessed 11 August 2012.

OECD (2005) *Economic Outlook* No. 78. Paris: OECD.

Østrup, F. (2010) 'Finanskrisen: Årsager og hjælpepakker', in Weise, K. and Munkøe, M. (eds) *I orkanens øje: Erfaring fra og løsninger på den globale finanskrise*, København: Cevea.

Ravnholt, H. (1943) *Den Danske Andelsbevægelse*, Copenhagen: Danske Selskab.

Realkreditraadet (2010) *Boligmarkedsstatistikken.* http://www.realkreditraadet. dk/Statistikker.aspx. Accessed 9 September 2012.

——— (2011) 'Realkreditrådets uddybende kommentar til EU-udspil om CRD IV', Copenhagen, Realkreditraadet.

——— (2012) 'Classification of covered bonds'. http://www.realkreditraadet. dk/Current_issues/New_international_rules_%28Basel_III_-_CRD_

IV%29/%E2%80%A2_Classification_of_covered_bonds.aspx. Accessed 12 September 2012.

Rodrik, D. (2009) 'A Plan B for global finance', *The Economist.* http://www.economist.com/node/13278147/print. Accessed 16 August 2012.

Rogoff, K.S. and Reinhart, C.M. (2009) *This Time Is Different*, Princeton: Princeton University Press.

Roubini, N. (2008) 'A conversation with Nouriel Roubini', Charlie Rose. http://www.charlierose.com/view/interview/9310. Accessed 25 September 2012.

Roxburgh, C., Lund, S., Atkins, C., Belot, S., Hu, W. W. and Pierce, M. S. (2009) 'Global capital markets: Entering a new era', McKinsey Global Institute. http://www.eclac.org/noticias/paginas/3/35143/Global-capital-markets.pdf. Accessed 30 January 2012.

Rupert, M. (1995) '(Re)Politicizing the global economy: liberal common sense and ideological struggle in the NAFTA debate', *Review of International Political Economy*, 2: 658–92.

Sachs, J. (2009) 'Our Wall-Street-besotted public policy', Real Clear Politics. http://www.realclearpolitics.com/articles/2009/03/making_rich_guys_richer.html. Accessed 25 September 2012.

Sarkozy, N. (2010) 40th World Economic forum – Opening speech by Nicolas Sarkozy, President of the Republic, Davos, 27 January 2010, FrenchEmbassy in London. http://www.ambafrance-uk.org/President-Sarkozy-s-opening-speech.html. Accessed 13 February 2013.

Schrøder, M. 2007. 'Bank: Ingen fare for subprime-krise i Danmark', København: epn.dk. http://epn.dk/brancher/finans/realkredit/article1133789.ece. Accessed 14 August 2012.

Schwartz, H. M. (2009) *Subprime Nation,* Ithaca: Cornell University Press.

Schwartz, H. M. and Seabrooke, L. (2009) 'Varieties of residential capitalism in the international political economy: old welfare states and the new politics of housing', in Schwartz, H. M. and Seabrooke, L. (eds) *The Politics of Housing Booms and Busts*, Basingstoke: Palgrave Macmillan.

Seabrooke, L. (2006) *The Social Sources of Financial Power: Domestic legitimacy and international financial orders*, Ithaca and London: Cornell University Press.

— (2008) 'Mediating private capital with public values: the everyday politics of mortgage bond systems in Denmark and the U.S.', Working Paper, Copenhagen: Copenhagen Business School.

— (2012) 'The everyday politics of homespun capital: economic patriotism in housing credit systems', *Journal of European Public Policy*, 19: 358–72.

Seabrooke, L. and Tsingou, E. (2009) 'Power elites and everyday politics in international financial reform', *International Political Sociology*, 3: 457–61.

Sharma, S. D. (2009) *China and India in the Age of Globalization,* Cambridge: Cambridge University Press.

Simmel, G. (1990[1907]) *The Philosophy of Money,* London: Routledge.

Sinclair, T. J. (2009) 'Let's get it right this time! Why regulation will not solve or prevent global financial crises', *International Political Sociology*, 3: 450–53.

— (2010) 'Round up the usual suspects: blame and the subprime crisis', *New Political Economy*, 15: 91–107.

Smith, T. (2009) 'Technological change in capitalism: some Marxian themes', *Cambridge Journal of Economics*, 34: 203–12.

Solomon, M. S. (2010) 'Critical ideas in times of crisis: reconsidering Smith, Marx, Keynes, and Hayek', *Globalizations*, 7: 127–35.

Stiglitz, J. (2008) 'Commentary: How to prevent the next Wall Street crisis', [CNN Politics. http://articles.cnn.com/2008-09-17/politics/stiglitz.crisis_1_housing-bubble-current-financial-turmoil-economy?_s=PM:POLITICS. Accessed 25 September 2012.

Swann, N. G. (2011) 'United States of America long-term rating lowered to 'AA+' due to political risks, rising debt burden; outlook negative', Toronto: Standard & Poor's. http://www.standardandpoors.com/ratings/articles/en/us/?assetID=1245316529563. Accessed 11 August 2012.

US Bureau of Labor Statistics (2011) *Labor Force Statistics from the Current Population Survey*, Washington DC: U.S. Bureau of Labor Statistics. http://data.bls.gov/timeseries/LNS14000000. Accessed 25 September 2012.

Valdez, S. and Molyneux, P. (2010) *An Introduction to Global Financial Markets*, London, Palgrave.

Valentin, K. (2008) *Hvad sker der med din økonomi, hvis rentefradraget fjernes?* København: Berlingske Tidende. http://kimvalentin.blogs.business.dk/2008/03/20/hvad-sker-der-med-din-%C3%B8konomi-hvis-rentefradraget-fjernes/. Accessed 17 September 2012.

Wallison, P. (2009) 'The true origins of this financial crisis', *American Spectator.* http://www.aei.org/files/2009/02/19/04-23894%20OTI%20Wallison-g.pdf. Accessed 17 August 2012.

Weber, M. (1949[1904]) 'Objectivity in social science', in Shils, E. A. and Finch, H. A. (eds) *The Methodology of the Social Sciences*, New York: The Free Press.

Wolverson, R. (2010) 'Confronting the China–U.S. economic imbalance', Council on Foreign Relations. http://www.cfr.org/china/confronting-china-us-economic-imbalance/p20758. Accessed 1 September 2012.

World Bank (2011) *World Development Indicators*, The World Bank. http://www.google.com/publicdata/explore?ds=d5bncppjof8f9_&ctype=l&strail=false&nselm=h&met_y=ny_gdp_mktp_cd&scale_y=lin&ind_y=false&rdim=country&idim=country:DNK&ifdim=country&tstart=-296528400000&tend=1281308400000&hl=en&dl=en&icfg&iconSize=0.5&uniSize=0.035. Accessed 9 September 2012.

chapter nine | conclusions: too little, too slow?

Manuela Moschella and Eleni Tsingou

> '*If there is a reproach to be made, it is that regulatory progress has not been faster.*'
>
> Andreas Dombret, member of the Executive Board of the Deutsche Bundesbank, speech delivered at the Global Seminar Financial Regulation – Bridging Global Differences, Salzburg, 16 August 2012.

Great expectations

As some time has now passed since the onset of the global financial crisis, it is far from controversial to claim that a crisis originating in the small subprime mortgage market in the United States triggered the worst global downturn since the Great Depression. In an echo of the early stages of the 1930s crisis, the world witnessed an unusually sharp drop in asset prices and output, followed by the failure and near-failure of prominent financial institutions, all of which culminated in generalised financial distress (Eichengreen 2012). Analogies with the early stages of the Great Depression were largely made to justify unconventional monetary policy by central banks: in order to prevent a repeat of the 1930s cascade of financial failures, monetary authorities around the world acted decisively in pumping in liquidity. Next to monetary policy, however, the other policy area where the Great Depression analogy has been most often invoked is that of financial regulation. Similarly to the 1930s, when a regulatory clampdown on banking activity was adopted to restore confidence in the US financial sector, the crisis that started in 2007 raised expectations of a profound overhaul of the financial system and its global interconnectedness, that is, the factors that were understood to be at the heart of the crisis. Public mobilisation against the banks and the pronouncements of key leaders and regulators – which did not shy away from comparing the post-crisis environment to the 'Bretton Woods moment' that materialised as a reaction to the depression of the 1930s – were all signs that a quick and substantial (re)regulation of the global financial sector was on the agenda and about to take place.

However, this book offers a sober assessment of the way in which policy-makers exploited the window of opportunity provided by the crisis. Rather than being a decisive intervention to fix the problems exposed by the crisis, the post-crisis regulatory reform process has proceeded quite slowly and by way of marginal adjustments. If the conventional wisdom holds that turning points, such as an external shock, usually bring major intellectual reassessment and policy changes, the cases in this book in fact show that the 'external shock' of the crisis has not led to such a comprehensive overhaul. Rather than rapidly lurching forward on the heels of economic disruptions and popular discontent, the key feature of the regulatory reform has been its incremental, non-paradigm-changing dynamic.

While incremental change is neither wrong nor bad in principle, it is nonetheless problematic for the post-crisis regulatory agenda. The problem derives from the fact that, as political scientists know quite well, a window of opportunity does not stay open for long and – when it shuts down – it is difficult to restore the conditions favourable to change that were seemingly possible before. This is exactly the risk that is materialising as the centre of the crisis moves from the financial sector to the sovereign-debt market. As the overriding focus of policy-makers is shifting to Europe's financial turmoil and the impact it could have on the rest of the world, it has not been uncommon to hear calls to water down or delay regulatory reform. An excessive regulatory pressure, so the argument goes, could put at risk the global economic recovery, exactly at a time when the euro crisis is already impairing global growth prospects.

However, and in spite of the fact that the sovereign-debt crisis in Europe is a major source of risk to global stability, it would be dangerous to slow further the financial regulatory-reform process. To start with, the same sovereign-debt crisis, which is driven not least by systemic problems in some countries' banking systems, underscores the urgent need to make the financial system more resilient. Furthermore, the financial sector is still a major source of potential risk. For instance, many banks remain highly leveraged, including those that appear well capitalised (BIS 2012: 5) and the level of risk in the banks that were saved by public money is also growing (Brei and Gadanecz 2012). In short, the 'problems with banks' are far from having been solved (Rethel and Sinclair 2012). On top of that, there is also mounting evidence that innovative products are already being developed to circumvent some of the new regulations (IMF 2012). Last, but not least, the financial scandals of the last few years, from the fraud allegations on mortgage-backed securities to the mismanagement of the Libor-setting process, have not undermined but reinforced the case for speedier and more comprehensive regulation.

The chapters collected in this volume have investigated why 'the regulatory progress has not been faster', in the words of Andreas Dombret, member of the Executive Board of the Deutsche Bundesbank, in the epigraph to this concluding chapter. Specifically, we addressed the question of why the regulatory-reform process has been incremental although the conditions were in place for a more decisive and radical outcome. Indeed, as clarified in the Introduction to this volume, the crisis opened a window of opportunity for rapid and radical reform, by significantly changing the institutional context in which financial policy-making takes place: public mobilisation and the shift in the locus of the financial debate from technical to political bodies such as the G20 were all factors that would lead us to expect the kind of punctuated change that is associated with quick and profound policy changes.

In unveiling the factors that prevented a punctuated-type of change from occurring, we set out to make both empirical and theoretical contributions. At the empirical level, our study maps and assesses the changes that have taken place in a number of crucial areas of financial governance, including financial supervision (Baker), offshore financial centres and shadow banking (Rixen), accounting

(Botzem), banking governance infrastructure (Carstensen) and banking and derivatives regulation (Quaglia, Pagliari and Young), the rules that apply to hedge funds and credit-rating agencies in the European Union (EU) internal market (Quaglia) and those that govern mortgage-related markets and products (Kjar). While these case studies do not exhaust the regulatory-reform agenda, they cover important or contentious reforms that highlight activity at various levels of governance, provide a contrast between pre and post-crisis debates, and allow investigation of the role played by a wide range of actors, from those that operate in the private sector to those in the official community. Furthermore, they provide a comparison of the dynamics of change across governance levels and also in several areas that are important to the workings of global finance, while going beyond the usual banking/securities/insurance subsector analyses often employed when studying financial regulation (e.g. Singer 2007). By mapping what has changed in these sectors, we also provide a complementary analysis to those economic studies that have thus far investigated the progress that has been made in making markets and institutions more transparent, less complex, and less leveraged (e.g. IMF 2012).

Furthermore, the contributions collected in this book provide a theoretically informed analysis of the changes that have taken place thus far. In particular, we deliberately decided not to elaborate new concepts and theories. In contrast, we opted to build on the insights developed within the historical institutionalist literature, which has long focused on processes of incremental, path-dependent change, and to exploit this opportunity for fruitful cross-fertilisation by expanding those insights and combining them with those developed in international political economy (IPE) scholarship.

The resulting theoretical model suggested in this volume builds on recent versions of historical institutionalism (HI), in that it incorporates the importance of normative underpinning and, above all, redresses the balance between agents and institutions by taking a more agent-centred perspective that emphasises the microfoundations of political actors' preferences (e.g. Fioretos 2011: 373–6; Mahoney and Thelen 2010). Attention to these microfoundations is crucial to the processes of change examined in this book: as constraints and opportunities in the global financial institutional framework changed following the crisis, the calculations of political actors also adapted and evolved. The ways in which they evolved, however, and the way in which they were translated into operational practices, were both facilitated *and* constrained by previous developments in the multiple institutions that make up global financial governance. Temporality and sequence, institutional density, positions of power across actors and within networks, as well as knowledge patterns: these were all factors that mediated the impact of the exogenous shock of the crisis, diverting responses towards an incremental dynamic. In other words, echoing findings at the domestic level, where historically grown institutions largely mediate globalisation forces, explaining the lack of policy convergence,[1] in this study, the historically grown features of global

---

1. On the differences in national policy responses to external, common challenges *see*, among

financial governance mediated the impact of the crisis and explain the lack of profound overhaul in its aftermath.

Adopting this theoretical framework, as will be clarified below, all the chapters in this volume shed light on how incremental change is the result of the activity of change-actors and/or veto-players that operate within the constraints and possibilities defined by the institutional characteristics that global financial governance has acquired over time. They were crucial in tilting financial regulation towards a dynamic of incremental change because they shaped micro-level incentives for change-actors and veto-players to change (or reproduce) existing financial rules and institutions. It is also important to note that, as suggested in the Introduction to this volume, change-actors and veto-players did not necessarily perform different roles in the post-crisis regulatory reform process – sponsoring change and opposing it respectively. The empirical evidence is far more mixed, showing that the same set of political actors can act as both change-agents and veto-players.

In what follows, we review the key findings that can be extrapolated from the empirical chapters, assessing the extent to which they lend support to the theoretical propositions staked out in the Introduction. Subsequently, we move to speculate on the implications of the post-crisis reform process for global financial governance. In this section, we also engage with the observation that incrementalism is mainly instrumental and serves to preserve the status quo. Finally, we reflect on other challenges for the regulatory-reform agenda and suggest some themes for future research, especially in a comparative perspective.

Summary of the findings and their implications

What change?

One of the primary contributions of the chapters collected in this volume is that of identifying and mapping the dynamics of change and the types of change that have been adopted across a number of key financial sub-sectors. While all cases show evidence of some change and reform, the scope, pace and expected outcome of such reform all point to the significance of incrementalism in understanding the process.

To start with, in spite of the evident policy failures exposed by the crisis, and of the popular anger and political support for more wide-ranging reforms, the changes adopted thus far are mainly concentrated at the level of policy instruments and settings. In the immediate aftermath of the onset of the crisis, as evidenced by the pronouncements of the G20, there was a general focus on big policy areas, covering all facets of financial activity. As reform proposals materialised, the agenda was either rendered more modest or the tasks simplified. This is especially notable in Quaglia's analysis, as it provides a bird's-eye view of the changing

---

others, Berger and Dore (1996); Schmidt (2002); Soederberg *et al.* (2005).

European regulatory landscape. Instead of comprehensive reform, we see changes in policy instruments and adjustments to the level of regulation and composition of the regulators. As such, Quaglia stresses that we need to see the full picture before we can determine that the overall reform, while incremental, can indeed amount to more than the sum of its parts. The empirical cases in this volume also show contrasting examples in the *potential* importance of changes in governance settings and infrastructure. Whereas Rixen, in his analysis of changes in the regulation of offshore finance, maintains that reform activity is merely symbolic with few meaningful consequences, Carstensen, in his discussion of cross-border resolution-regimes shows that rationalising bank-resolution infrastructure can potentially have wide-ranging consequences, as can be seen in the discussions of a European banking union.

Changes at the level of policy goals have been quite rare, if not altogether absent. This is especially the case in the mortgage-services industry, as can be seen in Kjar's contribution, and that despite its central role as a crisis trigger. The main exception in the empirical analyses of this volume is the ideational change in the adoption of a macroprudential regulation (MPR) agenda and discourse by regulators and supervisors: this change is the one area of reform that most closely resembles paradigmatic change, in Hall's terminology (1993). However, although Baker accounts for this development in terms of a shift in the policy paradigm, his assessment of the shift from micro- to macroprudential regulation also shows how this development is closely linked to pre-existing knowledge among regulatory-circle insiders; macroprudential ideas are driven by policy entrepreneurs who hold privileged positions in the relevant institutional settings and did so in the pre-crisis period. Finally, another important category of change that we can extrapolate from the empirical chapters pertains to the procedures according to which rules are created. In this context, Quaglia shows that a pooling of sovereignty is taking place in the post-crisis regulatory framework at the European level, whereas Botzem provides examples of how changes in the composition of the International Accounting Standards Board (IASB) enabled that professional community to claim that change was taking place despite the absence of wholesale shifts in accounting governance.

While virtually all contributions shed light on the incremental changes that have taken place thus far, a comparative look at the chapters allows us to see some important differences. In particular, under the rubric of incremental change, it is possible to distinguish between areas in which change has been characterised by cautiousness and timid advances and areas in which change has been symbolic at best, offering little scope for further reform or change in practices at a later date.[2]

The changes in offshore and shadow-banking regulation, as well as those in accounting standards, match this idea of merely symbolic change quite well. In

---

2. Symbolic change is akin to the 'hypocrisy' that many international bureaucracies display when they face external pressures for change that are not in line with dominant internal culture and preferences. For a detailed discussion of such hypocrisy, *see* in particular Weaver (2008).

Rixen's chapter, for instance, policy-makers (change-agents) tried to square the circle – between jurisdictional competition and financial-interest capture on the one hand and public demands for stricter regulation on the other – by resorting to incremental, but often ineffective and symbolic, reform measures. But policy-makers are not alone in pursuing symbolic adjustments. Private-sector actors also moved in this direction, in order to manage or control the process of regulatory change. In line with one of the key findings of HI, actors who stood to lose from more rapid intervention intervened to 'manage change', that is, control it. So, as Botzem shows, the IASB's reaction to the financial crisis can be interpreted as a strategic response combining avoidance of confrontation, reframing criticism and carefully renewing organisational leadership.

Symbolic change can also be the result when different dynamics are at play. As Kjar shows in the case of the reform of mortgage-services industry, the domestic setting made veto-players of the constituency of home-owners in the US and Denmark, rendering change insignificant and merely symbolic. In Kjar's case, the existence of 'economic patriots' who are reluctant to see changes in their domestic housing systems is aligned with the preferences of the mortgage industry for modest change.

As this overview of the changes mapped in the book reveals, one of the dominant features of the post-crisis financial regulatory process is the gap between what was possible and what actually took place: on the whole, political actors settled around adjustments in existing policy settings and instruments. In some cases, political actors even masked minor action under the rhetoric of major change. As such, though the authors in this volume do not automatically subscribe to a historical institutionalist approach, their findings directly speak to that research tradition. In particular, the contributions unveil the many ways in which change materialises without disruption through different types of incremental dynamics (Streeck and Thelen 2005).[3] So, what explains this big gap between possibility and action? What accounts for the emergence of different types of incremental change?

Not punctuated, nor paradigmatic: accounting for incremental change

In the Introduction to this volume, in order to explain the prevalence of incremental change, we suggested investigating the interaction between evolving institutional frameworks and the microlevel, agent-driven processes that create incentives for changing (or reproducing) existing financial rules. The contributing authors followed this lead in their empirical analyses. In doing so, they brought to the surface how the institutional and normative features that global financial governance has acquired over time interacted with the agency of different political

---

3.   For an analysis of different incremental changes and the distinction between change patterns that can be characterised as layering and those that can be characterised as conversion, *see*, in particular, Mahoney and Thelen (2010) and Streeck and Thelen (2005). For an application of these concepts to the patterns of change at the international level, *see* Moschella and Vetterlein (2013).

actors. This interaction gave rise to a type of change that was more constrained than would have been plausibly expected from the post-crisis environment. In what follows, we review and examine the institutional and normative features that channelled change in an incremental direction as well as the political actors that set in motion the process of change and shaped it along the way. While we focus on each dimension separately for analytical purposes, it is important to remember that they are flip-sides of the same coin: the post-crisis incremental dynamic cannot be successfully explained by focusing on one without the other.

In the first place, we find that specific institutional features pushed the reform process in an incremental direction. The findings of the chapters lend support to the propositions set out in the Introduction that the relevant institutional constraints on major, rapid change can be traced back to different levels of analysis – the intergovernmental, domestic and transnational levels. The common denominator here is that the relevant institutional constraints were the result of long-term processes in global financial governance. The distribution of power among states (with no one state in a dominant institutional position); various domestic vested interests and national economic structures; the density and complexity of the sites of authority in global financial governance; and the embeddedness of specific policy ideas on how to govern financial markets were all factors that were the result of institutional legacies of long-term political battles and previous rounds of reforms. In other words, temporality is crucial to understanding why the specific institutional features took the shape they did when the financial crisis broke. These institutional features weakened the push for reform following the onset of the crisis.

At the intergovernmental level, the importance of these institutional factors is most clear when looking at the cleavages among the states involved in the negotiations on regulatory reform at the EU level or in discussions on overhauling offshore and shadow-banking governance arrangements. With no clear leaders and too-diffuse state power, ambitious reform proposals were watered down. Indeed, regulatory change was possible to the extent to which it did not produce rules that significantly departed from those in place in the few, dominant financial markets. Quaglia's empirical case shows that pre-crisis 'market-making' and 'market-shaping' coalitions endured and were at the centre of post-crisis reform compromises and consensus (similar dynamics within the EU are also at play in the analysis of Carstensen in this volume). On the other hand, Rixen provides an account of how, when it came to offshore and shadow-banking regulation, there was ultimately a lack of interest in clear action among the main state actors in financial governance, who were unable to overcome issues of jurisdictional competition.

Domestic factors are also relevant in explaining the prevailing pattern of incremental change. Interest-group lobbying and the structure of domestic economies have been of particular importance. Indeed, in line with our theoretical expectations, political actors who stood to lose from the outcome of the regulatory process took action to preserve their interests and the investments made in existing regulatory designs. This is exactly the case of the financial industry. Pagliari and

Young's chapter clearly shows how the domestic financial industry in the United States influenced the pattern of regulatory reform of derivatives. It also explains, however, that this influence was conditional on the industry's capacity to adjust its advocacy strategies in response to changes in the regulatory environment triggered by the crisis. In particular, financial institutions aligned their interests and preferences to those of a wider range of corporate stakeholders, moving the focus away from calls to 'punish the financial sector' and emphasising the importance of not harming 'corporate America' instead. It was the mobilisation of corporate end-users of financial products, and in this case derivatives, that helped the financial industry to slow down more ambitious reforms in this area. We thus have a case of vested interests maintaining their privileged position and weakening regulatory reforms.

Domestic considerations were also a key determinant of the incremental pattern of change for a number of regulatory reforms debated at the international level, for which the variety of domestic financial systems mattered. In particular, whether a system is more market-based or bank-based had an impact on the regulatory process, affecting both preferences and coalitions at the international level. This is evident, for instance, in the division between the US and UK, on the one hand, and continental EU countries on the other, in the negotiations on Basel III first, and the CRD IV later. Reflecting the organisation of their domestic markets, continental EU countries acted to defend the specific structure of national financial markets, arguing that 'traditional' (continental) banks engaged in less risky trade-finance/financial activities. They thus opposed the leverage ratio, asked for a modification of certain aspects of the liquidity rules and wanted a longer transition period (Quaglia in this volume, *see also* Howarth and Quaglia 2013). Elsewhere, we observe seemingly different systems, such as those of the US and Denmark, exhibiting similar resilience in keeping their housing-finance systems – and the practices of mortgage providers in particular – relatively unchanged (Kjar in this volume).

Among the domestic factors that pushed the regulatory reform process in an incremental direction, capacity problems in domestic administration were also important, as Baker's chapter reveals. In this case, the translation of macroprudential concepts into operational practices has been slowed down by lack of data and the need for a period of experimentation and trials. Anticipating future implementation problems, regulators converged on more incremental measures while keeping a long-term macroprudential agenda alive.

Other factors that help explain the post-crisis incremental dynamics can be found at the transnational level and, in particular, in the specific institutional configuration that global financial governance has acquired over time. Echoing historical institutionalist insights on institutional density and complementarity, as discussed in the Introduction to this volume, a number of case studies show that the institutional landscape, which consists of several club-like and expert-driven institutions (*see also* Tsingou 2012), creates positive feedback effects and increasing returns for political actors operating in such a fragmented landscape (Rixen this volume). Under these conditions, incentives for radical change are limited, at best, and change may be driven mostly by concerns for efficiency (Carstensen in this volume). Indeed, actors who enjoy positive returns from existing institutional designs are more inclined to adopt only those rules that are compatible with existing ones. The incremental dynamics in accounting regulation are a case in point. As Botzem's chapter shows, the IASB's institutional configuration, which values expertise and favours isolation from public pressures, was the most powerful obstacle to a profound post-crisis overhaul. Since the organisation is able to define what counts as expertise and exercise social closure, the only change that can materialise – and the one that actually materialised after the crisis – is limited and highly controlled. This dynamic ensures that the functioning and expert legitimacy of the institution are not called into question.

Another key factor that can help account for the substantial continuity in global regulation can be traced back to the normative framework. Baker's analysis of the inclusion of macroprudential ideas in the reform process shows that, while the inclusion of these ideas as policy itself is new, we need to consider that these ideas were theorised and debated (albeit in small circles) prior to the crisis. Adoption has been gradual and is happening in parallel with adjustments to existing microprudential principles. As such, MPR is 'new' thinking that does not, even in ideational terms, fully replace 'old' thinking. In a different case, Carstensen, examining the development of resolution-regimes in the aftermath of the crisis, points to the contradictions between ideational consensus in principle and the difficulty of reconciling ideas of 'universality' and 'territoriality' in practice.

Although the institutional and normative characteristics summarised thus far are certainly key factors in explaining the incrementalism of the post-crisis reform process, the role of actors engaged in the reform process as change-agents and veto-players needs to be further investigated. In order to explain change, we should also focus on 'the microlevel processes that create incentives for individuals to reproduce (or not) designs during and after [critical historical] junctures' (Fioretos 2011: 375–6). Further we should recognise the dynamic relationship between structures and agency without privileging one over the other. Botzem makes this point in his analysis of the IASB in this volume, noting that simply referring to the institutional characteristics of the IASB is not sufficient to explain how the organisation reacted to the crisis. A thorough explanation of change instead requires us to focus on how powerful actors inside the IASB organised, mediated and actively managed change.

Building on the importance of combining an agent-centred approach with the more traditional insights of historical institutionalism, all chapters take as a starting a point the identification of key actors who support/advocate (change-agents) and oppose change (veto-players) within the distinct constraints and opportunities provided by the institutional environment in which they operate. In this context, actors' motivations and, more importantly to the purposes of this study, actors' reform strategies are endogenous to the distinct institutional context.

The findings of the empirical chapters reveal that the key political actors who support or oppose change include both state and non-state actors, officials and private-sector representatives. Furthermore, in line with our theoretical expectations, the identity of change-agents and veto-players cannot be anticipated *ex ante* because it is not fixed. The same actor can play the role of change-agent or veto-player according to the institutional context in which they operate. For instance, government actors acted as change-agents for certain reforms and as veto-players in others. This is particularly evident in the chapter on post-crisis EU regulation (Quaglia in this volume). Whereas the main political cleavage was between the Anglo-Saxon countries and the continental EU countries in the case of banking regulation, with the former acting as change-agents and the latter as veto-players, these roles were less stable as the regulatory process moved to other financial sectors. Quaglia shows that, instead, in the cases of the regulation of credit-rating agencies and hedge funds in Europe, France and Germany were the main sponsors of the new rules, acting as agents of change, with the UK and some Nordic countries such as Sweden and Finland performing veto-player roles. The importance of differentiating between types of public actors and their potential roles in pushing or stalling reform also comes through in the empirical cases, most notably in Carstensen's analysis of post-crisis bank-resolution regimes. Carstensen shows that, while there has been much change-agent activity from the European Commission on cross-border resolution thinking and policy, national authorities are more reluctant to push through ambitious implementation of these ideas (Carstensen in this volume).

The private sector, too, has acted both as change-agent and veto-player according to the sector or issue area under regulation. In Carstensen's analysis, for instance, the private sector as represented by the Institute of International Finance is a clear change-agent in promoting internationalisation of the regime. Elsewhere, however, the interests of the financial industry follow veto-player characteristics. This is notable in the example of derivatives regulation in the US (Pagliari and Young in this volume) and mortgage-providers in the US and Denmark (Kjar in this volume) but also in the governance of accounting standards, where the IASB strategically defined rules for 'normal' times (Botzem in this volume). As such, the findings from the empirical cases warn us to keep an open mind about who wants change and in whose interests it is to stall it and to recognise the issue-specific dynamics and different tactics and motivations at play.

In conclusion, our study, like most HI, gives significant attention to historical contextualisation and temporality, the notion that the timing and sequence of events shape political trajectories by conditioning the interests of and options available to actors in contemporary reform processes (Pierson 2000, 2004). At the same time, however, we stressed the importance of a careful examination of agency within the institutional constraints and opportunities that political actors face in their activity. Despite some expectations for bigger and speedier changes, the activity, motivations and strategies of change-actors and veto-players has been heavily informed by the deep-seated institutional characteristics that global financial governance has acquired over the past two decades, trapping change in an incremental dynamic.

Incrementalism as a regime-preserving strategy?
The unpredictability and complexity of the post-crisis politics of financial reform

To summarise the main message of this book, as supported by the solid empirical findings reviewed above, we can say that the onset of the crisis created apparent conditions for quick, paradigm-altering change in how global finance is governed. All the textbook factors for such change were indeed in place: from the large-scale implications of regulatory failures to the politicisation of previously technical issues and changes in the policy-making context. In spite of this window of opportunity, however, global financial governance has been fixed largely at the margins via small, incremental changes in key regulatory areas. In short, the great expectations for change have been largely disappointed. The distinct institutional characteristics of global financial governance reduced the room for manoeuvre of the political actors pushing for change and even foreclosed the range of possible options for regulatory reform. The institutional features that global financial governance has acquired over the past two decades strengthened the hands of veto-players, transforming them into *de facto* change-agents, in control of the pace and content of the regulatory-reform process. Cautious advances and regulatory gaps have been the ultimate result – a situation that is miles away from a profound rethinking and restructuring of how global finance is regulated.

Given the state of affairs in financial regulation several years from the start of the crisis, we can raise the question of whether the incremental policy-making mode that we describe in this book adds up to any more than a regime-preserving strategy. In other words, is it possible to conclude from our analysis that the process of change has altered 'something' just to ensure that things stay as they were before the crisis? Is incrementalism just a cover for conservative forces, both among change-agents and veto-players, to maintain the status quo? And does that mean that the long-term consequences of this round of reform will be negligible for the future of global financial governance?

The most immediate – but an inaccurate – reading of our findings suggests a positive answer to these questions. Indeed, as the findings have shown, more often than not the regulatory-reform process has accommodated the requests of political actors who wanted to preserve (and not change) the existing financial regime. By building a coalition with corporate end-users, the financial industry succeeded in containing the regulation of the derivatives market – thus preserving their profitable activities in this market. Likewise, change-agents within the IASB managed the regulatory reform process in a way that maintained the primacy of professional, private expertise in setting global accounting rules. The incrementalism of banking reforms, including those of the shadow-banking sector, was strongly supported by those governments that wanted to preserve the competitive advantage of their domestic financial industries. A regime-preserving orientation can also be detected among the most outspoken change-agents: for instance, while the Bank for International Settlements (BIS) and several prominent economists forcefully advocated the adoption of MPR, the debate has evolved in a way that preserves the centrality of unelected technocrats in shaping the rules for financial markets.

Although these findings clearly show that long-term trends, entrenched positions and crystallised power constellations in global financial governance severely constrained the politics of post-crisis reform, we argue that the incremental dynamics of change that have been analysed in this volume cannot easily be dismissed as mere regime-preservation. This argument rests on both empirical and theoretical observations.

At the empirical level, several findings indicate that the incremental dynamic that characterised the post-crisis regulatory reform is not solely a strategy for preserving the status quo but also a necessary strategy for altering the status quo and entrenching change. For instance, in the case of macroprudential regulation, economists in key international regulatory agencies deliberately decided to embark on a slow-moving experimentation with the new regulatory ideas, in order to collect the necessary evidence both to win the policy debate among technocrats and gather support from political leaders and the wider public. Elsewhere, the financial industry did not strongly oppose some key regulatory proposals because of their incremental nature: opposition was less decisive than in the recent past as proposed reforms included long and delayed implementation phases, allowing for more time to adapt to new rules but also, to organise a long-term lobbying effort.

In short, change-agents settled on a no-radical-change solution in order to win consensus or overcome institutional constraints. Veto-players also accepted – albeit grudgingly – incremental reforms because they thought that their incremental nature would push back the moment at which the effects of reform would be felt. The anticipation of inconsistencies in the timetable for reform, for example, with policy-makers reneging on their policy decisions or rethinking them as a result of lobbying pressures, made incremental reforms acceptable even to those actors who would have otherwise opposed them. While these incremental changes are a 'second-best option' from the perspective of those who wanted more radical transformation, their long-term effects should not be underestimated, as the following theoretical observations contend.

Indeed, at the theoretical level, the ambiguity of the new rules and the unintended consequences of the post-crisis round of reforms are likely to undermine the regime-preserving nature that incrementalism is often said to have. To start with, although the reforms can be read as an attempt to produce stability in an unstable world by formalising risks and ambiguities (Best 2005; Blyth 2006), new rules still need to be reproduced in practice by agents applying them to their specific – and changing – situations (Streeck and Thelen 2005). Wolfgang Streeck (2011: 664) summarises the logic behind the processes of change that take place due to the 'imperfect reproduction of existing rules':

> the conditions under which social rules are supposed to apply are inevitably unique and varying in time, due to the fact that the world is more complex than the principles we have devised to make it predictable. This forces actors to apply rules creatively, actualizing and modifying them in the process.

In short, there is an inherent ambiguity in the rules that guide behaviour. This suggests that the rules that have just been created will be in need of (re)interpretion, especially in such evolving contexts as financial markets. Their reproduction and practical application are thus not given but subject to interpretation by relevant actors. Given the need for interpretation and reproduction, even the most 'incremental', managed changes adopted thus far provide actors with room for manoeuvre, to develop new interpretations about how a specific rule should work under changed circumstances or about how a specific aspect of the world economy should be (re)interpreted. As Mahoney and Thelen (2010: 11) put it, 'actors with divergent interests will contest the openings this ambiguity provides because matters of interpretation and implementation can have profound consequences for resource allocations and substantive outcomes.' This, in turn, can bring about a more profound type of change than the one that it is possible to envisage from today's perspective.

Next to the ambiguity inherent in the new financial rules, another consideration that speaks against the equation incrementalism = conservatism derives from the application of the notion of unintended consequences. As HI scholarship has long demonstrated, change cannot be conceived as a dichotomous variable but it is better conceptualised as a continuous interaction between continuity and change (Thelen 1999). It is this blend of elements of continuity and change that allows for unexpected consequences to arise. Once some elements of change are brought into well defined institutional designs, the consequences are not easy to anticipate. For instance, it is not uncommon that rapid and substantive policy shifts are triggered by the slow, cumulative effects of previous policy changes (Haydu 1998; Howlett 2009; Kay 2007).

This may materialise in the area of global financial governance. Although the reforms that have been adopted thus far are small, slow adjustments to existing rules and institutions, these can set the stage for bigger ones. It is already possible to speculate on some developments that may bring about these big, unintended consequences.

For instance, the unintended effects of the rules adopted today may spring from wrong incentives and negative spillover effects. Banking regulation can serve as a prime example here. Indeed, one of the immediate threats is that of regulatory arbitrage, as stricter rules imposed on banks via Basel III create incentives for activities and risks to be moved from the core of the financial system to the non-bank financial sector, where the new rules do not apply. As already noted, there is mounting evidence that innovative products are already being developed to circumvent some new regulations (IMF 2012). In short, today's regulation may create the conditions for increased risks tomorrow. As these risks become clear – or lead to a new crisis – the case for more stringent regulation in today's overlooked markets will become a pressing concern.

A similar trend towards more decisive regulation than is currently the case may be triggered by the lack of regulation as some markets and products have escaped the attention of regulators and policy-makers. This challenge is not new to scholars of financial regulation: financial regulation – as most other forms of regulation – is usually reactive, rearward-looking. Like generals who keep on fighting the last war, after a crisis starts, policy-makers and regulators have an incentive to regulate the areas that are perceived to be at the origin of the crisis. However, given the speed of financial innovation and the scope of financial interconnectedness, it is likely that today's reforms (and lack thereof) won't stand up to the test of the next crisis, triggering a new round of regulatory reform. Although the regulatory actions that have been adopted so far are largely incremental, they have, nonetheless, set in motion a dynamic of change that is largely unpredictable, especially in light of evolving conditions in financial markets. In this situation, political actors will not be sure to have total control of the outcome of the regulatory-reform process.

This unpredictability is further discernible from the new alliances that have been built as a reaction to the crisis. In particular, the financial-industry–corporate coalition is more unstable than the coalition made up only of financial firms, which had dominated the reform process since the late 1990s. Although the two groups' interests converged around the need to mitigate the effects of too-stringent regulation of derivatives markets and products, the foundations upon which this alliance is based are shaky, at best. The two groups represent constituencies with dramatically divergent preferences that reflect the different distributional implications of cross-border capital flows (Frieden 1991; Goodman and Pauly 1993). Furthermore, the presumed conservative character of current incremental reform is also called into question by growing divergences within the financial industry. Rather than showing it to be monolithic, the crisis has exposed deep fault lines between different parts of the financial industry, nationally and globally (Helleiner and Pagliari 2011: 184). As a result, and in spite of its incremental nature, the post-crisis regulatory-reform process does not guarantee a 'lock-in' effect based on the reproduction of the status quo and its privileges.

Based on the above observations, it would be premature, we submit, to dismiss the result of post-crisis regulatory reforms out of hand. Under the dominant incremental dynamics highlighted in our case studies, there are important elements of novelty that may, in the long run, bring about a more profound overhaul of the way global finance is governed. This conclusion is not dictated by optimism about the reform process. It is based on a careful analysis of empirical findings and theoretical insights.

So, in our view, the main problem with post-crisis regulatory reform lies not so much in the presumed conservatism associated with the incremental dynamic of change. More disturbing are incrementalism's complexity effects. Rather than dismantling old rules and replacing them with new ones, the incremental regulatory process has proceeded through small adjustments, modifications and rule extensions. However, as new rules have been layered on old ones (as in the case of banking regulation, with the adoption of Basel III, *see* Baker in this volume) or existing supervisory tools have been redirected to new purposes (as with the emerging consensus on how to resolve distressed financial institutions, *see* Carstensen in this volume), the resulting outcome has been a complicated regulatory web that gives extra work to regulatory authorities in adequately assessing risks in global financial markets, while multiplying the possibilities for private actors to play with these same rules.

Andrew Haldane, Executive Director of Financial Stability at the Bank of England, has powerfully summarised the potential negative effects of this layering-cum-complexity process by examining the new banking regulations embodied in the Basel III accord. In a paper presented at Jackson Hole in August 2012, titled 'The dog and the frisbee', Haldane (2012) explained that dogs do not need to understand the physics behind a frisbee's trajectory in order to catch it. Similarly, capital standards are better when they are higher and blunter than when they are lower and more sophisticated. The complex maths, models and risk-weighting that underpin current banking regulation are easier for banks to game than simple rules. Furthermore, complex rules do not help regulators either. Haldane illustrated this point by comparing predictions about the chances of failure for a sample of 100 global banks in 2006, based on the simple ratios of assets/equity, with the corresponding complex, Basel-III-style, risk-weighted one. The simple metric won decisively over the more sophisticated risk-weighted system.

So the major risk stemming from the incremental dynamic of the post-crisis financial regulatory-reform is not so much its potential conservatism as the complexity it has helped create: given the inability to bring about a major overhaul of global financial regulation, change-agents and veto-players have created a regulatory system that reproduces and amplifies some of the mistakes of the recent past. In particular, this pattern of incremental reproduction has increased the complexity of the regulatory environment. This could help private-sector actors escape the rules that have just been created and may put an excessive burden on the public authorities in charge of supervising the new system.

The politics of global financial regulatory reforms: a prospective research agenda

Several years into regulatory negotiations and reforms, the time has come to start reflecting on the main challenges that policy-makers and regulators around the world will face as a result of the reforms that have been adopted thus far. In particular, it is possible to think of at least two main challenges whose investigation will be of primary importance for scholars interested in the politics of financial regulatory reforms. These challenges pertain to the problem of implementation and to the relationship between advanced economies and emerging markets in the governance of the global financial system.

The first challenge is associated with the implementation of the measures whose origins and adoption have been traced here. By the time we started working on this book, the greatest challenge to the post-crisis reform-process came from co-ordination and co-operation problems among the actors involved in the negotiations – not only governments but also regulatory agencies and private-sector actors. That is to say, the main problem was that of overcoming the cognitive limitations, mutual distrust and conflicting interests that hinder the adoption of consensus solutions. Given this overriding concern and considering that many regulatory reforms have only recently been adopted or remain under examination, the chapters in this book have analysed the politics of the post-crisis regulatory reform by focusing solely on the stages of rule-formulation, negotiation and decision. We opted not to cover in our analysis the other important stages of the regulatory process, namely rule-implementation, -monitoring and -diffusion. It is important to note, however, that issues related to implementation – such as the presence of necessary organisational capacity and networks to implement a specific regulatory reform – loom large during the process of regulatory-formulation, negotiation, and decision. For instance, Baker's case study in this volume shows that the political actors involved in the development of the macroprudential regulatory framework (mainly economists from key domestic and international regulatory agencies) have been cautious in pushing through the new framework because of the need to test new ideas and develop appropriate organisational capacities in domestic agencies.

In short, thus far, we have treated implementation problems as one of the independent variables that help explain the incremental pattern of the post-crisis regulatory reform. When political actors anticipated implementation problems, they settled on minor, slow-moving regulatory solutions. However, implementation problems can also be treated as the dependent variable to be studied. That is to say, we can ask what factors and conditions favour (or hinder) the implementation of new regulations. And this is one of the most pressing issues that the international community will face in the next stage of the post-crisis reform process. So, although the empirical chapters have bracketed this important issue, in these conclusions, we can start reflecting on what the major implementation problems are and what research areas they open up.

To start with, implementation problems are likely to differ according to whether implementation is required at the international or domestic level. At the international level, implementation will require either the development of new skills and bureaucratic practices by the regulatory agencies that will have to perform new tasks or the development of co-operative practices among international regulatory bodies. For instance, the implementation of the macroprudential framework requires regulatory bodies such as the BIS, the Financial Stability Board (FSB) and the International Monetary Fund (IMF) to develop common understandings of the measures that will make up the MPR policy toolkit. Furthermore, the implementation of MPR ideas is closely related to the development of new methodologies and data sets, for assessing risks from a macro, systemic perspective. In other words, the shift to a systemic oversight approach requests a demanding organisational effort from the international bodies that will undertake it – it requires these bodies to develop resources for collecting and pooling information on a wide range of sources of financial risk. A systemic approach to financial surveillance also requires the development and operationalisation of new standards against which to assess domestic policies (on these issues *see also* Baker 2013; Moschella 2011). In order to ensure the implementation of agreed-upon measures, international regulators will also need new powers. The Secretary-General of the International Organisation of Securities Commission (IOSCO), David Wright, has already made this point explicitly, noting that, in order to be successful, the watchdog would need more deterrents at its disposal. In his words, 'It's all very well setting up principles but we have to implement them globally. Our role at IOSCO will increase. Imagine a world where there are 15–20 major financial markets with nobody at global level able to enforce [regulation].' (Sullivan 2012).

Implementation of some of the new reforms will also require the deepening of inter-institutional co-operation among several regulatory bodies. For instance, the transformation of the FSF into the FSB has also been marked by an increased, formal role for the FSB in overseeing the activities of the other standard-setting bodies. In particular, the FSB has been delegated the power to 'undertake joint strategic reviews of and coordinate the policy development work of the international standard setting bodies to ensure their work is timely, coordinated, focused on priorities and addressing gaps' (FSB Charter, Article 2). For this new power to be effectively implemented, however, the FSB will need to interact more closely with the other standard-setting bodies in order to assess their progress. Similarly, the post-crisis 'data initiative', which has been adopted at the prompting of G20 leaders to fill in data-gaps on key financial-sector vulnerabilities relevant for financial-stability analysis, is closely dependent on the collaboration of several international bodies. For instance, the Interagency Group on Economic and Financial Statistics (IAG), which was established at the end of 2008 to co-ordinate work on the improvement of economic and financial statistics among international agencies, includes the BIS, the European Central Bank (ECB), Eurostat, the IMF, the OECD, the UN, and the World Bank. The collaboration of the FSB and the IMF is another prime example of the way in which inter-institutional co-ordination will impinge on implementation efforts. Indeed, both bodies have been mandated to carry out an Early Warning Exercise (EWE) to detect vulnerabilities in the global financial system. The successful implementation of the newly launched EWE will closely depend on how well the two bodies co-ordinate their surveillance activities.

The implementation of the regulatory reforms adopted thus far will also face domestic-level problems. The starting point here is that, much like other global regulation, the effectiveness of the rules governing global finance closely depends on domestic regulatory regimes (Mattli and Woods 2009: 3; on global regulation *see also* Büthe and Mattli 2011 and Djelic and Sahlin-Andersson 2006). This is particularly the case because much global financial regulation is best characterised as soft law. As the empirical findings here collected have shown, post-crisis regulatory reform has not deviated from this general reliance on soft law. As a result, the conditions present at the domestic level will be crucial for financial regulation to become binding. Hence, differences in domestic financial markets and regulatory structures, existing legislation and regulators' organisational capacities will certainly play a key role in the pace and content of implementation efforts. Differing conditions across domestic regulatory settings pose the risk of uneven or partial implementation of the regulatory reforms adopted thus far. Fragmentation and potential regulatory arbitrage effects cannot be ruled out. As Quaglia notes in this volume, 'in the case of the new pieces of [EU] legislation, their effects will very much depend on how they are implemented in the member states.' Variation in domestic conditions also poses the risk of delays in implementation. This is particularly the case in those jurisdictions where the domestic implementation process opens up several access points for the lobbying of the financial sector, with the United States being an apt case in point (*cf.* Singer 2007; *see also* Connaughton 2012). These observations point to the need for scholars interested in the politics of financial reform to monitor how the implementation of the important – although incremental – reforms will unfold in the next few months and years. Furthermore, this is exactly the area in which cross-fertilisation between IPE and comparative political economy could prove the most promising. That is, in order to make sense of future implementation patterns, we need both an understanding of the distinctiveness of global financial rules and also of the varieties of national regulatory structures which 'mediate' the international rules.

Next to implementation problems, another serious challenge for the future of the post-crisis regulatory process comes from the rise to prominence of emerging-market countries in the international financial regulatory debate. Emerging markets have a key interest in ensuring that their economic achievements are not undermined by global financial instability, as has been the case since the start of the crisis. In spite of the decoupling hypothesis, positing the resilience of emerging markets in the face of financial shocks in advanced economies, emerging markets have been put under severe pressure by developments in the more advanced financial markets. In particular, while emerging markets had to cope with severe capital outflows caused by the process of global de-leveraging in the early stages of the crisis, in the final quarter of 2009, easing in monetary conditions in the advanced economies pushed capital flows in the opposite direction. Since then, in order to prevent currency appreciation and asset bubbles, several emerging countries, such as Brazil, Chile and Peru, have heavily intervened in their currency markets, reviving memories of currency wars '('Trade war looming, warns Brazil', *Financial Times*, 10 January 2011).

A more assertive role for emerging-market countries in the international financial regulatory-reform agenda should therefore not be surprising. For instance, these countries are likely to be key players in the debate on the legitimation of the use capital controls (Gallagher, Griffith-Jones and Ocampo 2011). This group of countries also has key interests in other items on the international regulatory agenda, from measures to ensure the safety of banking systems to those to curb speculation on commodity and food prices.[4] Emerging-market countries' potentially growing assertiveness is also justified in light of the discrediting of advanced economies' financial systems as a result of the crisis. It is now abundantly clear that, although many factors contributed to the crisis, weak regulation played a primary role. Indeed, the countries where the global financial crisis originated had weaker regulation and supervisory practices (for example, less stringent definitions of capital, less stringent provisioning requirements, and greater reliance on banks' own risk-assessment), as well as less scope for market incentives (for example, lower quality of financial information made publicly available, more generous deposit-insurance coverage) (World Bank 2012: ch. 2). In short, the

---

4. For the role of the US in the regulation of agricultural derivatives markets *see* Clapp and Helleiner (2012).

crisis hit hardest the countries where regulation was weaker – and the weakest regulated countries were among the advanced economies, in contrast to what had happened in the 1990s. Emerging markets could thus play a more decisive role in the post-crisis financial regulatory-reform process. This is especially the case for the BRICS, whose financial support has been courted more or less explicitly by several advanced economies, especially in Europe.

One important future line of research thus lies in shedding light on the role of emerging markets in the international regulatory debate and its likely trajectory and implications. In this connection, it will be increasingly important to know more about the domestic political economies of these emerging players in global financial governance. In other words, while the literature on global financial governance and regulation has primarily focused on the political-economic characteristics of the advanced economies in general and key jurisdictions in particular (such as the US and the EU), future studies can no longer ignore political-economic developments in emerging-market countries. Besides, we need to know more about interest-group politics, regulatory practices and ideas in these countries to make sense of their role in the global financial regulatory debate. This knowledge will be all the more useful in light of changes in the membership of several regulatory committees in the wake of the crisis. Indeed, since 2008, the Basel Committee for Banking Supervision (BCBS) expanded from 13 member-countries (all developed economies) to 27 (of which ten are emerging economies). The Committee on the Global Financial System expanded from 13 to 22 countries, including Brazil, China, Hong Kong, India, Mexico, Singapore, and South Korea. The shift from the Financial Stability Forum (FSF) to the FSB has also been accompanied by membership expansion from 11 to 24 countries, of which ten are emerging economies, in addition to Hong Kong, Singapore, and South Korea. Additionally, in December 2010, the IMF adopted a significant realignment of its quota shares. Although the reform has not yet been approved by the majority required for it to enter into force, once enacted, it will result in the presence of the four largest emerging economies (Brazil, China, India and Russia) among the Fund's ten largest shareholders.

This membership expansion brings with it a potential risk of heterogeneity of preferences among the actors that are involved in financial negotiations – a development that stands in stark contrast to the prevailing homogeneity that has characterised global financial governance over the past two decades (Helleiner and Pagliari 2011: 183). Future research will thus need to investigate whether such heterogeneity will be an asset in improving the rules that govern global finance or an obstacle to making decisions.

Finally, another great puzzle for future research on global financial governance relates to the role of states and public authorities *vis-à-vis* that of markets (Germain 2010) and the resilience of pre-crisis economic ideas and, in particular, those associated with the neoliberal orthodoxy. The failure to abandon the economic-theoretical basis of financial governance, in spite of the events that have unfolded since 2007, is indeed one the great mysteries of the post-crisis debate (*cf.* Crouch 2011). Our analysis, and the empirical insights of this volume, show a great deal of nuance on this issue, including the importance of differentiating between form and policy content when discussing financial reforms. As such, future research may also focus on whether incrementalism and layering have altered neoliberal-ideas-derived practices in financial governance. Finally, following regulatory outcomes in the issue-areas studied in this book (and others) will lead to a clearer understanding of whether we can expect any further shifts in the make-up of the governors of finance, with technocratic expert networks coming to share governing space with new actors and with the post-crisis politicisation of finance leading to more ingrained practices of public scrutiny.

References

Baker, A. (2013) 'The new political economy of the macroprudential ideational shift', *New Political Economy* 18(1): 112-139.

Bank for International Settlements (2012) *Annual Report*, Basel: Bank for International Settlements.

Berger, S. and Dore, R. (eds) (1996) *National Diversity and Global Capitalism*, Ithaca: Cornell University Press.

Best, J. (2005) *The Limits of Transparency: Ambiguity and the history of international finance*, Ithaca: Cornell University Press.

—— (2010) 'The limits of financial risk management: or what we didn't learn from the Asian crisis', *New Political Economy*, 15(1): 29–49.

Blyth, M. (2006) 'Great punctuations: prediction, randomness, and the evolution of comparative political science', *American Political Science Review*, 100(4): 493–99.

Brei, M. and Gadanecz, B. (2012) 'Public recapitalisations and bank risk: evidence from loan spreads and leverage', BIS Working Papers, 83, July.

Büthe, T. and Mattli, W. (2011) *The New Global Rulers: The privatization of regulation in the world economy*, Princeton, NJ: Princeton University Press.

Clapp, J. and Helleiner, E. (2012) 'Troubled futures? The global food crisis and the politics of agricultural derivatives regulation', *Review of International Political Economy*, 19(2): 181–207.

Clegg, L. and Moschella, M. (forthcoming) 'The managers of information: international organizations, data, and financial stability', in Porter, T. (ed.), *The Fate of Transnational Financial Regulation in the Wake of the 2007/8 Global Financial Crisis*, London: Routledge.

Connaughton, J. (2012) *The Payoff: Why Wall Street always wins*, Westport CT: Prospecta Press.

Crouch, C. (2011) *The Strange Non-Death of Neoliberalism*, London: Polity.

Djelic, M. L. and Sahlin-Andersson, K. (eds) (2006) *Transnational Governance: Institutional dynamics of regulation*, Cambridge: Cambridge University Press.

Eichengreen, B. (2012) 'Economic history and economic policy', *The Journal of Economic History*, 72(2): 289–307.

Fioretos, O. (2011) 'Historical institutionalism in international relations', *International Organization*, 65(2): 367–99.

Frieden, J. A. (1991) 'Invested interest: the politics of national economic policies in a world of global finance', *International Organization*, 45(4): 425–45.

Gallagher, K. P., Griffith-Jones, S. and Ocampo, J. A. (2011) 'Capital account regulations for stability and development: a new approach', *The Frederick S. Pardee Center For the Study of the Longer-Range Future*, November.

Germain, R. (2010), *Global Politics and Financial Governance*, Basingstoke: Palgrave Macmillan.

Goodman, J. B. and Pauly, L. W. (1993) 'The obsolescence of capital controls? Economic management in an age of global markets', *World Politics*, 46(1): 50–82.

Haldane, A. G. (2012) 'The dog and the frisbee', speech given at the Federal Reserve Bank of Kansas City's 36th economic policy symposium, The Changing Policy Landscape, Jackson Hole, Wyoming, 31 August 2012.

Haydu, J. (1998) 'Making use of the past: time periods as cases to compare and as sequences of problem solving', *American Journal of Sociology*, 104(2): 339–71.

Helleiner, E. and Pagliari, S. (2011) 'The end of an era in international financial regulation? A postcrisis research agenda', *International Organization*, 65(3): 169–200.

Howarth, D. and Quaglia, L. (forthcoming), 'Banking on stability: the political economy of new capital requirements in the European Union', *Journal of European Integration*.

Howarth, D. and Quaglia, L. (2013) 'Banking on stability: the political economy of new capital requirements in the European Union', *Journal of European Integration*, 35(3): 333-346.

International Monetary Fund (2012) 'The reform agenda: an interim report on progress towards a safer financial system', in *IMF, Global Financial Stability Report*, October edition, Washington, DC: International Monetary Fund.

Kay, A. (2007) 'Tense layering and synthetic policy paradigms: the politics of health insurance in Australia', *Australian Journal of Political Science*, 42(4): 579–91.

Mahoney, J. and Thelen, K. (2010) 'A theory of gradual institutional change', in Mahoney, J. and Thelen, K. (eds), *Explaining Institutional Change: Ambiguity, agency, and power*, Cambridge: Cambridge University Press, 1–37.

—   (2010) *Explaining Institutional Change: Ambiguity, agency, and power*, Cambridge: Cambridge University Press.

Mattli, W. and Woods, N. (2009) 'In whose benefit? explaining regulatory change in global politics', in W. Mattli and N. Woods (eds), *The Politics of Global Regulation*, Princeton NJ: Princeton University Press, 1–43.

Moschella, M. (2011) 'Lagged learning and the response to equilibrium shock. The global financial crisis and IMF surveillance', *Journal of Public Policy*, 31(2): 1–21.

Moschella, M. and Vetterlein, A. (2013) 'International organizations and organizational fields: explaining policy change in the IMF, *European Political Science Review* DOI: 10.1017/S175577391200029X. ISSN.

Posner, E. (2007) 'Financial transformation in the European Union', in McNamara, K. and Meunier, S. (eds), *Making History: European integration and institutional change at fifty*, Oxford: Oxford University Press, 139–56.

Rethel, L. and Sinclair, T. J. (2012) *The Problem with Banks*, London: Zed Books.

Schmidt, V. A. (2002) *The Future of European Capitalism*, Oxford: Oxford University Press.

Singer, D. A. (2007) *Regulating Capital: Setting standards for the international financial system*, Ithaca: Cornell University Press.

Soederberg S., Menz, G. and Cerny, P. G. (eds) (2005) *Internalizing Globalization: The rise of neoliberalism and the decline of national varieties of capitalism*, London: Palgrave Macmillan.

Streeck, W. (2011) 'Institutions in history: bringing capitalism back in', in Morgan, G., Campbell, J. L., Crouch, C., Pedersen, O. K. and Whitley, R. (eds), *The Oxford Handbook of Comparative Institutional Analysis*, Oxford: Oxford University Press, 659–86.

Streeck, W. and Thelen, K. (2005) 'Introduction: institutional change in advanced political economies', in Streeck, W. and Thelen, K. (eds), *Beyond Continuity: Institutional change in advanced political economies*, Oxford: Oxford University Press, 1–39.

Sullivan, R. (2012) 'Securities watchdogs need more powers', *Financial Times*, 21 October 2012. http://www.ft.com/cms/s/0/97db3064-193c-11e2-9b3e-00144feabdc0.html#axzz2KhyXzuTN. Accessed 12 February 2013.

Thelen, K. (1999) 'Historical institutionalism and comparative politics', *Annual Review of Political Science*, 2: 369–404.

Tsingou, E. (2012) *Power Elites: Club model politics and the construction of global financial governance.* Unpublished manuscript, Department of Business and Politics, Copenhagen Business School.

Weaver, C. (2008) *Hypocrisy Trap: The World Bank and the poverty of reform*, Princeton: Princeton University Press.

World Bank (2012) *Global Economic Prospect – January Edition*, Washington, DC: The World Bank.

— (2012b) *Global Financial Development Report. Rethinking the role of the state in finance*, Washington, DC: The World Bank.

| index

www.ingramcontent.com/pod-product-compliance
Lightning Source LLC
Chambersburg PA
CBHW072117020426
42334CB00018B/1623